W9-CEI-860

WRITING HYPERTEXT AND LEARNING
CONCEPTUAL AND EMPIRICAL APPROACHES

ADVANCES IN LEARNING AND INSTRUCTION SERIES

Series Editors:
S. Strauss, E. De Corte, R. Wegerif, K. Littleton
Further details: http://www.socscinet.com/education

Published

VAN SOMEREN, REIMANN, BOSHUIZEN & DE JONG
Learning with Multiple Representations

DILLENBOURG
Collaborative Learning: Cognitive and Computational Approaches

BLISS, SÄLJÖ & LIGHT
Learning Sites: Social and Technological Resources for Learning

KAYSER & VOSNIADOU
Modelling Changes in Understanding

SCHNOTZ, VOSNIADOU & CARRETERO
New Perspectives on Conceptual Change

KOZULIN & RAND
Experience of Mediated Learning

ROUET, LEVONEN & BIARDEAU
Multimedia Learning: Cognitive and Instructional Issues

GARRISON & ARCHER
A Transactional Perspective on Teaching and Learning

COWIE & AALSVOORT
Social Interaction in Learning and Instruction

VOLET & JÄRVELÄ
Motivation in Learning Contexts

Forthcoming Titles
SMITH
Reasoning by Mathematical Induction in Children's Arithmetic

Related journals — sample copies available online from:
http://www.elsevier.com

Learning and Instruction
International Journal of Educational Research
Computers and Education
Computers and Human Behavior
Learning and Individual Differences

WRITING HYPERTEXT AND LEARNING

CONCEPTUAL AND EMPIRICAL APPROACHES

EDITED BY

RAINER BROMME

Psychology Department, University of Muenster, Germany

ELMAR STAHL

Psychology Department, University of Muenster, Germany

Published in Association with the European Association
for Learning and Instruction

2002

Pergamon
An imprint of Elsevier Science

Amsterdam – Boston – London – New York – Oxford – Paris
San Diego – San Francisco – Singapore – Sydney – Tokyo

ELSEVIER SCIENCE Ltd
The Boulevard, Langford Lane
Kidlington, Oxford OX5 1GB, UK

Notice

No responsibility is assumed by the Publisher for any injury and/or damage to persons or property as a matter of products liability, negligence or otherwise, or from any use or operation of any methods, products, instructions or ideas contained in the material herein. Because of rapid advances in the medical sciences, in particular, independent verification of diagnoses and drug dosages should be made.

First edition 2002

Library of Congress Cataloging in Publication Data
A catalog record from the Library of Congress has been applied for.

British Library Cataloguing in Publication Data
A catalogue record from the British Library has been applied for.

ISBN: 0–08–043987–X

♾ The paper used in this publication meets the requirements of ANSI/NISO Z39.48–1992 (Permanence of Paper).
Printed in The Netherlands.

Contents

Figures

Tables

Contributors

Michael Armbruster   Fakultät für Mathematik, Technische Universität Chemnitz, Chemnitz, Germany

Beatriz Barquero   Applied Cognitive Psychology and Media Psychology, University of Tuebingen, Tübingen, Germany

Carl Bereiter   Ontario Institute for Studies in Education, University of Toronto, Toronto, Ontario, Canada

Huub van den Bergh   Utrecht Institute of Linguistics, University of Utrecht, The Netherlands

Martine A. H. Braaksma   Graduate School of Teaching and Learning, University of Amsterdam, Amsterdam, The Netherlands

Rainer Bromme   University of Muenster, Psychology Department, Münster, Germany

Michel Couzijn   Graduate School of Teaching and Learning, University of Amsterdam, Amsterdam, The Netherlands

Ingo Dahn   Institut für Wissensmedien, Universität Koblenz-Landau, Koblenz, Germany

Andrew Dillon   HCI Lab, SLIS, Indiana University, Indiana, USA

Alessandra Fasulo   University of Rome "La Sapienza", Roma, Italy

Ulrich Furbach   Institut für Wissensmedien, Universität Koblenz-Landau, Koblenz, Germany

Gert Rijlaarsdam   Graduate School of Teaching and Learning, University of Amsterdam, Amsterdam, The Netherlands

Gerhard Schwabe   Institut für Wissensmedien, Universität Koblenz-Landau, Koblenz, Germany

Stephan Schwan | Applied Cognitive Psychology and Media Psychology, University of Tuebingen, Tübingen, Germany

Elmar Stahl | University of Muenster, Psychology Department, Münster, Germany

Alessandra Talamo | University of Rome "La Sapienza", Roma, Italy

Karsten D. Wolf | Lehrstuhl für Wirtschaftspädagogik, Otto-Friedrich-Universität, Bamberg, Germany

Carmen Zahn | Applied Cognitive Psychology and Media Psychology, University of Tuebingen, Tübingen, Germany

Chapter 1

Writing and Learning: Hypertext as a Renewal of an Old and Close Relationship — Introduction and Overview

Rainer Bromme and Elmar Stahl

Introduction

Once the basic idea of hypertext had spread rapidly throughout the world via the WWW, navigation in hypertexts and the reception of hypertexts soon became objects of empirical research among psychologists, cognitive scientists, and educational researchers. A fair amount of knowledge has now been acquired. This has led the expectations regarding promoting learning via the *reception* of hypertexts to become more modest and, as a result, more realistic. One thing that has become clear is that the most important requirement for successful learning via the reception of hypertexts is an active and goal-oriented approach to them.

This finding leads directly to the following question: Which learning effects can be anticipated from writing[1] hypertexts? This focus on *producing* hypertext is in line with the view on hypertext emphasized by its so-called "founders," Bush, Nelson, and

---

[1] Two terminological clarifications are necessary: The notion of *writing* hypertext is used in the following in a broad, and, so to speak, figurative sense, that is, it encompasses all productive activities with hypertexts. It includes the learner producing a hypertext from scratch (i.e., writing node texts and linking them) as well as rearranging existing hypertexts by setting new links, integrating new nodes, or transforming given traditional text into a hypertext. It is important to stress that when "production" is used in the following, this does not necessarily mean that all of these steps are involved.

Throughout this introduction, we use the notion of hyper*text*. However, this naturally also encompasses electronic documents that include other forms of representation in a hypermedia environment. We are sticking to the term "text" only because the process of writing traditional texts and research on it provides a good background that might help to illuminate the potentials and limitations of the new media. We shall use the notion of hypermedia, hypervideo, and so forth only when the context makes it necessary to focus the reader on different modalities (pictures, movies, etc.) to text.

Engelbart. Alongside the potential of fast access to large amounts of information, they stressed the opportunity for users to construct their own hypertexts to fit their own individual demands (Landow, 1994). Now that easy-to-use software for the production of hypertexts (HTML editors) has become so widely available, the technical obstacles impeding the use of hypertext writing in teaching and learning have vanished. Nonetheless, there is still very little research on this topic.

The present book contributes to this new research topic. It includes laboratory experiments, studies on the production of hypertexts in the context of educational institutions, and reports on software environments designed for the production of hypertext. Because the field of research is so new, the book also includes some mainly theoretical and developmentally oriented contributions alongside the empirical chapters. Nonetheless, all chapters refer to empirical data (without being restricted to any specific methodological approach).

Before presenting the individual chapters, we should like to sketch why we expect the production of hypertext documents to be able to promote learning. Starting points are research on the reception of hypertexts and research on traditional writing. Both research traditions form the backdrop for discussing our assumptions about producing hypertext as a way of promoting learning processes.

Research on the Reception of Hypertexts: Design as Such Does not Matter

At first glance, research on learning through the *reception* of hypertexts offers hardly any cause to hope that this medium might encourage learning in any particular way, in other words, any better than traditional media. Dillon and Gabbard's (1998) overview shows that when hypertext documents are compared directly with traditional texts, there are only a few cases in which the former contribute to better learning outcomes. Put briefly, hypertexts improve learning only when they deal with information that is more difficult to present on paper (e.g., movement sequences) or when they are used for learning tasks in which large amounts of information have to be inspected in a search for specific information. Despite widespread expectations regarding learning with hypertext, the opportunity to explore more freely (to deviate from a set sequence of processing) does not generally promote learning. It is only an advantage for those learners who possess sufficient prior knowledge and a suitable learning style to structure their work. This is often beyond the ability of other learners.

Dillon and Gabbard (1998) concluded that design variables have to be viewed in relation to learner variables; in other words, how the design of the hypertext software impacts on learning outcome depends on the learner's prior knowledge and individual learning style. While learner variables are crucial, they compose only a part of the conditions that are important for successful learning. Such interindividual differences between learners are only so important because learning outcome depends decisively on how the information presented is received and integrated into existing knowledge; in other words, what is important are the internal and external activities of the learner in his or her interaction with the contents of learning. As a result, the inconsistent and, in many studies, also negative findings on the impact of this technology on learning are only disappointing at first glance. If the technology is designed or implemented in such a way that learners can exploit it actively in accordance with their prior knowledge and learning habits, much better outcomes can be anticipated. Nonetheless, at present, it has to be stated that this is still more of a well-founded programmatic expectation than an observation based on a number of empirically evaluated examples. "Obviously, combining the technology with innovative classroom use, discretionary collaboration and self-paced learning may offer further advantages, but as yet such scenarios remain largely unstudied" (Dillon & Gabbard, 1998, p. 345). However, this expectation is justified insofar as it can be taken as confirmed that active learning leads to a more thorough processing of the learning materials and to better retention than a more passive, receptive learning, always assuming that the learner possesses the necessary learning strategies and prior knowledge (Kintsch, 1998).

The production of hypertexts — according to our hypothesis — is one way of enabling learners to deal with information actively and thereby encourage learning and comprehension of their contents.

Nonetheless, the production of hypertexts is not a final solution to the problem of designing learning environments. What it does offer is a promising starting point for the design as well as the study of learning through working with hypermedia. Naturally, it would be illusory to anticipate a stronger learning effect of the production of hypertexts per se compared with hypertext reception without taking the context conditions into account. Just as active variants of hypertext reception are also possible, the opposite case of a "passive" production of hypertexts is also conceivable. The production of hypertexts can also facilitate learning only when it is embedded within an appropriate learning scenario, and learners possess the necessary prior knowledge and attitudes for learning. To improve our understanding of these conditions, it is necessary to carry out studies like those presented in the following chapters.

The Psychology of Writing

Why should the production of hypertexts facilitate learning? When answering this question, it is helpful to look at the psychological models of traditional writing. There are two reasons for this: First, working steps from conventional and traditional writing are also necessary for the production of hypertexts when, for example, texts have to be produced for individual nodes. Second, psychological models of writing provide a good heuristic for a theoretical analysis of the specific conditions and processes of producing hypertext — partially in agreement with, and partially contradictory to writing traditional text.

The most widespread model of writing presented by Hayes and Flower (1980) describes it as a problem-solving process. The writer has to bring a certain thought content into a written form while continuously interacting with that which has been written so far. Hayes and Flower (1980) view writing as a goal-directed process. According to Hayes' (1996) revised version of the model, authors perform three interacting activities: They have to interact with the text passages that they have already written as well as unfamiliar texts (e.g., a writing task that is also given as a text or a text that has to be commented upon) and relate these to their existing internal representations. It is not just the content of the text that is important here, but also the spatial arrangement of information, for example, the graphic text design (*text interpretation*). Then, they have to plan their own text by selecting certain contents and linking them up with their knowledge about the appropriate text format (*reflection*), and, finally, they have to externalize the product of this reflection (*text production*) by writing it down or dictating it. However, the final formulation emerges only at the moment of writing. This is also influenced by, for example, the grammatical constraints of the phrases that have already been commenced. These three processes interact closely with each other, because the writing process proceeds not only in partial cycles but can also be recursive. Writing in partial cycles means that writers do not simply plan their entire text, go on to formulate it, and then check the final product. It is far more the case that they also plan, formulate, and revise smaller sections such as individual paragraphs before going on to the next section or reprocessing previous sections.

Both writing and interpreting existing text passages requires at least four cognitive resources:[2] factual knowledge, lexical and syntactic knowledge, discourse knowledge, and strategic knowledge.

Factual knowledge does not just enable writers to specify the contents they intend to address, but can already suggest how these contents should be related to each other. *Lexical and syntactic knowledge* cover the rules for using single words and combining them into meaningful phrases. However, factual knowledge and lexical and syntactic knowledge alone do not suffice to write a comprehensible text. This also requires *discourse knowledge* about the rhetorical text format and the perspective of the intended audience. The *rhetorical text format* is also called the "genre." It concerns the structuring of the texts and the use of genre-typical terminology such as technical terms or metaphors. Research papers, emails, sermons, or detective stories are all examples of different text formats that impose specific constraints on their authors. Nonetheless, knowledge of text formats is still not enough for designing a text. Text formats still leave a great deal of scope in their design, or, in other words, they still require a number of decisions on the text generation. Moreover, there is also a need for knowledge about the audience, that is, the recipients of the text, their perspective on the topic (Schober, 1998), their interests, and their prior knowledge (see, also, Bromme *et al.*, 1999; Jucks, 2001). *Strategic knowledge* is reflected in, for example, the skills involved in defining the writing task precisely and monitoring one's own writing process.

Hayes' (1996) model regards these types of knowledge as cognitive resources that enable writing. At the same time, however, they impose constraints and do not just contain unlimited possibilities for writing. The affordance concept from the psychology of perception (Gibson, 1982) can be used to label these two necessary aspects in general terms: Affordances are order structures outside the scope of individual mental

---

[2] This is not an exclusive list of the types of knowledge necessary for writing, and it is also not completely in line with the terminology of Hayes and Flower (1980) or Hayes (1996). What it does do is name the domains that are important in the present context.

representation; they enable and simultaneously structure the perception of the environment. The affordances with which the individual writer has to deal are, however, of a social nature. This is why the writing process cannot be understood just by looking at the individual resources and activities of the writer. Writing is always embedded in a certain social and cultural context, not just because (in most cases) one writes for other people, but particularly because the knowledge required is shaped by the culture in which it is written. This is obvious for discourse knowledge and lexical and syntactic knowledge. However, factual knowledge is also shaped socially even when, for example, an author would view creative writing as his or her individual product. The process of writing can be understood only when attention is also paid to the technical tools. When persons write with a personal computer, the product differs from that written by hand; dictated products differ from those written personally.

Although the model of Hayes and Flower (1980) and Hayes (1996) does not address learning by writing, it does include a description of which types of existing knowledge need to be activated in the writing process for the writing task to be achieved. The model does not consider the opposite direction, namely, that the text producer's own content-related knowledge can also be modified by the writing process.[3] However, it can also be applied to the issue of learning by writing. The "reflection" in Hayes' model that leads to the selection of the contents to be written and their structuring in line with the writing task and discourse knowledge does not just involve modifications of the texts. It can also lead to modifications of the internal representations of their content. The model of Bereiter and Scardamalia (1987) focuses on such interactions between what they label the content problem space and the "rhetorical" problem space. Like Hayes and Flowers, they conceptualize writing as the outcome of linking together content-related and discourse-related knowledge. However, they distinguish between two theoretical writing styles: writing as "knowledge telling" and writing as "knowledge transforming." Unlike Hayes and Flower, they do not assume that every form of writing can be described as a complex problem-solving process, but that writing may well proceed automatically.

Bereiter and Scardamalia (1987) describe the knowledge-telling style in terms of how children develop the ability to write. The underlying strategy can be illustrated with the following quotation from a 12-year-old student:

> I have a whole bunch of ideas and write them down until my supply of ideas is exhausted. Then I might try to think of more ideas up to the point when you can't get any more ideas that are worth putting down on paper and then I would end it. (p. 9)

Discourse knowledge is used here as well, but it does not influence the development of ideas on the content. Experienced writers also use the "knowledge-telling" style

---

[3] It should be noted that at this point, and in this context, we are interested in the learning of the contents addressed in the text to be written and not the acquisition of the ability to write itself. This has to be emphasized, because the majority of psychological research on the relation between writing and learning focuses on the acquisition of the writing abilities.

when they are able to draw on existing links between content knowledge and discourse knowledge either from memory or from external sources (Torrance, 1996).

The "knowledge-transforming" writing style, in contrast, represents a more strongly problem-oriented and thereby more complex procedure. When applying this style, text producers become more involved with the texts they are producing. As Bereiter and Scardamalia (1987) point out, authors following this style:

> ... are used to considering whether the text they are writing says what they want it to say and whether they themselves believe what the text says. In the process, they are likely to consider not only changes in the text but also changes in what they want to say. Thus it is that writing can play a role in the development of their knowledge. (p. 11)

They illustrate the interaction between discourse knowledge and topic-related content knowledge with an example: an author is working on the clarity of her writing style, in other words, a problem involving her discourse knowledge. She notices that she can make her line of argument easier to understand if she gives a more precise definition of a term on which her argument is centered. To solve this problem, she has to relate the problem "defining the term" to the content-related knowledge. However, when defining this term, she realizes that it is not the core of her argument, and she needs to focus on another concept. This consideration of content calls for, in turn, a revision of the text written so far, so that the new concept can be assigned the central role she envisages. This then calls for revisions of content and so forth. This contin-uous interaction between the two knowledge domains does not just advance the text. By working through her knowledge, the author may discover aspects of the topic that she was previously unaware of (Eigler, 1997).

However, one precondition for such an interaction between content knowledge and discourse knowledge is a corresponding task presentation (Torrance, 1996) and the availability of strategic knowledge to balance the discourse- and content-related demands when producing the text. Knowledge-transforming in text production has to be imparted explicitly itself by teaching strategic knowledge and practicing its use. It is not simply induced by the presentation of an appropriate writing task.

The "Rhetorical" Format of Hypertexts: Affordances for Learning

We consider that Bereiter and Scardamalia's basic idea can be generalized to the writing of hypertexts. A software environment for the production of a hypertext permits certain processing stages for producing and linking the text material such as writing or import-ing texts for the nodes or setting links. These technical options are the affordances that make it possible to create the typical features of a hypertext. In this sense, one can talk about the rhetorical format of a hypertext.

Of course, hypertexts are not simply one variant of the various kinds of text (essay, sermon, short story). On the other hand, the basic idea that there is a typical rhetorical problem space for each kind of text can be transferred to the features of a hypertext resulting from the specificity of the hypertext environment. The following features of the text form hypertext are likely to support "knowledge-transforming" in the process of writing:

a) *Writing nodes* requires decisions about how areas of content and concepts should be distinguished from each other in order to enable their presentation as closed, separate units. The writing of nodes thus contributes to understanding the concepts and the subject matter of the field being processed.
b) *Establishing links* requires the writer to become aware of the semantically significant connections between the concepts and the subject-matter fields.
c) The *total structure* of the hypertext must be planned in order to achieve coherence and to adapt the document to its anticipated audience. The fact that a hypertext can be perused by the reader in different ways leads to one major change compared with the commonly used means of shaping traditional texts to establish coherence, namely, arranging the text elements in a linear order. As coherence in content is an essential prerequisite for text comprehension (Kintsch & van Dijk, 1978; Schnotz, 1994), the hypertext author is confronted with the task of providing flexible ways of reading without simultaneously producing a loss of coherence in content (Foltz, 1996). For the content of every node, it is necessary to reflect which kind of further information a reader might desire or be able to reach at this point in order to ensure that it is precisely this information that is made available via links. To plan the hypertext's total structure feasibly, the author must comprehend the content structure of the subject-matter field that has to be processed while simultaneously anticipating possible reader perspectives (Spiro *et al.*, 1991; Jacobson & Spiro, 1995).

The decisions described above, however, identify only the "affordances" for thought processes offered by the "cognitive tool" of hypertext. The cognitive processes described here represent the ideal case. Most learners will not exploit the particular opportunities for structuring hypertexts if they are not given explicit guidance. Hence, it cannot be assumed that the features of hypertexts mentioned above will be taken automatically as an opportunity to reflect on the subject matter to be learned (Bromme & Stahl, 1999). Whether these decisions are really made consciously and based on appropriate reflection depends on the learning scenario (i.e., subject matter, instructions, tasks, etc.) and on the learner him or herself.

The Chapters in the Book

Hence, "learning by writing hypertexts" is a topic of research and development that needs to be processed in a different way. It is necessary to gain experiences with suitable instruction scenarios by looking at examples of lessons in which learners actively construct or modify the hypertexts. There is also a need for both analytical and empirical inspection of the individual variables involved in producing hypertext documents. Finally, different technical options for the active production of hypertexts need to be tested. The chapters in this book provide examples for each of these approaches to this research topic.

The first three chapters link up directly with research on traditional writing while addressing — even so completely different — aspects of the interaction between the content problem space and the rhetoric problem space.

Martine Braaksma *et al.*, (Learning to Compose Hypertext and Linear Text: Transfer or Interference?) deal directly with the cognitive processes used when coping with the demand to structure hypertexts. In traditional writing, authors have to convert a complexity of ideas into a linear sequence while simultaneously conveying the (non-linear) coherence of the total text to the reader. Braaksma *et al.*, consider *linearization* to be the gist of traditional writing. They describe the non-linear organization (in, e.g., a concept map) as hierarchical without meaning a one-dimensional hierarchy. When producing hypertexts, the ideas are not organized already in the pattern according to which they should be linked together into a hypertext. As a result, hypertexts demand what they call *hierarchicalization*. To approach the gist of hypertext writing, they chose *hierarchicalization* as a central process, that is, converting a linearly presented line of thought into a hierarchical network of ideas or statements. They report a witty experiment, in which two core components of the construction of hypertexts are investigated: hierarchicalization and linearization. In one experimental condition, participants had to arrange a given traditional text hierarchically. In another, they had to transform a hierarchically arranged knowledge structure (presented in form of a concept map) into a linear text. Those who produce hypertexts at, for example, school also have to learn to produce linear texts there. Therefore, the authors also investigate whether there is a positive transfer between *linearization* and *hierarchicalization*, or whether they inhibit each other.

Rainer Bromme and Elmar Stahl (Learning by Producing Hypertext from Reader Perspectives: Cognitive Flexibility Theory Reconsidered) also deal directly with the interaction between the rhetorical and the content problem space. Anticipating the assumed reader perspective is a necessary precondition for tailoring a certain content to fit a certain audience. Because writers (unlike speakers in a vocal interaction, see Clark, 1996) receive no direct feedback from the recipient, in other words, text production cannot be adapted continuously to an interaction partner, they have to anticipate how to construct the text in both content and formal terms so that readers will be able to understand it (Traxler & Gernsbacher, 1993). Furthermore, both texts and hypertexts generally have completely different readers, and a good author must also take account of the possibility that there will also be different perspectives within the audience he or she wishes to address. Inspired by "Cognitive Flexibility Theory" (CFT, see Jacobson & Spiro, 1995), some researchers have assumed that hypertext environments are particularly appropriate for helping learners to handle knowledge from different perspectives (Rouet & Levonen, 1996; Dillon & Gabbard, 1998). If this basic idea from CFT is transferred to the production of hypertexts, it leads to the hypothesis that taking account of (several) reader perspectives will impact positively on learning in the author. The experiment reported here examines this assumption within the context of hypertext production. It analyzes how adopting two different anticipated reader perspectives influences the processes and the learning effects of hypertext writing. In two successive sessions, participants were asked to create hypertexts by linking given nodes on a certain topic they had to learn about. In the experimental group, the anticipated perspective of the readership for whom the texts were intended was manipulated in each session. The control group was given no explicit reader perspective. In this way, it was possible to study the impact of anticipating reader perspectives on the setting of links and the generation of the total structure of the hypertext. The chapter also contains analyses of the cognitive process of hypertext production assessed with the thinking-aloud method.

Andrew Dillon (Writing as Design: Hypermedia and the Shape of Information Space) also focuses on the interaction between the content addressed in a hypermedia document and the document's design. He tackles the question of how far the production of hypertexts resembles the design of user interfaces. He addresses two contradictory developments: On the one hand, the vast range of technical options already makes the design of electronic documents an original challenge to be coped with — alongside the creation of the text as such. A historical parallel to this is the development of document design in the production of conventional books, which, traditionally, was also separated from the author's tasks. On the other hand, the growing availability of technical options in document design is transforming it increasingly into an author's task, and, therefore, a new challenge to them in the production of both conventional books and electronic documents.

Dillon's chapter forms an interesting contrast to the approach chosen in the first part of this introductory chapter. This understood and discussed the production of hypertexts as part of the creative writing process. We had started out from the idea — addressed metaphorically — of a common identity between writing and the production of hypertexts, and then explored the differences step by step. Dillon takes the opposite approach: He starts out with the differences (writing versus design) and then analyzes the commonalities step by step. This leads him to a crucial question for future research on writing hypertexts: Through which features can the "genre" of hypertext documents actually be distinguished? Does the wide availability of design options for all comers lead to the emergence of a new genre that is specific for hypertext documents? Moreover, Dillon also makes an interesting point regarding further research on the development of specific genres: Whereas Hayes (1996) mentioned the long underestimation of *graphic* constraints in research on traditional writing, Dillon sees a risk that *linguistic* constraints will be underestimated in the context of hypertexts.

Whereas the concern up to now has been with producing hypertexts as a cognitive process, the next three chapters focus on the cooperative learning of students in and through the production of hypertexts. They provide indications on how instructional scenarios could be designed in order to stimulate learning through the production of hypertexts. These chapters also illustrate an aspect that was mentioned above in relation to traditional writing, namely, that writing is a social activity.

Carl Bereiter's chapter (Emergent Versus Presentational Hypertext) is based on more than 15 years' experience with the software environment CSILE (Computer-Supported Intentional Learning Environment). Although the technical option of constructing hypertexts has been integrated into CSILE only in recent years, it proves to be very suitable for supporting cooperative writing in a hypertext environment. Based on his (and M. Scardamalia's) experiences with CSILE, Bereiter argues that learning effects emerge particularly when the production of an electronic document is not in the fore, but when, while working on a certain topic, different students collect different pieces of information and then — virtually incidentally — network these. He calls this "emergent hypertext." The hypertext is, so to speak, the natural structure that emerges, mediated by a technological environment, when persons cooperate.

His short, but determined plea is founded on the observation that most written tasks given to students at school focus on the reproduction of knowledge. Bereiter calls this the traditional project idea. Projects are tasks in which students have to compile texts. Learning remains superficial in such tasks, because students concentrate more on the presentation of the material than on understanding it. However, if one confronts students with a certain topic or problem and informs them that the written report about it is assigned the role of a mere by-product of the task, then, although the resulting hypertext really is a mere by-product, learning will be stimulated.

In his chapter (Sleepy Links, Collaborative Grading and Trails — Shaping Hypertext Structures by Usage Processes), Karsten Wolf also points out how the hypertext that emerges goes beyond the plans and understanding of individual students in cooperative learning scenarios. While this provides an opportunity for surprising learning experiences, it also harbors risks such as the problem of entropy in link structures. The chapter presents a case report on a software environment (EduSerf). Wolf describes interesting technical possibilities for supporting the learner's structuring of the emerging hypertext and reducing link entropy. Nonetheless, he is also very aware that reflection on the interaction between the content knowledge and the discourse knowledge can be supported by technical features of the software but not replaced by them. He concludes with a discussion of the problems resulting from the use of an authoring tool in an educational setting and possible solutions: (a) some users participate more actively in the creation and construction of the hypertext, therefore enlarging their knowledge in a faster way than their co-learners; (b) not all of the contributions (new nodes) are of high quality; (c) the entropy of the system (the number of links) becomes larger; and (d) not all of the links make sense to the different users because of their different usage contexts.

Practice in dealing with the specific affordances of hypertexts can already start when students are relatively young. Alessandra Talamo and Alessandra Fasula (Opening Windows in Each Other's Minds: Social Sharing of Hypertext Models) explore the effects of the collaborative construction of a hypertext on reasoning skills in elementary school children. Ten-year-old children who had participated in a three-year project on the production of a hypertext presentation were compared in an experimental work session with control classes who simulated a hypertext production. Results revealed a marked effect of the experimental condition: Children involved in the hypertext project deployed different skills in the social organization of work, in the management of information, and in the construction of the final product. Interactional features indicate that children trained in hypertext construction exhibited a greater interdependence when working on the development of the task. At the beginning of this introduction, we have repeatedly described the interaction between the topic structure and the rhetoric structure of the hypertext to be constructed as the outcome of individual reflection — as a cognitive process. Talamo and Fasula's case study shows that when given a suitable learning task, this interaction (understood as a cognitive process) can be, so to speak, externalized (thus becoming a process of social interaction). The students discuss the relation between hierarchy and linearization, between topic structure and rhetoric structure, and they can anticipate potential reader perspectives by trying to understand those of their fellow students.

The following two chapters look at technological advances. They describe new technological possibilities, namely, a software environment for transforming linear textbooks into personalized hypertexts and the design of a type of hypermedium that is still uncommon: hypervideos.

Ingo Dahn *et al*. (Slicing Books — The Authors' Perspective) report on a new technology they have developed. This technology splits textbooks into small, self-coherent slices and then uses semantic links to make structural relationships such as "Slice A builds on Slice B" explicit. This approach allows the reader to create personalized textbooks. The creation of sliced books poses new challenges to authors and "sliced-book re-engineers." New tools support them during the creation of those features of electronic documents (multiple links, personalization) that are also specific for hypertext documents. Nonetheless, the author of the sliced book (who may be, but does not have to be the author of the original text being processed by the book-slicing software) has to make the final decision on the links between the slices — even when the software provides support. This makes it necessary to cope with at least two of the basic demands involved in writing hypertexts, namely, setting links and ensuring coherence by considering the potential audience of the new electronic document. The slicing software was not written originally to promote personal learning in the person making hypertexts from traditional textbooks. The idea had been to prepare hypertexts for other learners. However, it is to be anticipated that such a software can also be very helpful for the "slicers" themselves. Dahn and colleagues conclude by discussing instructional scenarios in which students transform a linear text into a multiply linked document together with their teacher and thereby gain a better understanding of the structure of the learning material.

Although many hypertext documents also contain short video clips, the fundamental structure is still the text from which links point to the picture sequences. In hypervideos, things are the other way round: One or more video sequences form what Carmen Zahn *et al*. call the backbone of the hypermedia document. Their chapter (Authoring Hypervideos: Design for Learning and Learning by Design) starts with a description of this new technology and of its possible educational benefits and drawbacks. Because it is a new technology with restricted availability, Zahn and her colleagues first have to report on learning with prefabricated hypervideos before turning to their production by learners. This technology naturally also confronts us with the question regarding the interaction between the content of learning and the design, in other words, the content-related and the rhetorical problem space. The authors report an empirical study in which participants with content-related expertise and participants with design expertise had to decide where to place links in hypervideos. In addition, novices (persons with no prior knowledge of either the knowledge domains or the design of hypervideos) reported where they would anticipate links from the perspective of learners. Results justified the anticipation that novices would also be capable of setting meaningful links. This is important, because it is has to be asked whether the approach of "learning through hypertext production" can be applied in any way at all to such a complex document as a hypervideo. The authors of this chapter deliver convincing arguments that this is possible, and they finish their chapter by sketching possible learning scenarios.

This book contains a number of completely different questions on how one can approach the production of hypertexts in research and development as well as a few answers. At the same time, it becomes clear that this is a research and development program that is only just beginning. In line with this, the final chapter discusses potential methods for further research.

Elmar Stahl presents three groups of "Methods for Assessing Cognitive Processes During the Construction of Hypertexts": analysis of observable production steps; assessing verbal data through the thinking-aloud or retrospection method; and authors' self-ratings during the construction process through a computer-assisted assessment. Naturally, these methods can be traced back to those developed for analyzing traditional writing and other cognitive performances. Nonetheless, the category systems for coding observable activities and protocolling thinking aloud are specific to hypertext production. The categories proposed here have proved their worth in several research projects (Bromme & Stahl, 2002; Stahl, 2001), and they can be used as a starting point when putting together specific category systems for further studies.

Author Note

We wish to thank Johanna Hohmeister, Julia Rottmann and Marc Stadtler for editorial assistance and Jonathan Harrow for native-speaker advice.

References

Bereiter, C., & Scardamalia, M. (1987). *The Psychology of Written Composition*. Hillsdale, NJ: Erlbaum.

Bromme, R., Nückles, M., & Rambow, R. (1999). Adaptivity and anticipation in expert-laypeople communication. In: S. E. Brennan, A. Giboin, and D. Traum (eds), *Psychological Models of Communication in Collaborative Systems. AAAI Fall Symposium Series*. Menlo Park, CA: AAAI.

Bromme, R., & Stahl, E. (1999). Spatial metaphors and writing hypertexts: Studies within schools. *European Journal of Psychology of Education, 14*, 267–281.

Bromme, R., & Stahl, E. (2002). Is a hypertext a book or a space? Metaphorical introductions for learning through hypertext writing. (*Manuscript, submitted for publication*).

Clark, H. H. (1996). *Using Language*. Cambridge: University Press.

Dillon, A., & Gabbard, R. (1998). Hypermedia as an educational technology: A review of the quantitative research literature on learner comprehension, control, and style. *Review of Educational Research, 68*, 322–349.

Eigler, G. (1997). Textproduktion als konstruktiver Prozeß [Text production as a cognitive process]. In: F. E. Weinert (ed.), *Psychologie des Unterrichts und der Schule* [Psychology of instruction and of schools]. *Enzyklopädie der Psychologie, Serie Pädagogische Psychologie* [Encyclopedia of psychology, educational psychology series], Vol. 3 (pp. 365–394). Göttingen: Hogrefe.

Foltz, P. W. (1996). Comprehension, coherence, and strategies in hypertext and linear text. In: J.-F. Rouet, J. J. Levonen, A. Dillon, and R. J. Spiro (eds), *Hypertext and Cognition* (pp. 109–136). Mahwah, NJ: Erlbaum.

Gibson, J. (1982). *Wahrnehmung und Umwelt* [Perception and environment]. München: Urban & Schwarzenberg.

Hayes, J. R. (1996). A new framework for understanding cognition and affect in writing. In: C. M. Levy, and S. Ransdell (eds), *The Science of Writing: Theories, Methods, Individual Differences, and Applications* (pp. 1–27). Mahwah, NJ: Erlbaum.

Hayes, J. R., & Flower, L. S. (1980). Identifying the organisation of writing processes. In: L. W. Gregg, and E. R. Steinberg (eds), *Cognitive Processes in Writing* (pp. 3–30). Mahwah, NJ.: Erlbaum.

Jacobson, M. J., & Spiro, R. J. (1995). Hypertext learning environments, cognitive flexibility, and the transfer of complex knowledge: An empirical investigation. *Journal of Educational Computing Research, 12*, 301–333.

Jucks, I. (2001). *Was verstehen Laien? Die Verständlichkeit von Fachtexten aus der Sicht von Computer-Experten* [What do laypersons understand? The intelligibility of specialist texts from the perspective of computer experts]. Münster: Waxmann.

Landow, G. P. (1994). What's a critic to do? Critical theory in the age of hypertext. In: G. P. Landow (ed.), *Hyper/Text/Theory* (pp. 1–48). London: Johns Hopkins.

Kintsch, W. (1998). *Comprehension: A Paradigm for Cognition.* New York: Cambridge University Press.

Kintsch, W., & van Dijk, T. A. (1978). Toward a model of text comprehension and production. *Psychological Review, 85*, 363–394.

Rouet, J.-F., & Levonen, J. J. (1996). Studying and learning with hypertext: Empirical studies and their implications. In: J.-F. Rouet, J. J. Levonen, A. Dillon, and R. J. Spiro (eds), *Hypertext and Cognition* (pp. 9–23). Mahwah, NJ: Erlbaum.

Schnotz, W. (1994). *Aufbau von Wissensstrukturen. Untersuchungen zur Kohärenzbildung beim Wissenserwerb mit Texten.* [Acquisition of knowledge structures. Studies on the formation of coherence during knowledge acquisition with texts]. Weinheim, Germany: Beltz.

Schober, M. F. (1998). Different kinds of conversational perspective-taking. In: S. R. Fussell and R. J. Kreuz (eds), *Social and Cognitive Approaches to Interpersonal Communication* (pp. 154–174). Mahwah, NJ: Erlbaum.

Spiro, R. J., Feltovich, P. J., Jacobson, M. J., & Coulson, R. L. (1991). Cognitive flexibility, constructivism and hypertext: Random access instruction for advanced knowledge acquisition in ill-structured domains. *Educational Technology, 31*, 24–33.

Stahl, E. (2001). *Hyper-Text-Schreiben. Die Auswirkungen verschiedener Instruktionen auf Lernprozesse beim Schreiben von Hypertext* [Writing-Hyper-Text. The impact of different instructions on learning by writing hypertext]. Münster: Waxmann.

Torrance, M. (1996). Is writing expertise like other kinds of expertise? In: G. Rijlaarsdam, H. van den Bergh, and M. Couzijn (eds), *Theories, Models and Methodology in Writing Research* (pp. 3–9). Amsterdam: Amsterdam University Press.

Traxler, M. J., & Gernsbacher, M. A. (1993). Improving written communication through perspective-taking. *Language and Cognitive Processes, 8*, 311–334.

Chapter 2

Learning to Compose Hypertext and Linear Text: Transfer or Interference?

Martine A. H. Braaksma, Gert Rijlaarsdam, Michel Couzijn, and Huub van den Bergh

The aim of this study was to identify a set of cognitive activities involved in the writing of hypertext by secondary school students. We also tried to determine the extent to which writing hypertext is different from writing linear texts. We focused on the most central, distinctive features of linear and hypertext writing. For linear text writing, this is a *linearization* process, for hypertext writing, this is a *hierarchicalization* process.

Results showed that processes dominated by Planning and Analysis are effective in writing hypertexts and linear texts, and that these processes occur more frequently in hypertext writing than in linear writing. We concluded that the inclusion of hypertext writing in school curricula may have a positive effect on the quality of linear text writing.

Introduction

Although hypertext is not a new phenomenon, it is fairly new in schools. The present use of hypertext in Dutch secondary schools is restricted to reading and information-gathering activities: for example, students use hypertexts when they accomplish study tasks for a variety of school subjects, when searching on the Internet, and when cutting and pasting articles and pictures. In most cases they present their findings in writing in a traditional, linear format. In some cases, they are stimulated to present their findings orally, using the blackboard, overhead transparencies, or presentation software such as PowerPoint for visual support.

The use of the information and communication technology has recently become part of the official curriculum in the Netherlands, and has been defined in so-called attainment targets and exam requirements[1] (Basisvorming, 1998–2003; Examen-programma Nederlands, 1998). Just as the media (i.e. radio, television, film) were adopted for classroom use some time after they had become familiar to students at home, we can now expect not only that students will use hypertexts, but that they will

Writing Hypertext and Learning: Conceptual and Empirical Approaches
Copyright © 2002 by Elsevier Science Ltd.
All rights of reproduction in any form reserved.
ISBN: 0-08-043987-X

[Footnote 1 appears on p. 16]

also have to learn about hypertext features and structures. Another route along which hypertext is being introduced to schools is in the design of the learning environment: more learning activities are currently taking place within hypertext environments, or even hypermedia environments. For this reason, attention might be focused on hypertext learning in classroom instruction.

In the recent years, user-friendly technology and software for the production and publication of hypertext have become available. We therefore expect that, within the next few years, writing hypertexts will become part of official school curricula. The question is how this branch of communication should be treated in classrooms. Is hypertext writing a totally new skill, one that may be related to other communication skills, but which is different nonetheless? Can we build upon these related skills? Or should we devote so much learning time to writing hypertext, that regular skills, such as writing skills, will be given less time than they need? Are we on the verge of a new "curriculum war," in which traditional skills have to "pay" for the new skills?

Not much research is available about the nature of hypertext writing. While there are some studies on the pedagogy of hypertext writing (e.g. Russell, 1998), most try to identify the learning effects of hypertext learning environments. In such cases, hypertext is used as an independent variable in the research design, not as a dependent variable. For instance, a study by Lohr *et al.* (1995) evaluated a hypertext model for teaching writing at junior high and high school levels, that elicited reactions to features embedded in the design (model stories, note cards, cut-and-paste-tools, etc.). The results varied greatly according to teachers' beliefs, and according to students and programme features.

Jacobson and Spiro (1995) studied the effects of a hypertextual learning environment, and found strong effects on certain transfer tasks. These studies tend to favor hypertextual learning environments. However, in a recent review of experimental studies of hypermedia learning environments, Dillon and Gabbard conclude that the

---

[1] Attainment targets and exam requirements of Dutch education with a reference to information technology and the use of hypertext:

K7–9, all levels (12–15 y.). The student:

- should be able to use information and communication technology (ICT) in order to process texts, collect information from databases, and communicate through networks;
- should be able to use text-processing programs for writing, revising, and formatting text.

K10–12, intermediate and high levels (16–18 y.). The student:

- should be able to collect information from texts, hypertexts, data, video and audio in (multimedia) files, databases, and information retrieval systems using a computer network;
- should be able to use automated retrieval systems in libraries and media collections;
- should be able to prepare (multimedia) presentations;
- should be able to collect, order, and formulate relevant content elements for oral presentations, using written, oral and audiovisual sources, including sources that must be approached by means of ICT;
- should be able to select, develop, and order relevant content elements from given and/or collected information, for the purpose of writing texts; the student may use written, oral and audiovisual sources, including sources that must be approached by means of ICT;
- should be able to use the potential of ICT — including text processing and telecommunication — for the purpose of formulating, revising, and presenting text;
- should be able to collect and select relevant background information about literary texts, using written, oral and audio-visual sources, including sources that must be approached by means of ICT.

effects of hypermedia are limited to tasks in which learners search for and manipulate information, and that the distribution of these effects differs across learners according to their ability level and learning style preferences (Dillon & Gabbard, 1998).

Not many studies address the cognitive strategies involved in learning in hypertext environments. Rouet (1994) has reported on two studies in which students searched through hypertext in order to answer various types of study questions. These activities significantly improved students' domain knowledge. Rouet's conclusion is that even inexperienced students may benefit from hypertext-based learning activities, but that the efficient use of hypertext requires specific cognitive skills. However, in another study he found no differential effect between studying hypertext and studying documents presented in a linear format (Britt *et al.*, 1996).

The aim of the present study is to identify a set of cognitive activities involved in the writing of hypertext by secondary school students. We also try to determine the extent to which writing hypertext is different from writing linear texts. There is a growing body of knowledge about the cognitive processes involved in writing (see edited volumes by Levy & Ransdell, 1996; Rijlaarsdam *et al.*, 1996). A variety of methods are being used to model the architecture of the writing process and its subprocesses. Alamargot and Chanquoy's (2001) review of the writing models — starting from the well-known model by Hayes and Flower — provide a rich insight into the progress made.

Our present analysis is based on research that we conducted previously in the same age group (about 14–15). In these studies we modeled students' writing processes empirically, using writing-aloud protocols, that we analyzed with an extensive coding scheme grounded in the Hayes and Flower model (1980). We identified the cognitive activities involved in several stages of the writing process. By relating these processes to the resulting text quality — essay scores — we identified more and less effective distributions of these cognitive activities across the process (for an overall study, see Breetvelt *et al.*, 1994; for the process of structuring, see Rijlaarsdam & van den Bergh, 1996; van den Bergh & Rijlaarsdam, 1996; for re-reading, see Breetvelt *et al.*, 1994; for several content generation processes, see van den Bergh & Rijlaarsdam, 1999; and for goal orientation, see van den Bergh & Rijlaarsdam, 2001).

Our present study of hypertext writing processes does not progress beyond a very basic level. In it, we compare the processes of two types of tasks that are not "natural" writing tasks, but which are constructed to elicit basic common activities in linear and hypertext writing. The choice of these tasks was based on a global analysis of hypertext writing in comparison of linear text writing (see next section). Furthermore, we try to identify writing processes of so-called "good novices," i.e. to establish which cognitive activities performed by secondary students are closely linked to higher end quality in linear and hypertext writing. This analysis may help us to detect the qualitative relationship between the two ways of writing, and the extent to which hypertext writing facilitates or hinders the development of linear writing, and vice versa.

It usually takes considerable time and effort for students to build up some expertise in the writing of linear texts. Similarly, it takes a long while to develop from an associative writer (as described in Bereiter and Scardamalia's "knowledge telling" model) into a writer who is able to restructure, build and convey knowledge during the writing process (Bereiter and Scardamalia's "knowledge transforming" model, 1987).

A significant problem for writers of this age is to write argumentative texts, which require them to present a network of linked ideas in a linear text — the problem being that the network is often unconscious, and is generated associatively rather than hierarchically (Coirier *et al.*, 1999). During the composing process, students develop (and re-develop) this network, and have to learn to signal the hierarchy in the linear text, for example by verbal markers and paragraphing. In doing so, they help their readers to understand the text, as it is the reader's task to deconstruct the linear text into an underlying hierarchical information structure (van Dijk & Kintsch, 1983).

Hypertext writing also requires a well-developed sense of structure. It relies heavily on the ordering and connecting of ideas (whether generated from memory or from elsewhere); in the case of written sources, it often requires a deconstruction of traditional, linearly presented information. In order to arrive at a well-constructed hypertext, an underlying hierarchical information structure needs to be established first. If there is a sound underlying hierarchy, the composing process for hypertext is more likely to succeed. In this sense, a requirement for composing hypertext is to make an in-depth analysis of the hierarchy without thinking in linear formats, and to structure the text in a *hierarchical* rather than *linear* fashion. Learning to compose hypertext may therefore help students become aware of hierarchical text structures. Paradoxically, this may in its turn contribute to their skill in composing linear texts, for which a hierarchical information structure also serves a good starting point.

The writing tasks we assigned to the students capitalized on two key cognitive processes. To approach linear text writing, we chose *linearization* as the key-process, i.e. converting a hierarchical network of ideas or statements into a linear text. To approach the gist of hypertext writing, we chose *hierarchicalization* as a central process, i.e. converting a linearly presented line of thoughts into a hierarchical network of ideas or statements. In our view, this activity is particularly important for the composition of hypertext.

This study may help us to understand some of the key difficulties students must overcome when they are learning to compose hypertext. We present a process analysis on the ways in which novices compose and analyze small argumentative texts. Our data analysis focuses on relationships between process variables and product quality, so that questions such as "which writing activities contribute more, and which less, to the quality of the resulting text?" can be answered. Understanding of these relationships will underlie a validated instructional design for composing hypertext.

Hypertext and Linear Text: A Global Analysis of Cognitive Activities

A significant problem in text composition is the linearization process (Coirier, 1996; Coirier *et al.*, 1999). Students develop their ideas, chiefly following associative paths. Next, one or more structuring processes may follow (see Figure 2.1).

Structuring involves clustering and ordering these ideas (Hayes & Flower, 1980; for an extensive review, see Alamargot & Chanquoy, 2001). Hayes and Flower described four relationships between ideas: *direct* ("Order with respect to a previously

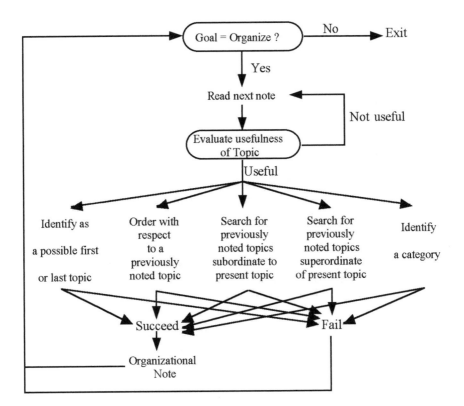

Figure 2.1: Framework for the sub-process "Organizing", adapted from Hayes and Flower (1980). Copyright © 1980 by Lawrence Erlbaum Associates. Adapted with permission.

noted topic"), *subordinated* ("Search for previously noted topics subordinate to present topic"), *superordinated* ("Search for previously noted topics superordinate to present topic"), or *hierarchically categorize* ("Identify a category").

Structuring is an important sub-process. As Rijlaarsdam and van den Bergh showed, it directly affects the final quality of argumentative texts (Rijlaarsdam & van den Bergh, 1996). However, structuring is also particularly difficult. There are in fact two types of structuring, one type following the other. First, to arrive at a writing plan, students must determine the structural relationships in a network of ideas. Next, they must transform this structure into a linear form (that is: into a logically and verbally coherent sequence), while still providing their readers with information on and explanations of their hierarchical structure — for instance, by using connectors and other structure markers. (This route is presented in Figure 2.2: starting at the bottom from the associative network of ideas, and moving via the writing plan to the upper left hand corner, where the writing process results in a linear text.) A reader of such linear text will have to deconstruct the linear form to form a hierarchy of connected ideas (resembling a hypertext: the upper right hand corner box). If the communication is without bias, this mental representation will successfully reflect the network of ideas with which the writer started.

In many instances, however, writers do not succeed in communicating their hierarchy of ideas to the reader without a certain measure of distortion. One possible cause of this is the necessary linearity of a text. Because ideas have to be sequenced in a linear way — with a succession of words, sentences, ideas and themes — and because content is generated in an associative fashion, writers tend to produce their texts via a "shortcut" route: in other words, ideas are written in the same order as that in which the writers generated them, without much re-structuring or re-ordering into a coherent writing plan.

One of the difficulties in teaching writing is to offer alternatives to this "shortcut" route, and to teach students to rework their ideas into a writing plan (whether mental or written), and then to teach the linearization process, i.e. to show students how they can sequence ideas in a linear fashion, and how they can use textual signs to guide readers in their process of reconstruction and regeneration, when the text can be converted into a hierarchical network of ideas. It may be decided to teach this process once students have achieved a writing plan.

What happens when students use the same network of ideas as a basis for writing a hypertext? They will again transform the network of ideas into a writing plan, by

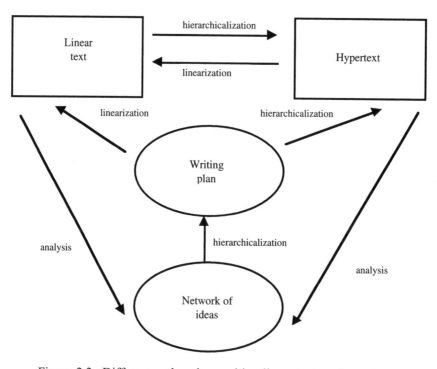

Figure 2.2: Different paths when writing linear texts or hypertexts.

articulating and structuring these ideas. But this time, the hypertext or "end product" may resemble the writing plan much more closely than it would when they were writing a linear text. When guided by the goal of producing a hypertext, the process of structuring textual units may remain more "natural". It is obvious that ideas still need to be clustered, and that some ideas, or clusters of ideas, will be subordinated, and others superordinated, and yet others co-ordinated. Thus, the process of clustering and relating ideas will remain a necessary step.

In the light of this analysis, the introduction of hypertext writing in schools raises a number of questions. From an educational perspective, one may ask whether the inclusion of such tasks inhibits or facilitates "normal", i.e. linear text writing. If students write more hypertexts and fewer linear texts, the influence of the lower number of linearization exercises may become noticeable. On the other hand, when students write hypertexts they will not be able to use the "shortcut" route, but will have to transform their associative ideas into some hierarchy of ideas, and this hierarchy of ideas into an apparent textual hierarchy. In this sense, they will spend more learning time on structuring information.

We thus have two contrasting potential effects of learning to write hypertext. So, will writing hypertext facilitate or hinder linear text writing? Most transfer theories would suggest that this will depend on the cognitive activities involved in these writing processes, and on whether students will perceive these activities to be similar. If they do consider them to be similar, transfer is more likely to occur.

In order to shed some light on the relationship between linear and hypertext writing, we set up a study, which was underlain by two questions:

1) To what extent is the writing of hypertext a new activity that needs to be learnt?
2) Does exercise in hypertext writing facilitate or interfere with writing linear texts?

Concerning the second question, we will address the issue whether hypertext writing helps students to unlearn the writing of linear texts via the "shortcut" route.

In our study, we focused on the most central, distinctive features of linear and hypertext writing. For linear text writing, this is the *linearization process*: i.e. transforming (subordinated, superordinated and co-ordinated) elements of the writing plan into linear text. For hypertext writing, the central feature is a *hierarchicalization process*: i.e. transforming into a hierarchical structure ideas that result from a generating process and are presented in a linear fashion. The following section describes in more detail the tasks we implemented in this study.

Method

We studied the writing processes of secondary students, each of whom wrote two short linear texts and made two short hierarchical schemes. Details of the method are provided below.

Participants

In total, 123 students participated in the study. One group of participants consisted of 69 students taken from twelve different groups in a multicultural school in Amsterdam. Their grade was K8, and their average age 14. From each class, the teacher selected the six most verbally skilled students for participation in the study. Another group of participants consisted of 54 students drawn from five different schools in the Amsterdam region. Their grade was K9, and their average age 15. All participants in this study took part on a volunteer basis; it was fully understood that the results of the study would not be part of the regular testing procedures at their schools.

Tasks

Students were asked to think aloud while solving two linearization tasks and two hierarchicalization tasks. A linearization task consisted of transforming a given argumentation scheme into a linear argumentative text. A hierarchicalization task consisted of transforming a given linear argumentative text into an argumentation scheme. In each case, students completed first a simpler task, and then a more complex task. No feedback was provided. Figure 2.3 shows a sample linearization task, and Figure 2.4 a sample hierarchicalization task. Argumentative texts were chosen because of the overt hierarchical relations between standpoint and arguments.

Task   Write a short argumentative text based on the following argumentation scheme. Make sure a reader understands the standpoint and arguments in your text.

Scheme

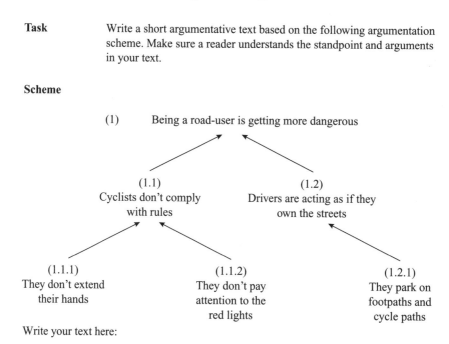

Write your text here:

Figure 2.3: Linearization task (traffic).

Task	Below you will find a short argumentative text. You are asked to draw the argumentation scheme of that text. Remember to put the text and the arrows in the right place.
Text	The dollar is considerably below the two guilders, thus it has a favorable exchange rate. Also on the moment, airplane tickets are very inexpensive. And the climate is also very nice, the temperature is approximately 20 degrees and there is hardly any rain. In short, it is a good moment to spend our holidays in the United States.

Figure 2.4: Hierarchicalization task (dollar).

Scores

Think-aloud protocols were typed, fragmented and scored. For scoring we used categories adapted from an instrument used in our previous writing process studies (Breetvelt *et al*., 1994; Breetvelt *et al*., 1994; van den Bergh *et al*., 1994; Rijlaarsdam & van den Bergh, 1996; van den Bergh & Rijlaarsdam, 1996, 1999, 2001). The categories used were Goal Orientation, Planning, Analysis, Pausing, Formulating, Writing, Evaluation, Re-reading, Revision, and Meta-Analysis. Most of the categories used for the analysis of the think-aloud protocols speak for themselves. However, as three — Analysis, Planning and Meta-Analysis — are more complex, we will briefly illustrate them here.

Analysis   This category is used when the student analyses the argumentation structure of the text or the scheme, labelling elements as standpoints, arguments, and so forth. For example: "Y is the standpoint." This utterance is coded as *Analysis*, as the student labels a fragment from the text or the scheme as a concept taken from argumentation theory.

Planning   Planning is used when an element indicates local planning. In other words, the student plans a step in the process, usually on the basis of an argumentation scheme (in which, for example, argumentation will follow an initial standpoint statement). The student coaches himself through the task, usually by uttering a temporal indication: "First I will . . .," "Then I must . . .," and "Now I'm going to . . . ." For example: "First, I'll start with the first argument." This phrase indicates that the student is probably using a known task scheme to perform the task.

Meta-Analysis   Meta-Analysis is used for a broad category of fragments in which the student monitors and regulates task execution: e.g. when stopping the process for some reason; when re-generating information on how to handle this kind of task (i.e. when generating the procedures); when making a remark on the level of difficulty of the task; or when remarking on his or her own ability. Problem definition, problem solution and checking the solution are also coded as Meta-Analysis.

Examples
   "OK, let's see whether I've included all the sentences."
   (On the last part of a task): . . . "So, now I've done all the arguments."
   "First, I'll read through the whole text."
   ". . . This is rather a difficult one . . . ."

We also scored the quality of the output of the writing processes: the argumentative texts and argumentation schemes. The output scores were obtained by coding the resulting texts and argumentation schemes on the aspects completeness, logical order, and use of connectives (or connecting arrows). A few weeks later, the students performed similar tasks under normal (i.e. non think-aloud) conditions. The quality of these tasks was also scored. Thus, in total we acquired four think-aloud protocols from each student, plus the quality scores of the resulting products, and quality scores of products from four similar tasks administered under "normal" conditions.

Two Illustrations

It is useful at this point to illustrate the tasks and the way in which the protocols were coded. The first example below (see Figure 2.5) shows a hierarchicalization task, in which the student reads a short text fragment in which several arguments and a standpoint are given. The task involves turning the information elements into a hierarchical argumentation structure (see Figure 2.4). By following the thinking-aloud protocol, the particular approach taken by this student becomes clear. The codes we used to describe the steps in the thinking process are noted in the second column.

This example shows a student who first analyses the standpoint, arguments and subordinate arguments (showing that he knows and identifies the ingredients), and then starts drawing the argumentation scheme, moving step by step, following an "internal plan."

The second example (see Figure 2.6) shows the execution of a linearization task. Here, the student is presented with a hierarchical argumentation scheme on paper (see Figure 2.3), which he has to transform into normal, linear text. The writing strategy of this student can be followed via the coded activities in the second column.

The student in this example first analyses the different ingredients of the argumentation scheme (standpoint, arguments, and subordinate arguments). Next, he thinks about the place he will put the standpoint. Deciding to end with it, he then writes the entire text without mentioning the ingredients until he comes to the standpoint. At that point, he plans the standpoint and writes it down.

Utterance in writing aloud process	Cognitive activity
The dollar is considerably below the two guilders, thus it has a favorable exchange rate. Also at the moment, airplane tickets are very inexpensive. And the climate is also very nice, the temperature is approximately 20 degrees and there is hardly any rain. In short, it is a good moment to spend our holidays in the United States	Reads text
Uhm, standpoint is	Analyzes standpoint
That we should go to the United States of America	Formulates standpoint before writing
Uhm, thus a couple of pro arguments	Analyzes arguments
The dollar has a favorable exchange rate	Formulates argument before writing
The climate is also very nice	Formulates argument before writing
The tickets are very inexpensive	Formulates argument before writing
And then two subordinate arguments	Plans subordinate arguments
The dollar is considerably below the two guilders	Analyzes subordinate argument
The temperature is approximately 20 degrees and there is hardly rain	Analyzes subordinate arguments
Thus, the standpoint	Plans standpoint
We should go to the United States of America	Formulates standpoint while writing
First argument is	Plans first argument
The dollar has a favorable exchange rate	Formulates argument while writing
That has a subordinate argument	Plans subordinate argument
The dollar is considerably below the two guilders	Formulates subordinate argument while writing
Uhm, and then there is another argument	Plans compound argumentation
The tickets are very inexpensive	Analyzes argument
The tickets are very inexpensive	Formulates argument while writing
And then the third argument	Plans compound argumentation
The climate is also very nice	Analyzes argument
The climate is also very nice	Formulates argument while writing
And two subordinate arguments	Plans subordinate arguments
The temperature is approximately 20 degrees	Analyzes subordinate argument
and	Formulates while writing
there is hardly rain	Formulates subordinate argument while writing
So, this is it	Stops/starts new cognitive activity

Figure 2.5: Example thinking-aloud protocol (dollar, hierarchicalization task).

Utterance in writing aloud process	Cognitive activity
Task.	Reads task
The standpoint is.	Analyzes standpoint
Being a road-user is getting more dangerous.	Reads scheme
Argument 1.1 is cyclists do not comply with the rules and that is because the cyclists don't extend their hands and cyclists don't pay attention to the red lights.	Analyzes arguments and subordinate arguments
And the argument 1.2 is drivers are acting if they own the streets and that is because the drivers park on footpath and cycle path.	Analyzes arguments and subordinate arguments
And now I am thinking if I will first take the argument and then the standpoint.	Plans
Then, it must be thus.	Analyzes connective
Cyclists do not comply with the rules.	Formulates before writing
Because they don't extend their hands.	Formulates argument before writing
Extend their hands.	Formulates subordinate argument while writing
And they don't pay attention to the red lights.	Formulates subordinate argument while writing
Further, drivers are acting if they own the streets because they park on footpath and cycle path.	Formulates argument and subordinate argument before writing
Further, drivers are acting if they own the streets because they park on footpath and cycle path.	Formulates argument and subordinate argument while writing
And then the standpoint.	Plans standpoint
Thus, being a road-user is getting more dangerous.	Analyzes standpoint
Thus, being a road-user is getting more dangerous.	Formulates standpoint while writing
Oke.	Stops/starts new cognitive activity

Figure 2.6: Example thinking-aloud protocol (traffic, linearization task).

Analyses

Test scores were obtained for the quality of the products, i.e. both for the lineariza-tion and the hierarchicalization tasks, and related to thinking processes, by calculating the correlations between quality scores and frequencies of writing sub-processes.

In order to answer question (1) (i.e. on the extent to which linear text writing and hypertext writing rely on the same cognitive activities) we compared the frequencies and proportions of cognitive activities for these two types of writing. Differences in sub-process frequencies and in the quantitative balance of these activities would reveal the ways in which the hypertext writing process differs from the linear writing process. Next, in order to establish which specific writing activities contribute most to "good hypertext writing" (i.e. rather than to "good linear writing"), we analyzed the relationship between process frequencies and the resulting text quality.

The second research question addressed the issue of transfer or inhibition between linear and hypertext writing. We answered this question by correlating sub-process frequencies for linearization tasks with quality measures of the "mirror tasks" (hierarchicalization). Similarly, we correlated sub-process frequencies for hierarchicalization tasks with quality measures of linearization tasks. Positive correlations are indicative of transfer of sub-processes.

Results

Processes in Text Writing and Hypertext Writing

Figure 2.7 shows the frequencies of the cognitive activities, as coded in the protocols, and distributed across writing tasks.

Figure 2.7 reveals that, on the whole, the hypertext writing tasks seemed to elicit more occurrences of various sub-processes than linear writing tasks did, even though, in structural terms, the tasks mirrored each other in argumentative complexity. Another observation is that on the whole, the metacognitive activities of Planning, Goal Orientation and Meta-Analysis are low-frequency activities,[2] although in hypertext writing the frequency is higher than in linear text writing. A modus effect was observed for all cognitive activities except Re-reading, revealing that hypertext writing elicits significantly more activities. An effect of task difficulty was also found: unsurprisingly, the more difficult task required a higher number of cognitive activities than the easier task. From Figure 2.7 we may therefore conclude that, while hypertext writing and linear text writing rely on the same set of cognitive activities, hypertext writing requires a different quantitative balance of these activities.

A second step in the search for similarities and differences between hypertext writing and linear text writing is to study the "arrangement" of the cognitive processes involved. The question is not just whether hypertext writing results in more cognitive activities, but whether the cognitive activities relate to each other in a different way than they do in linear text writing. An indication of such differences can be found when we compare the proportions of the cognitive activities. Table 2.1 shows the differences in relative occurrences of cognitive activities between linear text writing and hypertext writing.

Although the hypertext and linear writing tasks were similar in structural complexity, the role played by Goal Orientation, Planning, Analysis and Meta-Analysis

---

[2] The activity Revision occurred so rarely that we have neglected it altogether in this study.

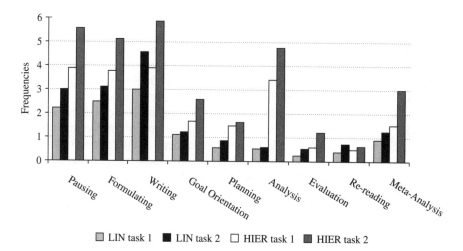

Figure 2.7: Task effects on the occurrence of cognitive activities of two types of tasks (LIN=linearization and HIER=hierarchicalization) and two levels of complexity (1 and 2).

was larger in the hypertext writing process, while linear text writing was defined by relatively more Writing and Re-reading activities. From a cognitive perspective, these differences are interesting. They suggest that metacognitive activities which are known to influence the quality of the writing product (e.g. Planning and Goal Orientation) are stimulated in hypertext writing. These metacognitive activities have been found to be important in carrying out complex tasks, as they guide task execution.

The question then arises of the extent to which these cognitive activities are related to the quality of the end product, i.e. the resulting text for a linear writing task,

Table 2.1: Relative occurrences of cognitive activities in hypertext writing and linear text writing (tested with logit scores).

Cognitive activities	Linear writing task	Hypertext writing task
Pausing		
Formulating		
Writing	+	
Goal Orientation		+
Planning		+
Analysis		+
Evaluation		
Re-reading	+	
Meta-Analysis		+

or the resulting hierarchical scheme for a hypertext writing task. The following section therefore shows whether or not there is a positive link between a higher frequency of a particular cognitive activity and the quality of the end product.

Profiles of Good Novices (Processes and the Quality of the End Product)

For the students in this study, writing hypertexts was a new task. In order to formulate a set of empirically based instructions for students, we wanted to know how "good novices" performed their task: in other words, we wanted to understand the mechanisms whereby certain students perform new tasks better than others.

For this reason, we will now compare the performance of two groups of students on two tasks. We will then present correlations between processes and texts.

Differences between Good and Weak Novices   Here, we present the result of an item in one of the hierarchicalization tasks. A decisive step in transforming a short argumentative text into a hierarchy is to identify the standpoint in the text. In both hierarchicalization tasks the problem was similar: in other words, while non-marked texts started with the standpoint, the standpoint in this case was somewhat hidden. For this reason, it was not possible for our students to work in a linear fashion by stating (for example), "The first statement in the text is always the standpoint, then I'll have an argument, etc." Instead, if — like most students — they decided to use a top-down approach to establishing the hierarchy, they first had to search the text for the standpoint. To distinguish activities that contribute to good hypertext writing, we divided the whole group into two parts: students who succeeded in identifying the standpoint correctly (55 percent) (the "good novices"), and those who did not (44 percent) (the "weak novices").

For both groups, the distribution of proportions follows more or less the same pattern (see Figure 2.8). However, "good novices" Planned and Analyzed significantly more. This finding indicates the importance of Analysis and Planning in effective hypertext

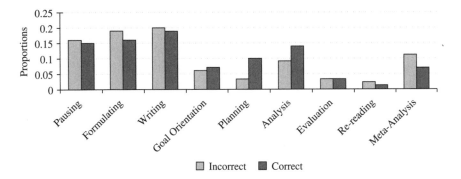

Figure 2.8: Hierarchicalization task. Differences between good and weak novices regarding writing sub-process frequencies (proportional).

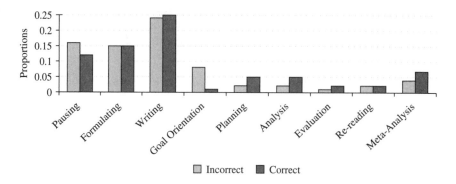

Figure 2.9: Linearization task. Differences between good and weak students regarding writing sub-process frequencies (proportional).

writing. As we have already seen in Table 2.1, students writing hypertext generally pay greater attention to Planning and Analysis. To this, we can now add that such students gained better results, or solved the hierarchicalization problem better.

In the linearization task, one of the most difficult items was to fit the subordinated argument from the hierarchical structure into the linear text. When, once again, we divide the group into two score groups on the basis of this item, we find that significantly higher proportions of Planning and Analysis coincide with better problem solving, i.e. better linear texts (see Figure 2.9).

In conclusion, we found that "good novices" in both hypertext writing and linear writing paid more attention to Planning and Analysis activities. If we consider this in the light of our previous finding that hypertext writing generally relies more on Planning and Analysis activities than does linear writing (see Table 2.1, above), we are inclined to conclude that learning to write hypertext may transfer more to linear writing than the other way around.

Correlational Perspective   In the preceding section we presented the proportions of processes which are related to correct outcomes of certain problems regarding hierarchicalization and linearization. We saw that solving difficult problems was related to proportions of Planning and Analysis. In Figure 2.7 and Table 2.1, we showed that these processes were more often found in hypertext writing tasks than in linear writing tasks. Taken together, these findings suggest that hypertext writing supports linear text writing, and that hypertext writing provides better and more natural opportunities to practice these cognitive activities.

To back up this claim with data, we correlated the occurrences of cognitive activities with the quality score for the resulting products. Product quality is defined as the extent to which the resulting text represented the original argumentation scheme (in linear text writing), or the scheme represented the original text (in hypertext writing). We coded according to strict criteria. For instance, when writing linear texts, the students had to use explicit connectives to connect the standpoint with the sub-ordinated arguments. If they connected a standpoint with an argument by using a comma, this was coded as incorrect.

As well as the direct relationship between a certain process and the quality of the resulting product, we wanted to assess the relationship between process activities and the quality of the resulting products of similar tasks under normal circumstances (i.e. no think-aloud conditions). When the frequency of a process activity is related to the quality of a product under normal conditions, the think-aloud condition no longer offers an alternative explanation for the observed relationship. To avoid possible effects of task content, a fully counterbalanced design was used: half of the students first performed task A, and performed task B three weeks later. The other half first performed task B, and performed task A three weeks later.

Table 2.2 presents the significance of correlations between cognitive activities in linear text writing and the resulting products ($p < 0.05$). The dominant finding shown in Table 2.2 is the positive correlation between Analysis and the resulting products, and the negative correlation between Formulating and these products. If the writing arrangement was dominated by the Analysis sub-process, the student produced better texts; however if the Formulating sub-process dominated, this resulted in weaker texts. Those relationships appear to be stable. When we correlated sub-processes during the writing-aloud sessions with the quality of a text written three weeks later, the relationship between the proportion of Analysis activities and linear text quality still proved to be both significant and positive. We conclude from Table 2.2 that, unlike the Formulating sub-process, Analysis plays an important part in effective linear writing tasks.

Table 2.2: Linear writing tasks. Significance of correlations between cognitive activities (proportions: logit scores) and the quality of the resulting product.

Cognitive activity	Linear writing task effect		Linear writing stability effect	
	Simple task	Complex task	Simple task	Complex task
Pausing				
Formulating		−		−
Writing	+			
Goal Orientation				
Planning			+	
Analysis	+		+	
Evaluation				−
Re-reading				
Meta-Analysis	+			

Table 2.3: Hypertext writing tasks. Significance of correlations between cognitive activities (proportions: logit scores) and the quality of the resulting product.

Cognitive activity	Hypertext writing Task effect		Hypertext writing Stability effect	
	Simple task	Complex task	Simple task	Complex task
Pausing				
Formulating				
Writing				
Goal Orientation				+
Planning		+		+
Analysis	+		+	
Evaluation				
Re-reading	−			
Meta-Analysis				

Table 2.3 shows the significance of correlations between cognitive activities in the process of hypertext writing and the quality of the resulting products. The table shows once again that Analysis is an important activity: the more it is performed, the better the resulting argumentation scheme. The same is true for Planning. Both effects were found to be stable: the same correlations can be found when we correlate the sub-processes with quality data acquired three weeks later. On the other hand, writing performances that include a lot of Re-reading activities usually end up producing worse results.

In sum, we conclude that Analysis and Planning are the most important activities in writing linear texts and in writing hypertext. Students who arrange their writing process by including many Analysis and Planning activities have a better chance of producing not only good linear texts, but also good hierarchical texts.

Transfer

In the section "processes in text writing and hypertext writing" we have shown that the linear writing task and the hypertext writing task can be described with the same set of cognitive activities. This opens the way to transfer: if a particular subset of cognitive activities is effectively trained in one type of task, this subset is a candidate for transfer to different-but-similar tasks. In this case, the question is whether Analysis and Planning activities — which we found to be effective during hypertext writing — transfer to linear text writing, or whether there is a transfer in the opposite direction, i.e. from linear to hypertext writing.

Table 2.4: Transfer from linear writing to hypertext writing. Significance of correlations between cognitive activities during linear writing tasks and the quality of the resulting argumentation scheme in hypertext writing tasks.

Cognitive activity	Hypertext writing task effect		Hypertext writing stability effect	
	Simple task	Complex task	Simple task	Complex task
Pausing				
Formulating	−		−	
Writing				
Goal Orientation				
Planning				
Analysis	+	+	+	+
Evaluation				
Re-reading			+	
Meta-Analysis	+			

In Tables 2.4 and 2.5, we present the significance of correlations between cognitive activities in one task, and the effect on the products resulting from the "mirrored" task.

When we combine Tables 2.2 and 2.4, we see that Analysis is an effective cognitive activity in linear writing, with two positive results: it enhances the quality of linear texts, and shows a positive transfer effect on the quality of hypertexts. Linear writing process arrangements that include many Analysis activities have a better chance to lead to good linear texts, and to be a better preparation for writing hypertexts.

Table 2.5 shows that undertaking a relatively large number of Analysis and Planning activities during hypertext writing has a transfer effect on writing performance in linear texts.

In sum, when we use the relative attention paid to certain activities in linear text writing and hypertext writing as an indication of the way students arrange their writing sub-processes, we conclude the following: (a) that hypertext writing requires more Planning and Analysis; (b) that these activities have a positive effect on the quality of the resulting hypertext; (c) that this effect is stable across time; and (d) that these activities transfer to the performance of a mirror task: linear writing. Linear writing processes should therefore make much use of Analysis rather than of Formulating: it yields good linear texts and is a good preparation for hypertext writing. Our study shows that Analysis and Planning are the key activities in writing linear and hypertexts, at least regarding the type of writing tasks that were used in this experiment.

Table 2.5: Transfer from hypertext writing to linear writing. Significance of correlations between cognitive activities during hypertext writing tasks and the quality of the resulting linear text in linear writing.

Cognitive activity	Linear writing task effect		Linear writing stability effect	
	Simple task	Complex task	Simple task	Complex task
Pausing				
Formulating				
Writing				
Goal Orientation	+		−	
Planning	+			+
Analysis	+	+		
Evaluation				
Re-reading	−		−	
Meta-Analysis				

Discussion

At the start of this study, we asked two questions:

1) To what extent is the writing of hypertext a new activity that needs to be learnt?
2) Does exercise in writing hypertexts facilitate or interfere with writing linear texts?

In order to answer the first question, we used protocol analysis to show the overlap in cognitive activities between linear and hypertext writing. This analysis showed that linearization and hierarchicalization tasks both rely on a particular set of cognitive activities, i.e. Planning, Analysis, Pausing, Formulating, Writing, Goal Orientation, Evaluation, Meta-Analysis, and Re-reading. However, linearization relies more on Writing and Re-reading than does hierarchicalization (which is taken here to represent hypertext writing). On the other hand, hierarchicalization (hypertext writing) requires relatively more Analysis, Planning and metacognitive activities (such as Goal Orientation and Meta-Analysis) than linearization does. Hypertext writing, in other words, relies on the same set of cognitive activities, but asks for another arrangement of these activities. Students must learn to make this new arrangement in an effective way.

To gain insight into the processes that contribute to the quality of the resulting products (i.e. texts and argumentation schemes), we correlated the product scores with the frequency of each cognitive activity. Results show that students who *Planned* and *Analyzed* more often produced better schemes in the hierarchicalization (hypertext) tasks. For linearization tasks, we found that *Analysis* was positively correlated to the quality of the linear text, and that *Formulating* was negatively correlated. Both in the case of both hypertext and linear writing, it seems that successful writing is underlain by a thorough analysis of ideas or given content. It also appears that hypertext writing demands more long-term planning of the whole hierarchical text structure.

The second question addresses the transfer or interference effects of linear and hypertext writing. In order to understand these effects, we correlated the proportions of sub-process frequencies in linearization tasks with output quality scores of the hierarchicalization tasks, and vice versa. We found that students who *Planned* and *Analyzed* more often during hierarchicalization tasks performed better on the linearization tasks. Besides, students who paid relatively more attention to *Analysis* when producing a linear text, performed better on the hierarchicalization tasks. Since we know that Analysis is a beneficial activity for both linear and hypertext writing, we conclude that this activity may account for positive transfer between the two types of writing. Besides, the activity Planning seems to be a good candidate for transfer from hypertext writing to linear writing.

We may conclude that processes dominated by *Planning* and *Analysis* are effective in writing hypertexts and linear texts. If hypertext processes naturally require processes of this sort (Table 2.1), it is reasonable to suppose that the inclusion of hypertext writing in the school curriculum will also have a positive effect on the quality of linear text writing processes and their products. If students learn how to write hypertexts, it may help them to unlearn their habit of unplanned linear writing (i.e. generating associative content, and then producing text while formulating — what we have called the "shortcut" route). Experience with hypertext writing may help students to achieve better writing plans for both linear text and hypertext.

The exact influence of hypertext writing on linear writing has to be studied in more detail. In the present study we used short tasks to reveal certain relationships between key processes in hypertext writing (hierarchicalization) and in linear writing (linearization). One of the obvious limitations of this study was the use of such tasks, which, due to their limited focus on these key-processes, cannot fully represent a complete and natural writing process. Nevertheless, it seems that implementing hypertext writing in the curriculum does not interfere with linear writing, but supports it. Analysis and ordering ideas is important in linear writing, but it appears to be more often elicited in hypertext writing. Experimental studies in which hypertext writing is taught, and in which the effects on linear writing are studied, should support this claim.

References

Alamargot, D., & Chanquoy, L. (Vol. eds) (2001). Through the models of writing. In: G. Rijlaarsdam (Series ed.), *Studies in Writing: Vol. 9. Through the Models of Writing.* Dordrecht: Kluwer Academic Press.

Basisvorming (1998–2003). *Kerndoelen voor de basisvorming* [Attainment targets for basic secondary education]. Enschede: SLO.

Bereiter, C., & Scardamalia, M. (1987). *The Psychology of Written Composition.* Hillsdale, NJ: Lawrence Erlbaum.

Breetvelt, I., van den Bergh, H., & Rijlaarsdam, G. (1994). Relations between writing processes and text quality: When and how? *Cognition and Instruction, 12*(2), 103–123.

Breetvelt, I., van den Bergh, H., & Rijlaarsdam, G. (1996). Rereading and generating and their relation to text quality. An application of multilevel analysis on writing process data. In: G. Rijlaarsdam, H. van den Bergh, and Couzijn (eds), *Theories, Models and Methodology in Writing Research* (pp. 10–21). Amsterdam: Amsterdam University Press.

Britt, A., Rouet, J. F., & Perfetti, C. A. (1996). Using hypertext to study and reason about historical evidence. In: J. F. Rouet, J. L. Levonen, A. Dillon, and R. J. Spiro (eds), *Hypertext and Cognition* (pp. 43–73). Mahwah, NJ: Lawrence Erlbaum Associates.

Coirier, P. (1996). Composing argumentative texts: Cognitive and/or textual complexity. In: G. Rijlaarsdam, H. van den Bergh, and M. Couzijn (eds), *Theories, Models and Methodology in Writing Research* (pp. 317–338). Amsterdam: Amsterdam University Press.

Coirier, P., Andriessen, J., & Chanquoy, L. (1999). From planning to translating: The specificity of argumentative writing. In: G. Rijlaarsdam, and E. Espéret (Series eds) and J. Andriessen, and P. Coirier (Vol. eds), *Studies in Writing: Vol. 5. The Foundations of Argumentative Text Processing* (pp. 1–28). Amsterdam: Amsterdam University Press.

Dillon, A., & Gabbard, R. (1998). Hypermedia as an educational technology: A review of the quantitative research literature on learner comprehension, control, and style. *Review of Educational Research, 68*(3), 322–349.

Examenprogramma Nederlands (1998). *Voorlichtingsbrochure Nederlands Examenprogramma* [Information Brochure Examination Programme Dutch Language and Culture]. Enschede: SLO.

Hayes, J. R., & Flower, L. S. (1980). Identifying the organization of writing processes. In: L. W. Gregg, and E. R. Steinberg (eds), *Cognitive Processes in Writing: An Interdisciplinary Approach* (pp. 3–30). Hillsdale, NJ: Lawrence Erlbaum.

Jacobson, M. J., & Spiro, R. J. (1995). Hypertext learning environments, cognitive flexibility, and the transfer of complex knowledge: An empirical investigation. *Journal of Educational Computing Research, 12*(4), 301–333.

Levy, C. M., & Ransdell, S. (eds) (1996). *The Science of Writing: Theories, Methods, Individual Differences and Applications.* Hillsdale, NJ: Erlbaum.

Lohr, L., Ross, S. M., & Morrison, G. R. (1995). Using a hypertext environment for teaching process writing — an evaluation study of three student groups. *Educational Technology Research and Development, 43*(2), 33–51.

Rijlaarsdam, G., & van den Bergh, H. (1996). The dynamics of composing — an agenda for research into an interactive compensatory model of writing: Many questions, some answers. In: C. M. Levy, and S. Ransdell (eds), *The Science of Writing: Theories, Methods, Individual Differences and Applications* (pp. 107–125). Hillsdale, NJ: Erlbaum.

Rijlaarsdam, G., van den Bergh, H., & Couzijn, M. (eds) (1996). *Current Trends in Writing Research: Effective Teaching and Learning of Writing.* Amsterdam: Amsterdam University Press.

Rouet, J. F. (1994). Question answering and learning with hypertext. *Lessons from Learning, 46*, 39–52.

Russell, G. (1998). Elements and implications of a hypertext pedagogy. *Computers & Education, 31*(2), 185–193.

van den Bergh, H., & Rijlaarsdam, G. (1996). The dynamics of composing: Modeling writing process data. In: C. M. Levy, and S. Ransdell (eds), *The Science of Writing: Theories, Methods, Individual Differences and Applications* (pp. 207–232). Hillsdale, NJ: Erlbaum.

van den Bergh, H., & Rijlaarsdam, G. (1999). The dynamics of idea generation during writing: An online study. In: G. Rijlaarsdam, and E. Espéret (Series eds) and M. Torrance, and

D. Galbraith (Vol. eds), *Studies in Writing: Vol. 3. Knowing What to Write: Cognitive Perspectives on Conceptual Processes in Text Production* (pp. 99–120). Amsterdam: Amsterdam University Press.

van den Bergh, H., & Rijlaarsdam, G. (2001). Changes in cognitive activities during the writing process, and relations with text quality. *Educational Psychology, 21*(4), 373–385.

van den Bergh, H., Rijlaarsdam, G., & Breetvelt, I. (1994). Revision process and text quality: An empirical study. In: G. Eigler, and T. Jechle (eds), *Writing: Current Trends in European Research* (pp. 133–148). Freiburg: Hochschul Verlag.

van Dijk, T. A., & W. Kintsch (1983). *Strategies of Discourse Comprehension.* New York: Academic Press.

Chapter 3

Learning by Producing Hypertext from Reader Perspectives: Cognitive Flexibility Theory Reconsidered

Rainer Bromme and Elmar Stahl

Cognitive Flexibility Theory (Jacobson & Spiro, 1995) postulates that learning with hypertexts stimulates the acquisition of flexible knowledge, because hypertext environments help learners to handle knowledge from different perspectives. The present experiment examines this assumption within the context of hypertext production. It studies how far adopting two different, anticipated reader perspectives influences the learning process induced by hypertext writing. In two successive sessions, 40 college students were asked to create hypertexts by linking given nodes on the topic of the Internet. In each session, the experimental group ($n = 20$), were told that the hypertexts should address one of two reader perspectives (interest in the historical development of the Internet or Internet services). Controls ($n = 20$) had to find an "optimal structure" during both sessions. Results showed both process and learning differences between the two groups. For instance, the experimental group exhibited significantly more knowledge about content relations and structures than the control group.

Introduction

Until quite recently, producing hypertexts was a specialized activity reserved for those who were, for example, specialists in web design. Nowadays, the situation has changed because of the wide availability of software for the production of web pages. If students at schools and universities can produce hypertext documents very easily, it is worth considering the learning effects of hypertext "writing," that is, the construction of hypertext documents. This question is the focus of a research project involving field studies in schools and universities (e.g., Bromme & Stahl, 1999) as well as laboratory experiments. The project has examined the effects of different instructions on the

Writing Hypertext and Learning: Conceptual and Empirical Approaches process of hypertext construction and on the resulting knowledge about the subject matter processed. In the following, we shall sketch our theoretical assumptions on how writing hypertexts might foster learning. Then, we shall present a study testing the effects of taking different reader perspectives into account when writing hypertext.

Knowledge Acquisition Through Producing Hypertexts

We consider that producing[1] hypertexts could have a particular learning effect. Producing a text in an unfamiliar text format represents a problem-solving process in which learners cannot simply fall back on previously acquired routines. Instead, producing hypertexts places particular constraints on the design of the documents that are due to features of the text format: the nodes, the links, and the non-linear structure. We assume that these constraints help to support a production process that promotes learning and can be equated with the "knowledge-transforming" described by Bereiter and Scardamalia (1987). The knowledge-transforming model refers to research on learning by writing traditional texts. It proposes that writing can contribute to knowledge acquisition only when the text is formulated within a continuous interaction between the content-related knowledge (on the topic addressed in the text) and the "rhetorical" knowledge (on the design of the text and, among others, its structure). This problem-oriented procedure (see also, Hayes & Flower, 1980, 1986; Kellogg, 1994; Hayes, 1996) requires text producers to reflect on and extend their own knowledge. This view on learning by writing is a helpful heuristic for examining conditions and processes of learning by producing hypertext.

In terms of this model, the following special features of hypertext could support the knowledge-transforming process:

1) Writing the individual node texts requires decisions on how to discriminate between concepts so that they can be presented as separately comprehensible text units. In this way, the formulation of node texts contributes to the understanding of concepts.
2) Thinking about the necessary links requires a processing of the semantic relations between the concepts explained in the individual node texts. A reflective application of links can thus contribute to the comprehension of semantic relations.
3) When planning the total structure of a hypertext, an author has to process the structure of its contents. Due to their non-linearity, hypertexts can be read in a variety of ways. Hence, an author has to anticipate possible reader goals or perspectives in order to create flexible reading paths. This may increase comprehension of the semantic structures of the content and a flexible use of the new knowledge.

---

[1] The notion of "producing" hypertext is used here in a broad sense. It is defined to encompass all activities of editing a hypertext, including writing a hypertext from scratch as well as rearranging existing hypertexts by setting new links, integrating new nodes, or transforming traditional texts to hypertexts.

Multiple Reader Perspectives and Non-linear Hypertext Structures

Of course, the processes described here represent an ideal case. Learners cannot be expected to profit "automatically" in this way from producing hypertexts (Bromme & Stahl, 1999). Therefore, it is necessary to test empirically how the particular "affordances" of hypertext environments might be conveyed to learners and stimulate their learning through hypertext production. The present experiment focuses on the opportunities for learning arising from the non-linear total structure of the hypertexts.

In order to plan the total structure of a hypertext, an author has to process the structure of its content. In most cases, semantically complex subject matters can be organized in different ways. Due to the non-linear structure of a hypertext, an author might offer the user a variety of ways to read through the nodes. Nonetheless, decisions about links need to be made prudently in order to ensure a coherent product. Since content coherence is a fundamental prerequisite for understanding texts (Kintsch & van Dijk, 1978; van Dijk & Kintsch, 1983; Schnotz, 1994; Kintsch, 1998), the hypertext producer has to balance flexible ways of reading the text against a possible loss of coherence (Foltz, 1996). Ideally, the author would inspect each node content and try to imagine which kind of further information a reader might desire or should be able to receive, and then set the links accordingly (Wingert, 1993). It can be assumed that authors who think about their hypertext product in this way would gain a deeper understanding of the subject matter at hand.

If, further to this, authors or learners are asked to take *different* reader perspectives into account, one can expect that knowledge will be acquired in a way that allows its flexible application.

This expectation is based on Cognitive Flexibility Theory (CFT, see, e.g., Spiro & Jehng, 1990; Spiro, Feltovich, Jacobson, & Coulson, 1991; Jacobson & Spiro, 1995). CFT deals with how knowledge about a complex and therefore hard-to-structure content domain can be acquired in a way that ensures its flexible use. The goal is to stimulate learning transfer and to avoid "inert knowledge," that is, knowledge a learner can reproduce, but fails to apply in new situations (Bereiter & Scardamalia, 1987; Renkl, 1996). Cognitive flexibility refers to this transfer of knowledge and is defined correspondingly as the ability to structure one's own knowledge in a variety of ways in adaptation to changing situational demands (Spiro & Jehng, 1990).

According to CFT, one reason for a lack of transfer can be inappropriate instruction methods that usually oversimplify complex contents (see, also, Spiro *et al.*, 1991; Jacobson & Spiro, 1995). Jacobson and Spiro (1995) therefore suggested instruction methods that emphasize the complexity and interconnections between the learning contents — through, for example, multiple representations of the domain. They viewed hypertexts as appropriate tools for this, because their structural features facilitate presentation of the same contents from different perspectives.

Although CFT is regarded as a promising approach for explicating the potential learning advantages of acquiring knowledge with hypertexts (Rouet & Levonen, 1996; Dillon & Gabbard, 1998), more experimental evidence is needed on its effectiveness. The only experiment testing the central assumption — learning by considering multiple perspectives — in hypertexts was carried out by Jacobson and Spiro (1995). Their experimental group read a hypertext repeatedly, but, each time, following a different given order of nodes emphasizing different thematic perspectives. This group was compared with two control groups (later joined together) who read the content in only one thematic order, and afterwards worked with a computer-based drill-and-practice program to ensure a deeper processing of the content. In a subsequent test on knowledge about *individual facts,* participants in the control groups scored significantly higher than those in the experimental group. However, the experimental group achieved significantly better results in a *transfer test,* in which participants had to write essays on given problems.

This experiment indicates that processing the same material from different perspectives may increase the acquisition of flexibly applicable knowledge. However, it examined the receptive handling of given hypertext structures. Asking the learner to *actively construct* a hypertext from different thematic perspectives would correspond to the core assumption of CFT. Because of the learner's more active role, which is in the spirit of the theory, one could even say that such a learning scenario fits CFT assumptions even better than the experimental design used by Jacobson and Spiro (1995) themselves.

Nonetheless, whether considering different assumed reader perspectives really does promote knowledge acquisition has to be examined experimentally. One could also counter that adopting specific perspectives would fail to exploit the particular opportunities of a hypertext: Adopting one perspective on an area of knowledge would mean emphasizing some relationships while neglecting others. This might reduce the total number of relationships recognized. When acquiring flexibly applicable knowledge, it might be better for learners to orient themselves toward the subject area "as such," and to bring to mind all relationships without having any constraints imposed through certain perspectives. If learners achieve the same depth of processing, they might be able to produce more relations within their mental representation. This, in turn, should result in an increased concept variety when applying the knowledge (in the sense of Barsalou (e.g., 1987; Barsalou & Medin, 1986) and Kintsch, 1998).

Research Question

Our experiment examines how the processes and products of hypertext construction are influenced by taking into account two reader perspectives, along with how hypertext construction impacts on the writer's acquisition of factual knowledge and transfer knowledge.

We examined this issue by focusing on the process of *setting* links. Participants were not asked to write nodes on their own, but to read and to process prepared nodes. Node writing was not included for both methodological and theoretical reasons: First, writing node texts would increase the variance of products (hypertexts) and of processes, and this might well make it harder to detect the effects we were interested in. Second, writing *and* linking nodes on a new subject matter would be too time consuming. (It could be argued that writing node texts for a hypertext always implies a need to think about the multitude of possible relations between the text nodes.

However, this aspect of node writing is also covered by the present task of setting links between existing nodes.) Hence, our main interest was in the effects of this *new* challenge resulting from the possibilities of presenting multiple subject matter structures.

The topic chosen for the present study was the domain of the Internet, that is, its history, its technology, and its services. The reader perspective was operationalized as a specific question or topic on which a fictitious reader would like to be informed. Therefore, we manipulated the adoption of perspectives in the instructions: the experimental group had to link the nodes from two assumed reader perspectives in succession. In the first session, they were asked to produce a hypertext for readers interested particularly in the *history of the Internet*; in the second session, for readers interested particularly in the *services offered by the Internet*. Members of the control group, in contrast, were told to structure the nodes into a hypertext in both sessions without any specific reader perspective being pointed out to them. They were asked to orient themselves toward the subject area as such and develop what they thought would be an "optimal structure" for fictitious readers who had to learn with the hypertexts. In the second sessions, participants in the control group were told they were getting a second chance to produce an improved hypertext starting with the same nodes as before.

Hence, the control group was not given a specific reader perspective, but were oriented toward the structure of the subject area alone. In a way, this meant that they had to develop their own perspective. There was one theoretical and one methodological reason for this approach: as already mentioned above, it is theoretically conceivable that adopting specific reader perspectives is disadvantageous for learning compared with a general orientation toward the subject area.

Adopting reader perspectives could lead learners to consider only those relationships that are relevant from those perspectives and neglect other relationships whose importance might be revealed from a unspecific orientation. Hence, an alternative hypothesis to CFT is that the author of a hypertext can learn a great deal about a subject area particularly because he or she has much less need to introduce a perspective than the author of a traditional text.

From a similar, but in this case, more methodologically formulated perspective, we also decided against giving the control group only one but the experimental group two different reader perspectives. As a result of this decision, we were unable to test empirically whether it is actually the provision of *several* perspectives that makes the critical difference. Such an approach would have disadvantaged the control group systematically in the knowledge and the transfer tests, because, in each case — as shown above — only a part of the relationships would have been emphasized and others pushed into the background (e.g., the historical relationships when the technical perspective is given). This would be a disadvantage in favor of our hypothesis and CFT, because the experimental group would be in the position of processing two perspectives that emphasized different relationships.

The advantage of our conservative approach is, above all, being able to clarify how far taking account of reader perspectives versus orientation toward the subject area structure offers a learning advantage during the production of hypertexts.

Method

Participants

Participants were 40 college students (20 per group) in the first three semesters of their studies. The experimental group contained 17 women and three men. Eleven members were majoring in psychology and nine were taking it as a minor. The control group contained 18 women and two men. Twelve members of this group were majoring in psychology and eight were taking it as a minor. Participation was voluntary and rewarded financially with 50 DM (about $20). A criterion for participation was no prior in-depth knowledge on the topic of the Internet and the concept of "hypertext." This was examined with a pretest.

Materials

Instruments Data were collected on a Power-Macintosh G3 connected to a 21-in monitor. The HTML editor selected for the production of the hypertexts was the software "AOLpress 2.0." This is an easy-to-learn graphics editor that can be used without any knowledge of HTML codes. The computer was connected to a video recorder with an external microphone, so that both participants' operations on the screen and their verbal statements could be recorded on the same tape. Paper and pens were provided in case participants needed to take notes.

Introductions to hypertexts and to the task Participants were familiarized with the new text format "hypertext" through a specially written introduction. Hypertexts were introduced with the metaphor of virtual information spaces; nodes, as individual information locations; and links, as pathways between these locations. The introduction was presented as a short hypertext containing approximately 1300 words. This introduction had been tested in a previous experiment. The space metaphor was used here because it has proved to be more suitable than a book metaphor (Bromme & Stahl, 2001).

Following this introduction, participants read the task instructions, which differed for the experimental group and the control group. In the first session, participants in the experimental group were asked to construct a hypertext for readers who were mainly interested in historical aspects of the Internet. In the second session on the following day, they had to construct a hypertext for readers who particularly wanted information about the services of the Internet. Participants in the control group were told to construct their first hypertext so that a fictitious readership would gain general information on the topic of the Internet without any particular interests being specified further (see above). In the second session, they were told that participants often like to rewrite their hypertexts, and that they now had an opportunity to improve the structure of their hypertext by linking the nodes again. This procedure was applied to ensure that the control group constructed hypertexts for the same total amount of time as the experimental group.

Exercises with the HTML editor Because participants were asked to link the presented nodes to a hypertext, they had to learn how to use the HTML editor to set their links. Therefore, each participant was given the opportunity to practice linking six nodes under supervision. The main topic of these nodes was "mammals." Twelve different links were set during the exercise. Each participant practiced setting links until the necessary commands had been mastered. No participant exhibited problems in learning the commands. These exercises were identical for both groups.

Nodes on the topic of the Internet The material to be processed consisted of 16 nodes on the topic of the Internet. Each node text used about 100 words to explain a concept taken from this domain. Topics were historical developments, technical basics, and services of the Internet.

The node texts were of sufficient semantic complexity to offer many potential links to other nodes. Two pilot studies had been conducted to check whether the text nodes as such were comprehensible and included enough variety of thematic relations for links to be set between them. The first pilot study, with 50 psychology students, tested the comprehensibility of 21 texts with a cloze procedure test (Groeben, 1982). In line with Groeben (1982, p. 68), a mean of 60 percent right solutions per text was defined as a criterion for appropriate comprehensibility. In the second pilot study, 25 psychology students drew concept maps of the relations between 21 text nodes. They were asked to mark all the semantic relations they could find between the node texts with arrows. The criterion for assessing the variety of realized relations was the number of relations found between nodes. On the basis of both pilot studies, 16 text nodes were selected from the texts that had been assigned relations to at least six other texts. These node texts formed a closed information set that could be linked together from various perspectives. For the three main topics (technology, history, and services), care was taken to ensure that each node could be integrated into a hypertext from each perspective. These node texts were presented on the computer as HTML files and as printouts on 16 file cards. Figure 3.1 presents an example of a node text.

NCP

Network Control Protocol. This protocol used to be responsible for the distribution of data packages in the ARPANET. To ensure a reliable data transfer, it confirmed the reception of every data package. In addition, the NCP controlled whether the data packages arrived without any errors by calculating a sum of the digits of the package contents and returning this to the sender. NCP was used by special computers comparable with "routers." To route the data packages toward the target computer correctly, it calculated the best connection – in terms of the current capacity of the different routes – every 0.7 s.

Figure 3.1: Example of a node text.

Procedure

Data were collected in two sessions each lasting 2 hours. Participants started by completing pretests on their knowledge of the Internet and computers. After having read the metaphor introduction, they received the instruction to construct a hypertext. Then, they were trained in the use of the HTML editor before receiving the 16 nodes (short texts) on file cards. After taking 15 minutes to read the texts and gain an overview of their content, participants also received the nodes as computer files. Then they had 60 minutes to link together the node texts and create their first hypertext.

In the second session, participants once again had 1 hour to link the nodes to a hypertext in line with the given instructions. They were not given the hypertext they had constructed on the previous day. The session ended with the knowledge tests. In both sessions, participants had to work for the whole 60 minutes. Some members of both groups said that they had finished their hypertext before the 60 minutes ended. In these cases, they were asked to navigate through their products, and to revise their hypertext document carefully. The two groups did not differ in this aspect.

Dependent Variables

The effects of the different instructions on hypertext production and on knowledge acquisition about the Internet were examined on four levels. If it was possible to deduce directed hypotheses from Cognitive Flexibility Theory, these are also presented along with the findings. However, parts of the analysis are exploratory, that is, we asked whether anticipating different reader perspectives would make any difference at all, without being able to predict the direction of this difference. The four levels of results are:

Structure of the constructed hypertexts   The participants' hypertexts were analyzed in terms of the set links (i.e., their number and the type of starting points) and their overall structure. We were interested in how far the instruction to adopt different reader perspectives would elicit different hypertext structures.

Analysis of the operations   The observable operations performed on the computer screen (i.e., setting links, opening nodes) were analyzed with a category system developed and applied in previous experiments.

Decision processes   Participants' decisions while constructing their hypertexts were assessed with a direct retrospection method (see, also, Kellogg, 1988, 1994). While constructing their hypertexts, participants were asked every 2 minutes (timed from the end of the previous answer) to report what they had just been thinking about. Their answers were analyzed with a category system developed and applied in previous experiments.

Knowledge acquisition   We assessed whether consideration of different reader perspectives had any effects on learning with a knowledge test that had already proved its worth in previous experiments. Its five subtests assess knowledge about the contents of individual nodes (content knowledge), knowledge about relations between nodes (relations knowledge), and transfer knowledge: The first subtest (10 multiple choice questions) on factual knowledge posed questions on the contents of the individual nodes. The second subtest contained 10 multiple-choice questions on the relations between concepts that had been explained in the different nodes. The third subtest consisted of four items presenting a logical relation (i.e., "is a"). Participants had to select from a number of given concepts (which were dealt with in the nodes) five pairs to which this kind of relation could apply. Transfer knowledge was assessed with two further subtests. Drawing on Jonassen (1993), we designed a subtest with 10 items asking participants to complete analogies between concepts. The missing concept could be chosen from a list of five. Finding these analogies can be viewed as a test of transfer knowledge, because participants needed to restructure their acquired knowledge in order to deal with the task successfully (Jonassen, 1993). The second subtest contained two open questions on the Internet that had to be answered in the form of short essays. Writing essays on given problems is a common means for assessing transfer knowledge (see, also, Jacobson & Spiro, 1995). To score the essays, we developed a list of important aspects that should be included in the answer. Participants received one point for each aspect they referred to. The maximum score for both essays combined was 16 points. Figure 3.2 presents examples of subtest items.

These tests were developed in the two pilot studies mentioned above through the application of a rational item analysis (Lienert & Raatz, 1994). The first pilot study tested and selected the items to assess content knowledge; the second, the items to assess relations and transfer knowledge.

The first subtest of these knowledge tests was used as a pretest to assess prior knowledge of the Internet. Prior knowledge of the concept "hypertext" was measured by expanding the test with a question asking participants to define a hypertext.

Additionally, each participant's general computer knowledge was assessed with a questionnaire, because familiarity with computers could be a relevant covariable influencing the construction of hypertexts and knowledge acquisition.

Results

Results are presented for the pretests and each of the above mentioned four types of dependent variable.

Pretests

The subtest used to examine the prior knowledge of the Internet revealed no significant differences between the groups (Mann-Whitney U Test: $z = -0.09$, $p > 0.20$). From a maximum of 10 points, the experimental group scored an average of 0.35 ($SD = 0.67$); the control group, 0.10 (SD = 0.31). Hence, participants exhibited no

Item from Subtest 1 (content knowledge):	Item from Subtest 2 (relations knowledge):
7) "NCP" stands for: ❑ A protocol serving as a basis for the World Wide Web (WWW) ❑ A service enabling synchronous communication between several users ❑ A protocol that used to be necessary for the allocation of data packets ❑ A service enabling the use of someone else's computer resources ❑ A protocol to copy programs from someone else's computers to one's own ❑ Don't know	Which kind of relation exists between these two concepts? 10) TCP — NCP ❑ TCP and NCP ensure data transport and data safety within the Internet ❑ TCP is a predecessor of NCP ❑ TCP is a successor of NCP ❑ TCP and NCP used to ensure data transport and data safety within the ARPANET ❑ TCP and NCP were replaced through IP ❑ Don't know

Item from Subtest 3 (relations knowledge):
1) Some of the following concepts can be paired, connected by the relation: "is a." Please find five pairs of concepts and their generic terms. Some concepts can be used repeatedly, others do not have to be included!

ARPANET — email — FTP — Gopher — Internet — IP — IRC — NCP — packet-oriented network — protocol

Item from Subtest 4 (transfer knowledge):	Item from Subtest 5 (transfer knowledge):
Please complete the following analogy: 2) ARPANET : Internet = Gopher : ? ❑ WWW ❑ NSFNET ❑ Telnet ❑ Internet Program ❑ IRC ❑ Don't know	The following question was embedded in a cover story: Please explain the technology of the Internet: "Given what you can do with the Internet, it seems to be quite interesting. But, from a technical point of view: How does it work?"

Figure 3.2: Examples of items from the five subtests assessing knowledge about contents of individual nodes (content knowledge), knowledge about relations between nodes (relations knowledge), and transfer knowledge.

prior knowledge of the theoretical aspects of the Internet, and there were no differences in prior knowledge between groups.

Seven participants in both groups tried to describe the concept "hypertext." They compared hypertexts with Internet pages or with texts that are connected via links. All definitions were short (a maximum of one sentence) and vague. There was no differentiation of the features "nodes" and "links," and no ideas were expressed on the overall structure of a hypertext. Hence, it was assumed that all participants had no in-depth prior knowledge about the concept of hypertext.

In the computer knowledge test, participants could score a maximum of 37 points. The experimental group scored an average of 15.85 (SD = 5.64); the control group, 13.55 (SD = 5.77). This difference was not significant, $t(38) = -1.3, p > 0.20$).

Structures of the Hypertexts

The hypertexts were analyzed in terms of the number of links, the type of concepts used as link points (i.e., the starting point when a link is set), and overall structure.

Hypothesis: Concerning the *overall number of links*, we assumed that participants in the experimental group would, in both sessions, only set links that would be relevant for the respective reader perspective. This, in turn, would result in a smaller overall number of links compared with the control group. The control group was expected to develop an idea about the overall structure of the semantic content including all relations that seemed to be important and therefore set significantly more links.

In the first session, the experimental group participants set an average of 1.89 (SD = 0.56) links per node compared with 2.19 (SD = 0.68) links per node in the control group. In the second session, participants in the experimental group placed an average of 2.40 (SD = 0.67) links per node; those in the control group, 2.60 (SD = 0.84).

An ANOVA with repeated measurements revealed no significant differences between the two groups, $F(1,38) = 1.68, p > 0.05$. However, significantly more links were set in the second session compared with the first, $F(1,1) = 2.12, p < 0.0001$. This was true for participants in the experimental group, $t(18) = -3.33, p < 0.01$, as well as in the control group, $t(18) = -3.21; p < 0.01$. Therefore, our hypothesis that the adoption of reader perspectives would result in fewer links could not be confirmed.

Hypothesis: Regarding the total *number of different links*, we anticipated a significantly higher number in the experimental group. The experimental group was required to write hypertexts by taking different anticipated reader perspectives into account (historical versus service aspects of the Internet). For both sessions, this should result in different relations being emphasized, which, in turn, should be reflected in a larger number of differing links. For the control group, we assumed that participants would set more identical links in both sessions, because they would pay more attention to the node contents and their potential semantic relations when writing their hypertexts.

The number of set links that were *not* identical across both sessions had an average

Table 3.1: Mean number of set links for each of the four categories of link points and the different instructions.

Link points	Experimental group		Control group	
Headings	37.35	(15.63)	51.75	(19.38)
Content-related	6.00	(4.18)	8.80	(5.53)
Self-created	9.25	(8.42)	6.45	(7.25)
Navigation links	4.90	(8.12)	3.25	(6.27)

Note. Standard deviations (*SD*) in parentheses. Means are for both hypertexts in each participant combined.

of 37.05 (*SD* = 11.89; 57 percent) in the experimental group compared with 24.15 (*SD* = 9.40; 34 percent) in controls. Therefore, and in line with our hypothesis, the experimental group set significantly more differing links in both sessions than the control group, $t(38) = 3.81, p < 0.001$.

A further difference was expected for the *kinds of starting words* participants used to set their links. We differentiated four kinds of link points for links: First, the participant could use words as link points that were also the headings of the target nodes. A link was classified to this category, when, for instance, the link point was "TCP" and the target node's heading was also "TCP." Second, content-related words could be used as link points, that is, concepts relating to both the contents of the starting node and target node. When, for example, both nodes contained a text passage about data transport, and the concept "data transport" was chosen as a link point, links would fall into this category. Third, participants could add words as link points themselves by writing short transitional passages leading to the target node and then using a concept from this newly created text as a link point. When a participant, for example, wanted to establish a link from the node "Internet" to the node "FTP," although this concept was not contained in the Internet node, they could write an additional text and then link it. The last category included navigation links like "proceed" or "back," which were inserted into the text without establishing a content relation to the target node. In this analysis, we categorized the total number of links set by each participant over both sessions. Table 3.1 gives an overview of the number of set links for each of the four categories.

A MANOVA across the four categories revealed significant differences between the two groups, $F(4,35) = 2.71, p < 0.05$ (Hotelling-Lawley Trace). Subsequent ANOVAs showed that this difference could be attributed to the control group using significantly more starting words that were also *headings* of target nodes, $F(1,38) = 6.69, p < 0.05$. No significant differences were found for *content-related starting words,* $F(1,38) = 3.26, p > 0.05, self-created link points, F(1,38) = 0.97, p > 0.05$, or *navigation links,* $F(1,38) = 1.98, p > 0.05$. Participants in the control group therefore showed a stronger tendency to accept those concepts as starting words that had been emphasized (as headings) in the node texts. Being required to adopt a certain reader perspective, in contrast, led the experimental group to restructure the contents independently and therefore create more transitions that were not suggested so obviously by the structure of individual nodes.

Analysis of the Total Structures of the Hypertexts

The total structures of the hypertexts were analyzed by classifying them as being either network-like or non-network-like. We tried to find an objective measure for this distinction that would not be dependent on the categorizations of raters. For a hypertext to be viewed as network-like, at least 60 percent of the processed nodes had to show links to at least three other nodes. The direction of the links — whether they proceeded from the nodes or pointed toward them — was not taken into account. When a hypertext revealed fewer links, it was labeled non-network-like. Experience in earlier experiments had shown that such a simple categorization was sufficient for the desired comparison of total structures (see Stahl, 2001). Figure 3.3 presents examples of a network-like and a non-network-like hypertext.

In the first hypertext construction session, there were seven hypertexts in the experimental group and 12 in the control group that exhibited a network-like structure. This difference failed to attain significance, $\chi^2(1) = 2.5$, $p > 0.05$. In the second session, there were 14 hypertexts with a network-like structure in both groups.

Hence, whereas there were hardly any changes between the first and second session in the control group, the number of hypertexts with a network-like structure doubled in the experimental group. A McNemar Test (with Yates' correction for continuity) showed that this difference was significant, $\chi^2(1) = 6.1$, $p < 0.05$.

Taken together, the adoption of different reader perspectives had a strong effect on the hypertext structures. In both sessions, the experimental group participants set significantly more different links than the control group. In line with this, the hypertext structures in the experimental group varied more strongly between the two sessions than those in the control group. Moreover, they used significantly fewer starting words corresponding to the headings of target nodes. This indicated clearly that participants in the experimental group tried to structure their hypertext so that it agreed with the demands of the respective reader perspective.

Analysis of Operations

Operations were analyzed in order to examine the effects on the construction process of taking into account different reader perspectives. The operations on the screen could be categorized into three groups: the first group contained operations to *navigate* through the hypertext. This was performed by opening node texts, activating links that were already set, as well as by using the "back" and "forward" keys. The second group contained operations related to the *setting of links*. This involved placing links, writing link points or short transitions, and deleting existing links. The third group was made

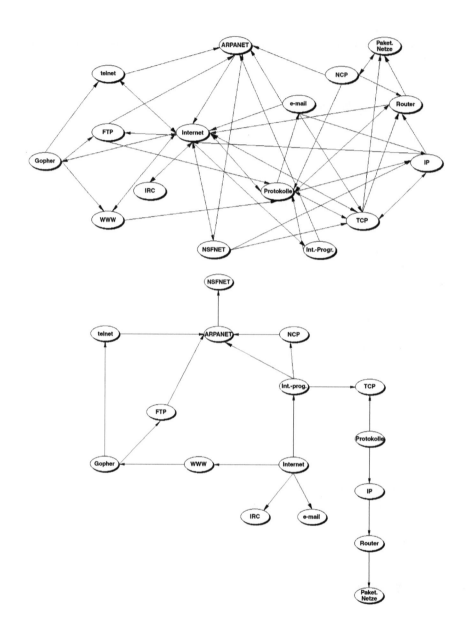

Figure 3.3: Examples of a network-like (top) and a non-network-like (bottom) hypertext.

up of "*internal activities.*" These were defined as periods during which participants read the node texts or planned the hypertext, in other words, when they were performing cognitive "operations."

The following presents the findings on operations to *set links*. Results on internal activities will not be presented, because these were practically reciprocal to the course of link-setting operations. Navigational operations are also not reported, because they were not influenced significantly by the instructions.

To examine whether the instructions had any effects on the operations to set links, the temporal courses of linking activities were calculated. The construction phase was divided into six 10-minute intervals. Figure 3.4 shows the temporal courses of link-setting operations for both groups split for the two sessions.

We assumed that the experimental group would plan the hypertext structures thoroughly in both sessions. This should be indicated in the courses of operations by fewer link-setting activities at the beginning of the sessions, as well as an increase in these operations over time. The control group, in contrast, was expected to show a stronger orientation toward the node contents and therefore spend less time on planning the structure. In other words, they were expected to start setting more links at the beginning of the sessions.

Separate ANOVAs with repeated measurements were calculated for both sessions. Significant differences were found only for the time variable in the first session (first session: $F(5,190) = 7.14$, $p < 0.0001$; second session: $F(5,190) = 1.60$, $p > 0.05$), whereas there was no difference for the group variable (first session: $F(1,38) = 0.05$, $p > 0.05$; second session: $F(1, 38) = 0.51$, $p > 0.05$).

However, both sessions revealed a significant difference in the interaction between group and time (first session: $F(5,190) = 5.19$, $p < 0.001$; second session: $F(5,190) = 3.28$, $p < 0.01$). This is reflected clearly in the graphs.

One possible explanation for those temporal courses lies in the planning strategies assumed in the two groups: In both sessions, the experimental group initially spent more time planning the structures of their hypertexts and therefore started linking nodes later. This would explain the increase in activities over time. In contrast, participants in the control group did not plan their structures in such detail, so they began setting their links earlier. Particularly in the second session, participants started setting most of the links during the first 30 minutes (see Figure 3.4). It can be assumed that they mostly adopted the hypertext structures they remembered from the previous day.

The analysis of operations reflected the differences in the courses of operations between the experimental and the control group. These differences can be explained by the more intense planning phase in the experimental group.

Decision Processes During Hypertext Construction

As a second way of examining construction processes, we analyzed participants' statements on their decisions and strategies. These statements were classified with a system of 13 categories. These categories can be grouped into six areas:

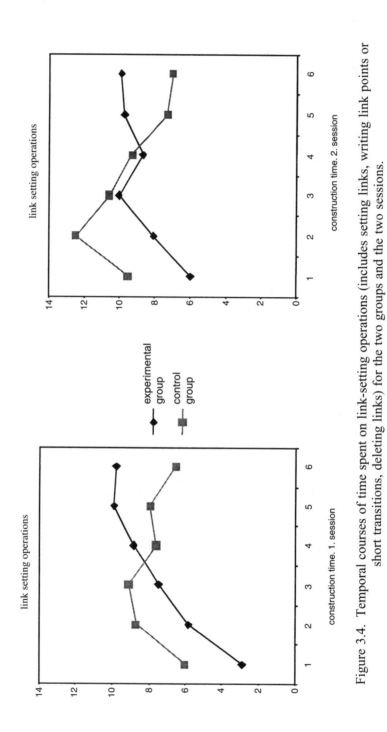

Figure 3.4. Temporal courses of time spent on link-setting operations (includes setting links, writing link points or short transitions, deleting links) for the two groups and the two sessions.

Content-related reflections This category included statements relating to the contents to be processed, that is, when participants were trying to understand the individual node contents and dealing with semantic relations and structures between the node contents.

Search processes Statements belonging to this category addressed the search for links between the nodes, for instance, when participants were scanning nodes for potential connection points or looking for a link point to place the link in a node.

Reflections on the structure of the hypertext This category was composed of statements on the structure of the hypertext, such as reflections on a starting node or the overall structure of the hypertext they had to produce.

Composing activities All statements not relating to reflections on content but to operations on the computer or technical aspects fell into this category.

General statements about one's own approach This category included statements in which participants reflected on their strategy or the task of constructing the hypertext.

Other statements This covered all statements that did not relate to the content or the construction of hypertexts.

Two independent raters categorized 10 participants' statements from both sessions. Longer statements relating to several categories were decomposed, and each part was categorized separately. Interrater agreement was 85 percent, which was in line with the results of previous experiments. Therefore, the statements of the remaining 30 participants were categorized by only one rater, because the procedure was very time-consuming. The following analyses refer to the number of statements the participants made summed across both sessions.

On average, the same number of statements were categorized in both groups (experimental group: $M = 61.15$; $SD = 5.22$; control group: $M = 62.15$; $SD = 6.57$).

If adopting a reader perspective — as assumed by the knowledge-transforming model — leads to an interaction between the reflection on the hypertext design and the structure of the content domain to be processed, the experimental group should make more statements on the structure of the hypertext as well as on the structure of the contents.

To examine this assumption, we calculated a MANOVA across the three relevant categories. Two of them related to the category reflections on the structure of the hypertexts: First, there was the category *statements on the starting node*. This contained statements referring to the selection of an appropriate node for the user's entry into the hypertext. Second, we analyzed the category *statements on the hypertext structure*, which included statements about the order of the nodes and about which kind of structure the hypertext should take. A further category took the content structures of the topic into account: *statements on content structures*. This contained

Table 3.2: Mean number of statements on the structure of the hypertext and its contents.

Category	Experimental group		Control group	
Starting nodes	1.95	(1.19)	1.10	(1.07)
Structure of hypertext	16.70	(7.59)	11.55	(7.27)
Content structure	4.10	(2.40)	2.65	(1.27)

Note. Standard deviations (*SD*) in parentheses. Means are calculated from the total number of statements for each participant across both sessions.

statements concerning content relations and content structures of the subject area. Table 3.2 gives an overview of the mean number of statements in each of the three categories.

As anticipated, the experimental group made significantly more statements on structures: $F(3,36) = 5.02$; $p < 0.01$ (Hotelling-Lawley Trace).

Subsequent ANOVAs revealed that the differences were significant for each of the three categories (statements on starting nodes: $F(1,38) = 5.63$; $p < 0.05$; reflections on the hypertext structure: $F(1,38) = 4.80$; $p < 0.05$; reflections on the content structures: $F(1,38) = 5.69$; $p < 0.05$).

The task of constructing a hypertext from two different reader perspectives therefore involved a more intense dealing with the hypertext structure. Furthermore, and in line with the knowledge-transforming model, the participants reflected more strongly on the semantic structures of the subject area they were dealing with.

Knowledge Acquisition

Participants scored an average of 36.67 (*SD* = 10.42) out of a possible 66 points in the knowledge test. Table 3.3 reports the distribution of results separately for both groups in the three areas of content knowledge, relations knowledge, and transfer knowledge as well as their overall scores.

Table 3.3: Mean scores on the knowledge tests for the different instructions.

	Experimental group		Control group	
Contents	6.55	(2.19)	6.75	(2.51)
Relations	18.75	(4.00)	16.60	(4.88)
Transfer	13.80	(4.98)	10.90	(4.76)
Total	39.10	(9.90)	34.25	(10.59)

Note. Standard deviations (*SD*) in parentheses.

Table 3.4: Ten-percent trimmed mean scores on the knowledge tests for the different instructions.

	Experimental group		**Control group**	
Contents	6.56	(1.63)	7.13	(1.75)
Relations	18.81	(3.12)	16.31	(3.84)
Transfer	14.00	(3.74)	10.88	(3.96)
Total	39.98	(6.41)	34.31	(7.66)

Note. Standard deviations *(SD)* in parentheses.

A MANOVA across the three *areas* revealed significant differences between the groups: $F(3,36) = 4.15$; $p < 0.05$ (Hotelling-Lawley Trace). Due to the large variances, subsequent ANOVAs revealed only a trend toward better results in the experimental group for transfer knowledge: $F(1,38) = 3.55$; $p = 0.067$, and knowledge about relations, $F(1,38) = 2.32$; $p = 0.14$. No significant differences were found for knowledge about facts: $F(1,38) = 0.07$; $p > 0.05$. In order to counter the heterogeneity of the results due to the different learning preconditions in the participants, the two best and two worst participants in each group were dropped before analyzing this difference more closely (10 percent trimmed mean, see Wilcox, 1998). These results are reported in Table 3.4.

A further MANOVA emphasized the significant differences between the groups more strongly, $F(3,28) = 5.70$, $p < 0.01$ (Hotelling-Lawley Trace). Whereas the groups continued not to differ in terms of content knowledge: $F(1,30) = 0.89$; $p > 0.05$, ANOVAs revealed that the experimental group tended to perform better on knowledge about relations: $F(1,30) = 4.08$; $p = 0.053$, and was significantly superior on transfer knowledge: $F(1,30) = 5.26$; $p < 0.05$.

General computer knowledge, which was controlled as a covariable, showed no systematic relations to knowledge acquisition.

Therefore — as anticipated in our hypothesis — the intervention of structuring the hypertext from two different perspectives supported knowledge gain particularly in terms of acquiring knowledge about relations and transfer knowledge.

Discussion

The aim of the present experiment is to examine whether taking on assumed reader perspectives influences the processes and products of hypertext construction and the resulting knowledge acquisition. We have analyzed how far allowing for multiple perspectives helps — in a way conducive to learning — participants to deal with the demands of hypertext design arising from its non-linear overall structure. In accordance with Cognitive Flexibility Theory (CFT), we anticipated that adopting multiple perspectives would support the acquisition of flexibly applicable knowledge.

Our results show that taking the two reader perspectives into account impacts significantly on the process of hypertext construction as well as on knowledge acquisition. The demand to create hypertexts for readers with different interests leads the experimental group (in contrast to the control group, who oriented themselves toward the subject matter as such) to consider the structure of the hypertext more intensively. Evidence for this conclusion can be found in the hypertext structures as well as in the process data.

The analysis of the hypertexts reveals that the two groups do not differ in the overall number of set links. However, in each of the two sessions, participants in the experimental group place a significantly larger number of different links compared with the control group. This is a clear indication that the control group mainly considers the node texts as such, which, in turn, leads to a more identical link-setting in both sessions. The experimental group, in contrast, tries to adjust hypertext structures to the anticipated readership, that is, to accommodate the material and the reader perspective. This is achieved by emphasizing different semantic relations and, therefore, different links in the two sessions. Across both sessions, participants in the experimental group reflect about a greater number of different semantic relations between the nodes while setting their links.

This interpretation is supported by the finding that participants in the control group produce an equal amount of network-like structures during both sessions, whereas the experimental group produces significantly fewer network-like structures during the first compared with the second session. As participants have to create a historical perspective in the first version and work on the services provide by the Internet in the second, these differences in structure make sense: presenting the history is easy to implement with more sequential structures illustrating the course of historical developments. In contrast, the presentation of the individual Internet services requires a greater variety of links in order to show, for example, in which of the different networks individual services can be used.

The increased reflection on the structures of hypertext and their contents is further indicated by the significantly lower use of starting words that are also headings of target nodes. Participants in the control group mostly use those concepts as links that are obviously emphasized in the texts. Apparently, this strategy does not suffice for taking on a particular reader perspective. Moreover, taking certain perspectives into account requires finding transitions that are not contained directly in the node texts.

The results of the analysis of operations also fits into this line of interpretation: the experimental group shows an increase in link-setting activities over time. One possible interpretation suggests a more precise and thorough planning of the hypertext structures at the beginning of the sessions, which implies a delayed link-setting. As the courses of operations in the experimental group are similar across both sessions, one can assume that, in both cases, the structure of the hypertexts is being planned in more detail. The temporal courses of activities in the control group, in contrast, indicate that these participants start setting links a lot earlier. This holds particularly for the second session. One reason could be that they remember many links from the previous day, still consider them useful, and, therefore, insert them once again.

Additional support for our interpretation comes from participants' retrospective statements on their decisions: being asked to adopt certain reader perspectives makes participants reflect a lot more on the structure of both the hypertexts and the contents they are dealing with. In the introduction, we argued that writing hypertexts may promote learning if the learner relates the content structures to the rhetorical structure of the respective text format (knowledge transforming, according to Bereiter and Scardamalia, 1987). The requirement to take an anticipated reader perspective into account apparently supports the process of linking the semantic and the rhetorical structure.

In line with the assumptions of CFT, the two groups differ significantly in their knowledge about relations and structures within the subject area. This is a prerequisite for knowledge transfer, which the experimental group achieves significantly better. Also in line with the results of Jacobson and Spiro (1995), no significant differences are found on knowledge about the contents of individual nodes, that is, simple factual knowledge. Therefore, it can be stated that our experiment provides further empirical evidence supporting CFT. Because we use a production task instead of a reception task, our study also demonstrates how the scope of this theory may be extended. CFT combines the adoption of multiple perspectives with hypermedia learning environments.

Our study has added an idea that is well-known in another strand of educational research: producing texts not only for oneself but for an "external" readership may improve the subject-matter understanding in the writer her- or himself (Bereiter & Scardamalia, 1987; Lumbelli, Paoletti, & Frausin, 1999). Of course, many open research questions have to be answered before this can be used as an instructional approach. Further studies could examine, for example, how detailed the explanation of the assumed reader perspective needs to be for learners constructing a hypertext.

Furthermore, our study does not clarify whether a weaker intervention (requiring participants to work from only one perspective) would already have facilitated learning more than not making such a demand. We argue that requiring only one perspective would probably lead participants to observe the variety of relations between the contents of the individual nodes too selectively. Naturally, this depends on the complexity of the semantic structures contained in the node texts. Future research can start here by varying this complexity and the number of reader perspectives required systematically.

Nevertheless, we can state that prescribing multiple reader perspectives proves to be an appropriate instruction that employs the non-linear structure of hypertexts in a way that can promote learning. Because hypertexts offer this opportunity in a simple way, with potential flexibility being a fundamental part of their format, writing hypertexts may well be a useful means of supporting the acquisition of flexibly applicable knowledge.

Author Note

The experiment here is part of a series of studies funded by the *Deutsche Forschungsgemeinschaft*. We wish to thank Christian Hövelmeyer and Raphael Jaron for their help in data collection and Jonathan Harrow for native-speaker advice.

References

Barsalou, L. W. (1987). The instability of graded structure: Implications for the nature of concepts. In: U. Neisser (ed.), *Concepts and Conceptual Development: Ecological and Intellectual Factors in Categorization* (pp. 101–140). Cambridge, England: Cambridge University Press.

Barsalou, L. W., & Medin, D. L. (1986). Concepts: Static definitions or context-dependent representations. *Cognitive Science, 6*, 187–202.

Bereiter, C., & Scardamalia, M. (1987). *The Psychology of Written Composition*. Mahwah, NJ: Erlbaum.

Bromme, R., & Stahl, E. (1999). Spatial metaphors and writing hypertexts: Study within schools. *European Journal of Psychology of Education, 14*, 267–281.

Bromme, R., & Stahl, E. (2001). The idea of "hypertext" and its implications on the process of hypertext writing. In: W. Frindte, T. Köhler, P. Marquet, and E. Nissen (eds), *IN-TELE 99 — Internet-Based Teaching and Learning 99, Vol. 3 Internet Communication* (pp. 302–308). Frankfurt am Main, Germany: Peter Lang.

Dillon, A., & Gabbard, R. (1998). Hypermedia as an educational technology: A review of the quantitative research literature on learner comprehension, control, and style. *Review of Educational Research, 68*, 322–349.

Foltz, P. W. (1996). Comprehension, coherence, and strategies in hypertext and linear text. In: J.-F. Rouet, J. J. Levonen, A. Dillon, and R. J. Spiro (eds), *Hypertext and Cognition* (pp. 109–136). Mahwah, NJ: Erlbaum.

Groeben, N. (1982). *Leserpsychologie: Textverständnis — Textverständlichkeit* [Reader psychology: Text comprehension — text comprehensibility]. Münster, Germany: Aschendorf.

Hayes, J. R. (1996). A new framework for understanding cognition and affect in writing. In: C. M. Levy, and S. Ransdell (eds), *The Science of Writing. Theories, Methods, Individual Differences, and Applications* (pp. 1–27). Mahwah, NJ: Erlbaum.

Hayes, J. R., & Flower, L. S. (1980). Identifying the organisation of writing processes. In: L. W. Gregg, and E. R. Steinberg (eds), *Cognitive Processes in Writing* (pp. 3–30). Mahwah, NJ: Erlbaum.

Hayes, J. R., & Flower, L. S. (1986). Writing research and the writer. *American Psychologist, 41*, 1106–1113.

Jacobson, M. J., & Spiro, R. J. (1995). Hypertext learning environments, cognitive flexibility, and the transfer of complex knowledge: An empirical investigation. *Journal of Educational Computing Research, 12*, 301–333.

Jonassen, D. H. (1993). Effects of semantically structured hypertext knowledge bases on users' knowledge structures. In: C. McKnight, A. Dillon, and J. Richardson (eds), *Hypertext: A Psychological Perspective* (pp. 153–168). New York: Ellis Horwood.

Kellogg, R. T. (1988). Attentional overload and writing performances: Effects of rough draft and outline strategies. *Journal of Experimental Psychology, 14*, 355–365.

Kellogg, R. T. (1994). *The Psychology of Writing*. New York: Oxford University Press.

Kintsch, W. (1998). *Comprehension: A Paradigma for Cognition*. New York: Cambridge University Press.

Kintsch, W., & van Dijk, T. A. (1978). Toward a model of text comprehension and production. *Psychological Review, 85*, 363–394.

Lienert, G. A., & Raatz, U. (1994). *Testaufbau und Testanalyse* [Test construction and analysis]. Weinheim: Beltz.

Lumbelli, L., Paoletti, G., & Frausin, T. (1999). Improving the ability to detect comprehension problems: From revising to writing. *Learning and Instruction, 9*, 143–166.

Renkl, A. (1996). Träges Wissen: Wenn Erlerntes nicht genutzt wird [Inert knowledge: When what is learned is not put to use]. *Psychologische Rundschau, 47*, 78–92.

Rouet, J.-F., & Levonen, J. J. (1996). Studying and learning with hypertext: Empirical studies and their implications. In: J.-F. Rouet, J. J. Levonen, A. Dillon, and R. J. Spiro (eds), *Hypertext and Cognition* (pp. 9–23). Mahwah, NJ: Erlbaum.

Schnotz, W. (1994). *Aufbau von Wissensstrukturen. Untersuchungen zur Kohärenzbildung beim Wissenserwerb mit Texten* [Acquisition of knowledge structures. Studies on the formation of coherence during knowledge acquisition with texts]. Weinheim, Germany: Beltz.

Spiro, R. J., Feltovich, P. J., Jacobson, M. J., & Coulson, R. L. (1991). Cognitive flexibility, constructivism and hypertext: Random access instruction for advanced knowledge acquisition in ill-structured domains. *Educational Technology, 31*, 24–33.

Spiro, R. J., & Jehng, J.-C. (1990). Cognitive flexibility and hypertext: Theory and technology for the nonlinear and multidimensional traversal of complex subject matter. In: D. Nix, and R. Spiro (eds), *Cognition, Education and Multimedia: Exploring Ideas in High Technology* (pp. 163–205). Hillsdale, NJ: Erlbaum.

Stahl, E. (2001). *Hyper-Text-Schreiben: Die Auswirkungen verschiedener Instruktionen auf Lernprozesse beim Schreiben von Hypertext* [Writing-Hyper-Text: Effects of different instructions on learning processes during the writing of hypertext]. Münster: Waxmann.

van Dijk, T. A., & Kintsch, W. (1983). *Strategies of Discourse Comprehension.* New York: Academic Press.

Wilcox, R. R. (1998). How many discoveries have been lost by ignoring modern statistical methods? *American Psychologist, 53*, 300–314.

Wingert, B. (1993). Äußerer und innerer Hypertext: Eine notwendige Differenzierung, verdeutlicht am Flusser-Hypertext [External and internal hypertext: A necessary differentiation as shown in Flusser hypertext]. *Nachrichten für Dokumentation, 1*, 29–36.

Chapter 4

Writing as Design: Hypermedia and the Shape of Information Space

Andrew Dillon

In the present chapter the act of writing hypertext is analyzed as a human task that needs to be studied for us to determine the best means of supporting it through technology. For this purpose, writing is conceptualized as a design task that extends normal composition-based analyses of text production (e.g., Hayes, 1996) to incorporate analyses more usually associated with user interface design. There are interesting parallels between these activities, such as their ill-structured nature, the shared central role of iteration, and the reliance on drafts or prototypes as generators of finished products.

In particular, the chapter examines the role of shape or structure in understanding how discourse communities create and consume information. The analysis of shape reveals the underlying socio-cognitive dimensions of an information architecture that can aid designers or writers of hypertext documents to produce more usable and acceptable digital forms.

The techniques involved in exploiting the power of the technology are likely to extend beyond those employed in "traditional" writing, and the manner in which we teach writing and teach design will be examined to develop parallels and suggest directions for further research.

Introduction

It is widely recognized by researchers and designers of hypermedia systems that the usability of digital documents is a crucial determinant of their acceptance and successful exploitation by users (Nielsen, 1995; Dillon, 1996). To this end, much effort is spent understanding the navigation features and underlying structure of hypermedia contents so as to support the user's comprehension of layout and content. For more than a decade, research effort has been spent on determining such aspects of usability as link density (Zhu, 1998), provision of maps or spatial organizers (Simpson &

Writing Hypertext and Learning: Conceptual and Empirical Approaches
ISBN: 0-08-043987-X

McKnight, 1989), user disorientation, and learning outcomes from the use of hypermedia (Dillon & Gabbard, 1998). The bulk of such work to date has come from the HCI (Human-Computer Interaction) and Education fields, which have treated the user largely as the recipient of the designed hypermedia, not its creator. Dedicated journals on hypermedia such as the *Journal of Educational Hypermedia and Multimedia* concentrate almost exclusively on such a view of this technology and its use.

In its extreme (and highly simplified) form, this view of hypermedia perpetuates a three-stakeholder model of hypermedia development and use: a writer, a designer, and a user. This model leaves out finer grain divisions of labor that abound in software design (such as editors, programmers, testers, media designers, etc.) but serves a purpose for the present chapter in emphasizing key roles. However it should be noted that recent developments in tool design (e.g., web-authoring tools such as FrontPage) offer a twist on this distinction by providing the equivalent of a design tool to an author.

The writer creates the content, ensuring appropriate level of argument, accuracy of material and logical sequencing of ideas. The expectation here is that the role embodies subject-matter expertise in the topic of the final hypermedia product. The designer's role is to enable the hypermedia to function as a working artifact. To this end she needs to be a competent user interface designer and to ensure that the presentation works on screen where mixed media, links, and navigation facilities must be provided. Finally, the user's role is often seen as passive recipient, who may actively explore an information space whose boundaries and form are determined by the others.

While there are many ways in which the responsibilities of each stakeholder might blur with another, it is the division between writing and design that particularly interests me, for two reasons. First, the content produced by a writer affords certain design manipulations by its very nature. Lengthy narratives afford different linking than expositional forms for example. The mixture of text and graphics is often determined by content not by capability of the delivery mechanism. Thus, there is a natural relationship between content and form that belies forced divisions of labor in software development. Second, writing is a communicative act that is predicated on mutual understanding between author and reader. Writers shape their output in anticipation of use, and users or readers themselves arrive at a document with many expectations of form and structure. As a result, I believe the classic model of hypermedia design is limited and needs to focus more on what I might call the mutual interdependence of creation and use.

So What is Different about Hypermedia?

One question we must ask ourselves is what makes hypermedia writing different from standard text production? It cannot just be the means of production since any published paper text goes through a sequence of processes as elaborate, if not a more elaborate, from conception to use, as most software products. Instead, it is the nature of hypermedia that causes people to think of it as distinct. By this I mean it is the capability for hypermedia to be linked and accessed in multiple ways, affording its creators (theoretically) with the means (and challenge) of by-passing many of the apparent rules of form that need to be followed more rigidly in linear (paper) writing (see Nielsen, 2000 for a strong advocacy of this position).

I find this an unsatisfying argument on several levels, not least because I have long argued that the supposed tyranny of the linear form in paper is more imaginary than real (Dillon, 1996). Furthermore, if pushed to the extreme, the creation of a hyper-media document could be seen as far simpler than a traditional paper one since it removes the burden from the author to determine the logical flow. Who needs a logical flow when multiple flows are enabled and encouraged? Of course this is a specious argument, though one might be forgiven for thinking that more than one hypermedia rhetorician or constructivist has advanced it as a reasonable position.

In reality, the process of authoring a hypermedia document seems to be deviate fairly little from the process of authoring any text, at least for experienced authors. Dillon (1993) reports two analyses of group authoring of technical reports. Both teams consisted of experienced authors, and one team was experienced in working together as a group on reports. Both groups had access to the latest technologies for authoring documents, including hypermedia tools, yet both adopted a round-robin approach characterized by the development of a writing plan, followed by turn-taking by each author. In effect, these authors wrote alone, on their normal text-editors, and passed their work on to the next author in line. This process continued until all were satisfied that the document was ready. There were few exchanges of information or sources of discussion in the hypermedia document space itself during production, suggesting that new authoring tools are as much shaped by the practices of authors, as they are mechanisms for new creative processes.

Whether this is in part due to the forceful carryover of experience on the part of the author, or, as some have suggested, it is a function of authors' lack of experience exploiting the nature of hypermedia for authoring purposes (Nielsen, 2000), remains an interesting question. In my view there are differences, but they are far subtler than would appear at first glance. It is not sufficiently the case that hypermedia is just text production with an extra design phase where links and layout are considered. Instead, I believe hypermedia authoring is text production with a need to reconsider how we convey and exploit structure beyond the cues that authors (and readers) have relied upon for centuries. The new medium offers new opportunities and requires us to focus more on human communication that might appear necessary from a software design perspective. I will return to this later in the chapter, but for now it is important to consider how hypermedia documents are currently produced.

Separating Design from Content: Hypermedia Production as an Engineering Process

In its extreme form, hypermedia design separates form from content. In other words, the material contained in the digital document is assumed to be the product of a subject matter expert, while the decisions about linking structure, navigation aids and screen layout are often considered the responsibility of the interface designer. In many ways this results from the natural evolution of roles from the print-based culture where typography, page layout, and document design were all responsibilities removed from the writer and handled by the publisher. However, it has reached its zenith in current engineering approaches to software development where developmental stages are mapped out in advance and roles in the process are allocated according to specialist knowledge. To this end, the writer is divorced from the final production of her work. Her role is one of content provision, and content is viewed as words and images to be shaped by others into a consumable hypermedia form. This is particularly true for example in educational software design where instructional specialists extract content from domain experts and often hand the design over to software engineers for development.

In part, there is value in this approach. Examination of the web reveals how poorly understood are the principles of linking and layout for screen by authors. Self-made websites often reflect poor choices of font, color, linking style and navigation aids. Yet such choices are the stock in trade of professional designers who (in theory) have built up a bedrock of empirical knowledge on how to design for use on screen. Hence, there appears to be a distinct role for specialists in user interface design who can work with any content to produce a usable form.

Such a division of roles seems natural since the design decisions to be made are not trivial. Indeed interface design problems constitute the single greatest failing of digital documents. Thus, there must be room for interface design in hypermedia production. However, while I would be the last person to reject such inputs, I do believe that the separation of content expertise from design decisions is itself a doomed strategy that can at best yield temporary benefits. Instead of treating the design phase as distinct from the content creation work, we should be trying harder to bring both camps together.

Writing as Viewed in the Hypermedia World

As stated previously, the major thrust of research into hypermedia has been the examination of user effects or the technical aspects of digital information systems. Where writing has been studied directly in hypermedia systems the emphasis has been more on its impact on literacy and rhetoric. Technical advocates have promised a social shift in literacy equivalent to the development of the printing press. Terms such as "cultural literacy", and "digital rhetoric" abound and we are supposed to be freed from the constraining need to write (and thereby think) linearly by the tyrannical force of an outmoded medium. To date, such arguments have rarely been supported by any empirical data from writers, and the little evidence we have suggests that hypertext-based authoring is neither empowering nor likely to produce radically different output. Authors studied by Dillon (1993) reported that they did not feel that hypermedia-authoring tools offered any significant advantages or caused them to engage in a different form of writing process.

There are other voices but they are isolates. Haselkorn (1988), in one of the earliest collections on hypertext, stated the following:

Writers will play a major role in the design and development of user interfaces. (. . .) Writer's involvement in user interface research, design and
development is a natural one. Clearly the writer who looks at the product
through the user's eyes and is also a communications specialist has much
to contribute to this area. (p. 9)

However, Haselkorn was talking more directly about the production of user documentation, and future role of technical writers, not specifically about the role of hypermedia content provider, though in many cases this distinction can be blurred.
Nevertheless, there is a paucity of work on the nature of the writing process in hypermedia terms, which perpetuates the idea that the creative act of authoring content is
somehow distinct from the design of hypermedia interfaces.

Writing as a Design Act

The traditional literature on the psychology of writing is itself far smaller than the
literature on the psychology of reading. Even within this literature, theoretical analyses
have been dominated by one cognitive model, that of Hayes and Flower (1980) which
for nearly 20 years dominated the psychological literature on this human activity.
Having been refined recently by Hayes (1996) this model is a natural starting point
for any serious examination of the cognition underlying hypermedia production.

Hayes' latest model is based on an individual–environmental analysis of the factors
shaping text production. At the individual level is seen the working memory, long-
term memory components of production, married to general cognitive processes of
interpretation and reflection, as well as motivational and affective components of goals
and beliefs. As such, this is a richer recognition of cognition than is typical in cognitive science analyses of human task performance.

At the environmental level Hayes proposes a distinction between the social environment (where audience expectations and co-authors influence the process) and the
physical environment of the means of production and the text produced so far. In so
doing he raises for examination elements of writing that have been known as important
by writers for years but have rarely been considered theoretically.

The implications of this model for hypermedia design are, in my view, intriguing.
Most noticeably, with the exception of the use of the word "text" in Hayes' model,
there is little to distinguish this model from a model of any design act at the cognitive level. Certainly, software design, as it has been studied, reveals similar reliance
on external or environmental drivers and constraints that are mediated by internal
processes of reflection and interpretation bounded by working and long-term memory
parameters (see, e.g., Dillon & Sweeney, 1988; Carroll, 1999).

There are many interesting parallels between these activities, such as their ill-
structured nature (no two writers or writing tasks follow the precise same path), the
shared central role of iteration, and the reliance on drafts or prototypes as generators
of finished products (see, e.g., Lawson's (1980) classic study of architectural design
reasoning). Indeed, within the field of human–computer interaction (HCI), iteration is

considered the single most important component of user-centered design. As such, Hayes' model of writing could serve as a general model of design at the individual level.

More directly, for hypermedia production, the revised model places great emphasis on contextual forces in the communicative process. According to Hayes, writers are imagining their audience's reaction to the text as they create it. The emphasis on communicative context appropriately draws attention to the important mediating effects of expectation on the part of the author (writing for a specific audience) and the reader (anticipating the pattern of organization the author will likely follow). Dillon (1995) invokes the term "shape" to describe this property of an information space and while the term has a somewhat elusive quality, it captures an essential element of the interactions people have in information space.

Shape: Structuring Information Space for Usability

In a world of multiple information types, stable patterns of presentation have emerged. Thus, newspapers follow conventions of layout and style and both writers and readers of a newspaper learn to identify these conventions and employ them in their inter-actions with this information space. By conventions I am referring specifically to the high level regularities of form that hold over frequent interactions (production and consumption). In studies of literature as found in the humanities the term "genre" is usually employed to describe this spread of regularities and of late there has been an interest in the emergence of digital genres (Dillon & Gushrowski, 2000).

In a paper world there is greater stability of form and most studies of communica-tive forms suggest that genres are slow-forming, often taking generations to stabilize. However, once in place, the notion of genre places largely unarticulated but never-theless strong pressure on the form of a document. Thus do we have genres for detective fiction, modern novels, popular science books, encyclopedias, etc. (and the role of genre is not limited to the written form, but extends to movies, plays, and docu-mentaries, etc.).

The value of genre springs from very real cognitive processes. Genres establish context for a reader with the result that anticipatory processes prime the reader, enabling faster comprehension. Over lengthy documents the genre can serve as a form of schematic representation or scaffold for long-term memory. Indeed, there is evidence that such forms tie closely to behavioral practices in a community (van Dijk & Kintsch, 1983). Genre also supports inference, allowing both readers to fill in gaps, and authors to avoid stating every detail.

An important issue is the linguistic basis of genre. By this I mean that many aspects of genre spring from the language used, not from visual or typographic aspects of the text. This is not to downplay visual or typographic elements, but I mean here to argue that language contains within itself many rich cues that are not immediately apparent when one talks of information design. In my view, hypermedia design has tended to be too quick to emphasize visuo-spatial properties at the expense of such linguistic attributes. We can see the power of linguistic cues in some recent experimental work in my lab.

Shape, as I have envisaged it, attempts to raise both the linguistic and visuo-spatial attributes of information to the fore and show how communities of practice (any group that shares points of reference and tasks, and exchanges information on regular basis) learn to interpret and expect such patterns in the information they share. For example, Dillon (2000) reported verbal protocols from novice and expert scientists reading isolated paragraphs of text from a scientific article. The stimulus materials here were screen-presented paragraphs of text, without graphics. We manipulated the presence or absence of key textual cues also, such as the use of formulae, statistical results and so forth. The subjects' task in the trial was to examine the text and categorize its location in the body of a scientific article as quickly as possible e.g., as belonging to the Introduction, Method, Results or Discussion section of an article. Paragraphs from more than one article were combined in these trials and obvious lead-in or follow-on sentences were removed. Even stripped of visual cues, experts were far more able to place correctly the isolates in a location within the text from which it was extracted than were novices. Examining the verbal protocols it was clear that novices relied on superficial cues in the text while the experts interpreted the text they read in terms of their expectations of what type of information they would find in that genre of document.

What this work points to is the need to consider writing itself as fundamentally a design process, the shaping of information to serve a communicative process. With the text that authors produce containing more than raw content, but qualities and cues that suggest order, layout, and context, the division of hypermedia production into content provision and interface design is, in my view, shortsighted.

Bridging Writing and Design — What is the Alternative?

Instead of enforcing a separation of content creation and interface design, I would challenge the very notion that these are best thought of as distinct. An alternative is to consider the content as a driver, containing within itself the very basis for an interface between author and reader. To put this in concrete terms for design practice, I would argue that we pay closer attention to the regularities of form and structure inherent in the content we seek to communicate and use these cues to drive the interface design. Exploiting the cues can support the provision of navigation aids, determine the amount of text to be shown on a single screen, suggest natural or cognitively compatible locations for links, and help provide the user with a path through the information space that may work for them. Indeed, it makes little sense to consider navigation at the document or unit level without an analysis of the very content that is typically performed by a writer in situ.

Content provides guidance on form, as a natural by-product of the means of communication we have evolved and exploit in the natural world. The analysis of shape reveals the underlying socio-cognitive dimensions of an information architecture that can aid designers or writers of hypertext documents to produce more usable and acceptable digital forms. The techniques involved in exploiting the power of the technology are likely to extend beyond those employed in "traditional" writing, and the manner in which we teach writing and teach design will have to change to accommodate this.

One objection to this approach, of course, lies in the role of tradition. It is fine for us to exploit tradition for designs intended to mirror the paper world (such as the case for online newspapers or e-journals, etc.) but surely, the objection runs, this limits what we can do with the new media. I would agree if all I was arguing for was a simple transfer of analog designs to digital form, but that is not what I seek. Indeed, there is ample evidence in the design world that merely copying paper forms in the digital environment results in poor usability. In fact, I would argue against such copying. What I do recommend is better understanding the basis on which the cognitive system recognizes and reacts to cues for form and structure in information spaces so that we can exploit these, not the superficial or surface level characteristics of look and layout that seems drive such transfers.

Beyond this however, how do we handle new forms of information, true digital genres that have no paper equivalent? Again, I believe this approach holds. It is true that the speed of genre formation in digital space is likely to increase. What once took decades to become part of a community of creation and consumption now may take much less time. Dillon and Gushrowski (2000) argued that home pages on the web might even be the first true digital genre. In their study, they examined a sampling of 100 personal home pages and extracted a ranked list of features. While there was much diversity in what could be found in these home pages, a core set of common features were observed (photographs of person, email address, etc.). The researchers then created a set of test pages that systematically varied the number of common and uncommon features on a page, and users were asked to rate each page for "typicality" and suitability as a home page design. Even though there is no formal definition of a "home page," and such pages have no real equivalent in the paper world, their data show an almost perfect correlation between ranking of suitability and the presence of commonly found features in the design. In other words, users agree very closely on what a home page should contain. As such, a genre has formed in real time very quickly.

Now if this speed of formation is typical, it also remains true that the cognitive processes underlying them are not altered by virtue of the medium of presentation. Regardless, readers exploit the same cues and stimuli, and seek to impose patterns, as always. Thus, even for new forms, the psychological principles remain the ones most important for us to understand. And it is precisely the human information-processing underlying these formations and abstractions that I believe is most important for us to research and explain. Furthermore, not only does this mean the questions are ultimately medium-independent, it also renders the research more urgent as digital forms are being proposed and created all around us nowadays. Whatever forms become standards now will have a far-reaching impact on users the world over, many of who have yet to use a digital document.

Training the Next Generation of Hypermedia Designers

I believe that the intellectual traditions that underlie current university training in the disciplines discussed in this chapter must undergo revolution. In a world transformed by the power of a new technology the values of a university are crucial, but we should not confuse values with disciplinary divides. There is no rule that says the division of intellectual labor seen appropriate in the 20th century must be fixed forever on our campuses. In truth, many universities are reflecting these changes and I see the emergence of new disciplines, such as information architecture, informatics, and interaction design as welcome signs of recognition for the theoretical and scholarly richness of the problems underlying media design.

I suspect that a new generation of hypermedia designers will emerge from existing training, but that over time, a new science of design will be seen as fundamental. In the interim, my advice to students is to choose programs that allow for intellectual curiosity and provide access to courses in computer science as well as psychology, fine arts as well as journalism, statistics as well as linguistics. For sure, there is no pure science of hypermedia design that one can now study, but there may be soon, and new technology will serve as the nexus between science and application in a manner that pushes the barriers of our scientific models.

Conclusion

Ivory, Sinha, and Hearst (2001) showed that content is key in award winning websites, not graphics or "cool" design features. Content provision is the role of the author and has traditionally been treated as distinct from "design." In this chapter I have proposed that this division is unhelpful, and furthermore, content contains the seeds of design that need to be nurtured if we are to enable cognitively compatible presentation of information to users. Production of hypermedia documents thus needs to focus more attention on the psychological processes underlying communication between members of speech communities, and less attention on feature-based analysis of hypermedia interfaces. Features, divorced from content, are meaningless and cannot be the basis for a meaningful interface design. Future digital forms of communication will succeed best where they exploit a rich cognition of communication and render the production of hypermedia as much a process of authorship as of screen design.

Author Note

I would like to thank Prof. Dr Rainer Bromme for his support and excellent feedback throughout this process. The chapter is greatly improved from his comments.

References

Carroll, J. (ed.) (1999). *Beyond the nurnberg funnel*. Cambridge, MA: MIT Press.
Dillon, A. (1993). How collaborative is collaborative writing? In: M. Sharples (ed.), *Computer-Supported Collaborative Writing* (pp. 69–86). London: Springer-Verlag.

Dillon, A. (1995). What is the shape of information? *SIGOIS Bulletin*, Special issue on digital libraries, *16*(2), 32–35.

Dillon, A. (1996). Myths, misconceptions and an alternative perspective on information usage and the electronic medium. In: J. F. Rouet, J. J. Levonen, A. Dillon, and R. J. Spiro (eds), *Hypertext and Cognition* (pp. 25–42). Mahwah, NJ: LEA.

Dillon, A. (2000). Spatial semantics and individual differences in the perception of shape in information space. *Journal of the American Society for Information Science*, *51*(6), 521–528.

Dillon, A., & Gabbard, R. (1998). Hypermedia as an educational technology: A review of the empirical literature on learner comprehension, control and style. *Review of Educational Research, 68*(3), 322, 349.

Dillon, A., & Gushrowski, B. (2000). Genres and the Web — is the home page the first digital genre? *Journal of the American Society for Information Science*, *51*(2), 202–205.

Dillon, A., & Sweeney, M. (1988). The application of cognitive psychology to CAD. In: D. Jones, and R. Winder (eds), *People and Computers IV* (pp. 477–488). Cambridge: Cambridge University Press.

Haselkorn, M. (1988). The future of writing for the computer industry. In: E. Barrett (ed.), *Text, Context and Hypertext: Writing With and For the Computer* (pp. 3–14). Cambridge, MA: MIT Press.

Hayes, J. (1996). A new framework for understanding cognition and affect in writing. In: C. Levy, and S. Ransdell (eds), *The Science of Writing: Theories, Methods, Individual Differences and Applications* (pp. 1–28). Mahwah, NJ: Lawrence Earlbaum Associates.

Hayes, J., & Flower, L. (1980). Identifying the organization of writing processes. In: L. Gregg, and R. Steinberg (eds), *Cognitive Processes in Writing* (pp. 3–30). Hillsdale, NJ: Lawrence Earlbaum Associates.

Ivory, M., Sinha, R., & Hearst, M. (2001). Empirically validated web page design metrics. *Proceedings of CHI'01*. New York: ACM Press.

Lawson, B. (1980). *How Designers Think*. London: Architectural Press.

Nielsen, J. (1995). *Hypertext and Multimedia: The Internet and Beyond*. New York: Academic Press.

Nielsen, J. (2000). *Designing Web Usability.* Indianapolis, IN: New Riders Publications.

Simpson, A., & McKnight, C. (1989). Navigation in hypertext: Structural cues and mental maps. In: R. McAleese, and C. Green (eds), *Hypertext: State of the Art* (pp. 73–83). Oxford: Intellect.

van Dijk, T., & Kintsch, W. (1983). *Strategies for Discourse Comprehension*. New York: Academic Press.

Zhu, E. (1998). Hypermedia interface design: The effects of number of links and granularity of nodes. *Journal of Educational Multimedia and Hypermedia*, *8*(3), 339–358.

Chapter 5

Emergent versus Presentational Hypertext

Carl Bereiter

There is a long tradition in North American education of what are called "projects" at the elementary level and later elevated to the status of "research papers." Although there are many variations, the essential steps are (a) collect information; (b) organize it; and (c) present it. As new media and information sources have appeared, these have been assimilated to this routine. The original tools for "projects" were pen, paper, scissors, and library paste. The traditional information source was the encyclopedia, supplemented by library books and old magazines — the latter serving as a source of illustrations. CD-ROMs and Internet documents have now become prominent as information sources; audio recording, video recording, Hypercard stacks, and now multimedia authoring tools have become popular as means of presentation. The essential steps remain the same, however. What is most significant from an educational standpoint is that the objective, as far as the students are concerned, is presentation. They collect and organize information in order to present it. Learning is a by-product of this presentational effort.

Project-Based Learning

The traditional "project" has been criticized for fostering the mere reproduction of information. With the rise of constructivism as an educational creed, this criticism has become more severe. The traditional "project" seems based on a view of knowledge as something external that is to be taken in, rather than as something to be constructed by the student. "Project-based learning" has gained popularity as an alternative that assigns the learners a more active and constructive role. Marx, Blumenfeld, Krajcik, and Soloway (1997) define it (with special but not limiting reference to science) as follows:

> Project-based science focuses on student-designed inquiry that is organized by investigations to answer driving questions, includes collaboration

Writing Hypertext and Learning: Conceptual and Empirical Approaches
Copyright © 2002 by Elsevier Science Ltd.
All rights of reproduction in any form reserved.
ISBN: 0-08-043987-X

among learners and others, the use of new technology, and the creation
of authentic artifacts that represent student understanding. (p. 341)

The principal change indicated in this definition is a shift from topic-based collection
of information to question-driven inquiry. Note, however, that the end-point is still a
presentation.

Although there are reports of high levels of motivation among students in project-
based learning, little attention has been given to what the students may be learning
apart from media production (McGrath *et al.*, 1996). Several accounts have appeared
in which creation of the product obliterated the inquiry. Yarnall and Kafai (1996) had
students who were studying oceans create educational computer games. Apparently all
the students' and even the teacher's attention became focused on game design and
only isolated facts about oceans made it into the process. Anderson, Holland, and
Palincsar (1997) report a case in which students were to prepare a poster and a presentation to explain a physical phenomenon they had been shown. The students divided
up tasks so that only one member of the group dealt with the explanatory problem
while the rest focused on the poster and presentation.

Various justifications for the production of artifacts and presentations have been
offered, ranging from high-flown constructivist pronouncements (e.g. Papert, 1993) to
the mundane acknowledgement that teachers need something to grade. In the definition set forth by Marx *et al.* (1997), however, it would seem that the essential character
of project-based learning lies in "investigations to answer driving questions" and the
collaborative character of these investigations. Of the remaining terms, "use of new
technology" would seem to be an irrelevant concession to modernity and "creation of
authentic artifacts that represent student understanding" an irrelevant concession to
tradition.

Emergent Hypertext

For the past 15 years we have been working on ways to move knowledge to the center
of educational activity rather than leaving it as a by-product of schoolwork. We have
accordingly been skeptical of movements like "writing across the curriculum",
"writing to learn," and "learning by hypermedia design" (Carver, Lehrer, Connell, &
Erickson, 1992) because, although they indicate a laudable concern with subject
matter, they continue to encourage the students to focus on presentation rather than on
knowledge advancement. The roots of this skepticism, however, lie farther back, in a
previous decade of research on writing (Bereiter & Scardamalia, 1987).

Dissatisfaction With School Writing

School writing instruction has been criticized for many years for its artificiality and
for the fact that the teacher is the only audience. These criticisms, of course, apply to
"projects" as well as shorter writing assignments and they can also apply to contem-

porary hypertext and multimedia production. Through the work of a number of educators such as James Brittain and Donald Graves, a new approach to school writing developed in which students write for each other in a kind of workshop arrangement, revise in the light of peer responses, and produce books that become part of the classroom library. This approach makes excellent sense for those kinds of writing, such as fiction and poetry, where producing a literary artifact is the appropriate goal. When the approach is applied to writing in subject-matter fields, however, it suffers from the same drawback I have been discussing: attention is focused on presentation rather than on the pursuit of knowledge and understanding.

Our own writing research did not focus on the written products so much as on the thinking that went on in their creation. We found that expert writers did, as is often claimed, improve their knowledge and understanding through the thinking that went on as they composed. This rarely happened with novice writers, however. They employed, often very efficiently, a strategy we called "knowledge telling," in which knowledge appropriate to the topic and genre was retrieved and expressed with little or no reflection (Scardamalia & Bereiter, 1987). We experienced some success in teaching reflective strategies to students (Scardamalia, Bereiter, & Steinbach, 1984), but it seemed that the nature of school writing would eventually defeat any such efforts; "knowledge telling" is highly adaptive in the ordinary school setting.

Development of CSILE

In order to make the pursuit of knowledge rather than media production the center of school activity, students had to be able to represent knowledge in ways that it could be worked on, to organize cooperative activities around the improvement of that knowledge, and to respond to one another's ideas as these were developing. These requirements point toward networked computers and a shared database. At the time the first version of CSILE (Computer Supported Intentional Learning Environments) went into classrooms, in 1986, hypertext was not a realistic possibility. Xerox PARC's Notecards had only recently appeared and it demanded such a large screen and so much computing power that its functionality seemed quite beyond our reach. But we did have commenting, which linked one note to another, and our graphics had a "zoom in" feature that enabled students to attach graphic notes to graphic notes in a branching hierarchy. With those few resources, we discovered that the students themselves were finding ways to create hypertext. But they were not deliberately producing hypertext documents. They were simply finding better ways to represent and work with knowledge.

As technology advanced we were able to incorporate more hypertext capabilities into CSILE. Knowledge Forum™, the current version, contains an abundance of ways to link, collect, synthesize, and create graphical views of database content. Yet it is not the software you would look for if you wanted to author a hypertext document. It is a knowledge-building, not an authoring environment. It is designed so that the hypertext grows up naturally as a result of operations carried out to advance inquiry. The "rise-above-it" note, for instance, is a note whose technical function is to remove other notes from viewing. This is not something a hypertext author would do, but it is a worthwhile operation when inquiry has proceeded to the point where a number of older ideas can now be subsumed under a more comprehensive or powerful explanation.

Results and Challenges

Hewitt (1998) has documented the changes that took place in one teacher's CSILE classroom over four years as he moved from a traditional "project" approach to one of problem-driven collaborative knowledge building. On a variety of measures the quality of process and content improved as these changes took place. Studies by Hakkarainen (1995) and Oshima (1997) have shown that CSILE students not only pursue questions of genuine scientific and scholarly significance, but that they make advances on them. Of relevance to the issue of "learning from creating hypertext," however, is the fact that teachers and students alike have shown a preference for a linear, discussion-like sequencing of notes, despite its obvious limitations for knowledge organization. We have taken this as a design challenge, and there are indications that enabling students to create meaningful higher-order views of the work that is going on gives them sufficient perspective that they are no longer so attracted to the one-thing-after-another construction of knowledge.

Conclusion

I recently acquired the CD-ROM version of a popular school encyclopedia. The content is quite similar to the 1967 print version of the same encyclopedia, which I also own, but the new version is hypertext. You can click on almost any word and go to a related article and there are also linked movies and graphics. I am sure this will greatly facilitate research and exploration for students. It certainly does for me. One carry-over from the old version is a topic outline attached to each major article, an outline clearly intended for students to use in doing "projects" or "research papers" on those topics. This outline organizes the student's report in advance, so that all the student has to do is retrieve information corresponding to the headings and write up the report. The result, of course, would not be a hypertext document. It would be a conventional, topically organized linear text. It is strange to see a modern digital encyclopedia supporting this archaic scholastic ritual. But would it be much of an advance if, instead, the encyclopedia came supplied with a tool for compiling a hypertext document? I am not sure it would be any advance at all.

The problem with the old "project" ritual was not its form, nor was it the source of information. Valuable research and inquiry can be done using an encyclopedia. The problem was its focus on the production of a document rather than on the solution of a problem or the advancement of understanding. There is a deeply held belief among educators that students must be given a concrete objective, something to produce in the end, that they cannot be expected to pursue cognitive objectives "in the abstract." We have devoted the better part of the past 15 years to showing that this is not true (cf. Bereiter & Scardamalia, 1989; Bereiter, Scardamalia, Cassells, & Hewitt, 1997). Students can become deeply engrossed in advancing their understanding of the world, and it is the ideal way to occupy school time. At some point they may decide that they have got hold of knowledge that is worth disseminating, if only to others in their class. That is the time for presentation, which may take many forms, one of which might be the production of a hypermedia document. But along the way, students can be helped in their knowledge building by computer supports that allow them to preserve, search, organize, and view their knowledge from different perspectives. This activity will also produce hypermedia, but it is an emergent of the knowledge building process itself. It should not be confused with presentational hypermedia.

References

Anderson, C. W., Holland, J. D., & Palincsar, A. S. (1997). Canonical and sociocultural approaches to research and reform in science education: The story of Juan and his group. *Elementary School Journal, 97*, 359–383.

Bereiter, C., & Scardamalia, M. (1987). *The Psychology of Written Composition*. Hillsdale, NJ: Lawrence Erlbaum Associates.

Bereiter, C., & Scardamalia, M. (1989). Intentional learning as a goal of instruction. In: L. B. Resnick (eds), *Knowing, Learning, and Instruction: Essays in Honor of Robert Glaser* (pp. 361–392). Hillsdale, NJ: Lawrence Erlbaum Associates.

Bereiter, C., Scardamalia, M., Cassells, C., & Hewitt, J. (1997). Postmodernism, knowledge building, and elementary science. *Elementary School Journal, 97*, 329–340.

Carver, S. M., Lehrer, R., Connell, T., & Erickson, J. (1992). Learning by hypermedia design: Issues of assessment and implementation. *Educational Psychologist, 27*(3), 385–404.

Hakkarainen, K. (1995, August). *Collaborative Inquiry in the Computer-Supported Intentional Learning Environments*. Poster session presented at biennial meeting of the European Association for Research on Learning and Instruction, Nijmegen, Netherlands.

Hewitt, J. (1998, April). *From a Focus on Tasks to a Focus on Knowledge: The Cultural Transformation of a Toronto Classroom*. Paper presented at the annual meeting of the American Educational Research Association, San Diego.

Marx, R. W., Blumenfeld, P. C., Krajcik, J. S., & Soloway, E. (1997). Enacting project-based science. *Elementary School Journal, 97*, 341–358.

McGrath, D., Cumaranatunge, C., Ji, M., Chen, H., Broce, W., & Wright, K. (1996). Multimedia science projects: Seven case studies. *Journal for Research on Computers in Education, 28*(5) Retrieved January 17, 2002, from http://www2.educ.ksu.edu/Projects/JRCE/v28-5/McGrath/article/main.htm

Oshima, J. (1997). Students' construction of scientific explanations in a collaborative hypermedia learning environment. In: R. Hall, N. Miyake, and N. Enyedy (eds), *Computer Support for Collaborative Learning '97*. Toronto: University of Toronto.

Papert, S. (1993). *The Children's Machine*. New York: Basic Books.

Scardamalia, M., & Bereiter, C. (1987). Knowledge telling and knowledge transforming in written composition. In: S. Rosenberg (ed.), *Advances in Applied Psycholinguistics: Vol. 2. Reading, Writing, and Language Learning* (pp. 142–175). Cambridge: Cambridge University Press.

Scardamalia, M., Bereiter, C., & Steinbach, R. (1984). Teachability of reflective processes in written composition. *Cognitive Science, 8*, 173–190.

Yarnall, L., & Kafai, Y. (1996, April). *Issues in Project-Based Science Activities: Children's Constructions of Ocean Software Games.* Paper presented at the annual meeting of the American Educational Research Association, New York.

Chapter 6

Sleepy Links, Collaborative Grading and Trails — Shaping Hypertext Structures by Usage Processes

Karsten D. Wolf

This chapter discusses three main topics concerning the educational use of hypertext authoring systems. First, an implementation of a networked authoring system is described. The main focus of the environment is to support the key activities in constructivist learning: creation, construction, communication, cooperation, and collaboration. Students are enabled to author hypermedia content easily. Second, the results from an evaluation of a pilot study are reported. Learning effects of writing hypertexts can be shown. Third, problems resulting from the use of an authoring tool in an educational setting and possible solutions are discussed: (a) some users participate more actively in the creation and construction of the hypertext, therefore enlarging their knowledge in a faster way than their co-learners; (b) not all of the contributions (new nodes) are of high quality; (c) the entropy of the system (the number of links) becomes larger; (d) not all of the links make sense to the different users because of their different usage contexts.

Introduction

The use of hypertext or hypermedia editors as "cognitive tools" (see Kommers, Jonassen, & Mayes, 1992) is spreading through constructivist learning environments. Students can create their own hypertexts, making their own knowledge structures more explicit and open to discussion. This process is assumed to enhance learning (Scardamalia, Bereiter, & Lamon, 1994). This chapter will investigate three main questions concerning the educational use of hypermedia authoring systems:

First, how to implement a networked authoring system that enables the students to create hypermedia by themselves without difficulty (section 2: *implementation*). Second, what evidence can be found to support the assumption that hypermedia

Writing Hypertext and Learning: Conceptual and Empirical Approaches
ISBN: 0-08-043987-X

authoring supports learning (section 3: *evaluation*). Last, what problems may emerge when students become authors, and how to solve them (section 4: *innovation*).

Implementation of the Authoring System

Constructivist learning environments can be defined as "a place where learners may work together and support each other as they use a variety of tools and information resources in their guided pursuit of learning goals and problem-solving activities" (Wilson, 1996, p. 5). The technical capabilities and the widespread infrastructure of the Internet is especially suitable to implement such a system (for a detailed discussion of the six new qualities of Internet based learning see Wolf, 1999).

This section first analyzes the functional demands for a constructivist learning environment. Following, an actual software implementation is described. Finally, the main features, which are associated with constructivist learning theories, will be discussed.

Key Activities of Constructivist Learning

Honebein (1996), building on work of Cunningham, Duffy, and Knuth (1993), asks for environments which:

- connect students with the knowledge construction process;
- provide students with experience with the knowledge construction process;
- provide experience in and appreciation for multiple perspectives and modes of representation;
- provide for collaboration. (Honebein, 1996, p. 11)

A basic assumption of pedagogical constructivism is that students' ideas should be tested against alternate views through social negotiation and collaborative learning groups (Honebein, 1996). Networked hypermedia authoring systems could meet these requirements.

In Wolf (1995) the author further elaborates the five key activities of constructivist learning (see Figure 6.1): A group of learners (possibly distributed across the globe) do:

Create   A basic element of a constructivist learning environment is to allow learners to create their own contents. By creating an external representation they make parts of their internal world model explicit. For example, these representations can be a presentation, a node in a hypertext or a physical model.

Construct   To prevent that students just accumulate unrelated bits of knowledge, they need to construct a deeper structure connecting their own representations as well as those of other students. They should identify parallels, connections, dependencies, and conclusions as well as omissions, contradictions, or errors. For example, in a hypertext this structure can be expressed with categorized links.

Communicate   A central functional element of teaching–learning-processes is the exchange of information, knowledge, experiences, opinions, and attitudes between learners with one another, as well as with the teacher. This can happen within a conversation, but it is also possible to use other media such as a text, illustration, physical model, or outlines — *public entities* in the sense of Papert (1991).

Cooperate   Learning is a process highly dependent on the willingness of the interaction partners to help each other. Asking for, receiving, and giving answers, help and guidance is a central learning activity. Cooperation can also mean to take over coresponsibility for other students' learning.

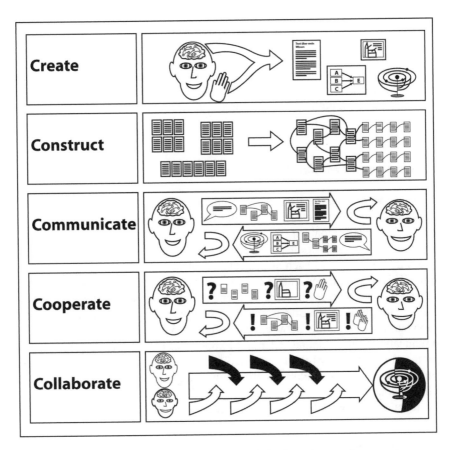

Figure 6.1: Key activities in constructivist learning environments
(5 Cs, see Wolf, 1995).

Collaborate   Collaboration means that two or more persons are jointly working to solve a problem or produce some entity, thus shouldering the responsibility for the result together. Both success and failure will be attributed to all members.

Creation and Construction are the basis for Communication, because exchange of knowledge cannot take place without contents. Cooperation is a special Communication process aimed at finding and giving help to co-learners. Collaboration is a joint process of creation, construction and communication in a group of people.

The technical infrastructure of the Internet supports this type of highly interconnected, networked environment, which has never before been possible to implement in a practical, efficient way. Net based learning environments allow to:

- connect the learners' minds in scaffolding a process of group thinking and problem solving;
- bring together the learners' actions in collaboratively creating artifacts such as presentations, documents, or solutions to problems.

By introducing such an environment, the role of the teachers and learners will naturally change. Teachers become scouts, consultants, trainers, mediators, referees, advocatus diaboli, and moderators. Students therefore become problem solvers, project managers, presenters, authors, experts, and evaluators (see Wolf, 2002 for a detailed description of these roles).

The Internet-based Learning Environment EduSerf

EduSerf has been designed from the ground up to support the key activities of constructivist learning, both in classroom work (internet augmented teaching) and in online learning.[1] The main goal of the system is *not* to *replace* teachers by a kind of web-based training but rather to *support* teachers and students in complex teaching–learning-arrangements such as projects, problem based learning or self-organized learning. This is done by providing the necessary infrastructure, without the drudgery that comes along with some necessary organizational tasks (hence the name Edu*Serf*).

The user interface of EduSerf is split into two parts (frames): on the *left side* there is a toolbar for navigating between the different parts of the system (DataCenter, CommunicationCenter, MediaCenter and ExpoCenter plus Search, Notebook, Administration and Help). Any of the four centers as well as the help, search, administration and notebook buttons is available with one mouse click. The *right side* always shows the chosen content or activity.

The functionality provided in the four centers is shown in Figure 6.3.

---

[1] EduSerf has been implemented with WebObjects 4.0/4.5 from Apple, a web application server. Earlier prototypes of EduSerf were called Webber and have been implemented in ScriptX 1.x (Kaleida Labs) and Frontier 4 & 5 (UserLand Software).

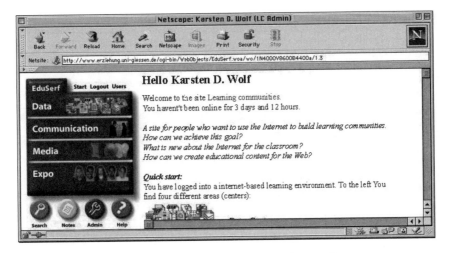

Figure 6.2: The EduSerf™ interface seen from a German user
(© kdw & w.i.s.e. 1998–2001, see http://www.eduserf.de).

Association of EduSerf Features with Constructivist Learning Theories

A central idea for the design of EduSerf is the creation of an environment for the collaborative writing of texts and the building of a joint knowledge base in the sense of *intentional learning* (Scardamalia *et al.*, 1994). The software enables users to create linear presentations, and non-linear hypertexts. These integrated authoring tools allow students both to document one's own learning process as well as to study by designing teaching and learning materials in the sense of Harel (1993). The results of this work are to be published in the learning community (*public entities* in *constructivism*, Papert, 1991) and are the focus of a content-based peer analysis.

Cognitive flexibility theory asks for a repeated traversal of a complex subject matter from multiple perspectives to gather and acquire a topic (Spiro, Feltovich, Jacobson, & Coulson, 1992). Expanding this idea, EduSerf expects students to *create* alternative representations (hypertext nodes) by themselves. In order to anchor the learning process (*generative learning*, Bransford, Sherwood, Hasselbring, Kinzer, & Williams, 1990), presentations of complex, ill-defined problems can be integrated into the learning environment.

EduSerf is to be understood as a cognitive tool (Jonassen & Carr, 1998) fostering meta-cognitive thinking processes such as setting goals, writing learning protocols and giving mutual feedback. These elaborative actions are supported by content editors (presentation editor, hypertext editor). Conversation and discourse tools are available, as well. Other thinking tools such as a scenario analysis in a spreadsheet document can be integrated into the environment using computer files.

In their discussion of knowledge management systems, Brown and Duguid (1991) propose to support and coordinate knowledge exchange on a personal level. EduSerf

Communication Center: *Communicate & Cooperate*
Personal Email: Read emails and send new emails to the other members of the learning environment. **Announcements:** Read and create new announcements for groups of users. **Calendar:** Manage dates and milestones for groups and individual users. **Newsgroups:** Discuss, inquire, ask and answer questions in threaded newsgroups.

Expo Center: *Plan, Solve Problems, Collaborate, Document and Present*
Welcome: Self-description of the user and the groups. Information about the projects and the site. **Commented WWW-linklist:** Create, manage and structure commented lists of WWW bookmarks (favourites) on personal, group and project level. Automatic ordering of the links by usage frequency. **Goals of project and groups:** Define goals for the project and the group. Create reports about the achieved progress toward the goals. **Problem tasks in the project:** Present a problem for the project, define tasks and room for maneuvre, offer starting points, close problems as solved. **Learning protocols:** Put down in a protocol, who has done what, what has been achieved and learned, where problems were discovered, what has to be done next. **Presentations:** Create web-based presentations based on templates. Add comments to charts to start content based discussions. **Guestbooks:** Direct open feedback to projects, groups or persons.

Media Center: *Create, Construct, Cooperate, Collaborate*
Contents and Representations: Define thematic areas, create and edit hypermedia documents, build a hyperstructure.

Data Center: *Create, Cooperate, Collaborate*
Folders: Organize computer files and share them with other users in your group, project or site-wide. **Files:** Save and share computer files and manage different file versions.

Figure 6.3: Overview of the functions found in the four centers of EduSerf.

put this *heter*archical organizational structure into practice in the form of problem-oriented projects.

Learning from Authoring: Results from a Pilot Study

EduSerf has been evaluated to test the basic assumption of constructivist learning theory that the knowledge construction process of students enhances their learning.

The pilot study took place in a graduate course with the topic "Internet-based learning in apprenticeship and training." The students worked individually or in groups through three phases (see Figure 6.4). In the first phase the students conducted a web research for a self-chosen problem and created a commented WWW link list. In the second phase they created a presentation to answer their own questions. Finally, they

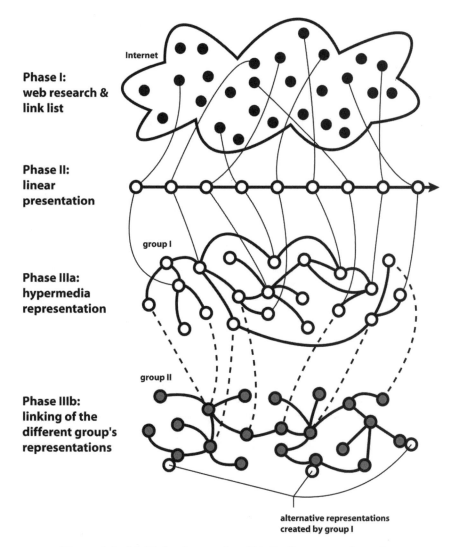

Phase I:
web research &
link list

Internet

Phase II:
linear
presentation

Phase IIIa:
hypermedia
representation

group I

Phase IIIb:
linking of the
different group's
representations

group II

alternative representations
created by group I

Figure 6.4: Multiple phases of an EduSerf augmented seminar.

extended their presentation into a richly linked hypertext. A detailed description of the evaluation can be found in Wolf (2002). In this section some results concerning learning effects shall be reported.

The Internet-augmented seminar focused on the domain-specific improvement of the learners' *complex problem solving ability* (CPSA). To measure the CPSA the author used two special problem cases (AIT = analytical ideal types of problem solving; Sembill, 1992). The students had to solve these cases in a pencil-and-paper method (see Figure 6.5). The CPSA/*quantity* score measures the breadth and depth of the students' solutions, and the CPSA/*quality* score appraises the excellence of the

Dear Participant,

Please try to put yourself in the following situation:
You have your Masters Degree, and are now an assistant to a senior advisor in a consulting firm. Your boss has to give a presentation to a client firm (an advertising agency) next week. But suddenly an emergency with a very important client in London comes up, and your Boss gives you the following task (flight ticket and suitcase clinched in hand):

"Next week we have a presentation at Cyber Ad advertising agency. They design Internet ads. Outside of that they concern themselves with the professional design of websites for firms. Cyber Ad works a lot with freelancers (specialists sign on for only special projects), and students (particularly design and physics) together. Through this arises a high fluctuation, in which a traditional furthering of education is made seemingly impossible.

So, the boss attended the Lotus-conference, and is totally crazy about net-based learning environments. He would like to know from us, if net-based education can be specifically converted for his company, and how it can be structured, in order to get results.

And no technological jargon! You've worked with pedagogy before, right? Weren't you talking one time about that seminar "Further education with the Internet"? Right, I estimate, this will be your first test. Fax me your ideas, I'm at my hotel in London until Monday. I'll work them through and come to the airport Monday evening. Pick me up there. Then I'll give you the sketches for the presentation, so that you can have them done by Tuesday morning. Alright? Doesn't matter, I have to go. Bye"

Develop a problem solution for Cyber Ad. Consider, which information is important for the comprehension and clarity of your ideas. Write everything down, which seems necessary or important for a good solution. The fax costs are insignificant . . .
You have 25 minutes to work out the problem!

Figure 6.5: Complex problem case (AIT case) — first test (Wolf, 1998).

solution. To determine how much the students learned from the hypertexts of the other students, an additional *cross-knowledge test* was conducted.[2]

The first test was taken after an introduction to the seminar contents (4 hours of lecture and presentations). The second test was taken one month after the end of the seminar. The students could clearly improve their content specific problem solving ability (see Figure 6.6) after working with EduSerf for around 4 months.

Pre-knowledge is known as one of the strongest predictors of students' performance (Dochy, 1992; Vosniadou, 1992). A higher CPSA/quantity score at the beginning of

---

[2] In the cross-knowledge test a question was added for each topic created by a student.

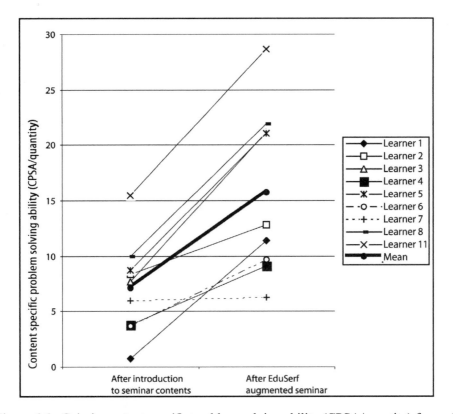

Figure 6.6: Gain in content specific problem solving ability (CPSA/quantity) for each learner (TN): mean difference = 7.80, Std. Error = 1.67, *t*-Ratio = 4.66, Prob > $t = 0.001$.

the seminar correlates with a higher score at the end (0.87**). The gain in complex problem solving capability (difference CPSA/quantity) is moderated by the quality of the first CPSA (pre CPSA/quantity; see Table 6.1). Nonetheless, the average growth of more than two standard deviations in the problem solving ability is a strong sign of a major learning success. As can be seen in Figure 6.6, nearly all students improved their CPSA/quantity.

In the correlation structure of the usage quantity (see Table 6.1) it is important to notice that the *usage quantity of creation* correlates with the post CPSA/quantity score (0.82*).

More active usage (such as information retrieval, creation and communication) goes together with a better score in the cross-knowledge test and partly with the quantitative CPSA score, but not with the *quality* of the problem solution. Only the *usage quality* correlates strongly with the *quality of the problem solving*.

Overall, the *use of a hypertext* editor in this setting has therefore *supported learning*.

Table 6.1: Correlation matrix of learning and usage in EduSerf.

	Cross-knowledge test	Post CPSA/ quantity	Difference CPSA/ quantity	Post CPSA/ quality
	mean = 9.75 std. dev.= 3.69 span = 4–14	mean= 15.76 std. dev.= 7.60 span = 6–29	mean = 7.80 std. dev.= 4.73 span = 0–13	mean = 33.75 std. dev.= 19.49 span = 6–60
Intelligence and pre-knowledge				
Picture–Word–Test (IQ-Test)	−0.05 (0.901)	0.05 (0.912)	−0.15 (0.728)	−0.38 (0.359)
Computer pre-knowledge	0.75* (0.031)	0.17 (0.681)	−0.13 (0.762)	−0.17 (0.683)
Internet pre-knowledge	0.126 (0.766)	0.54 (0.171)	0.36 (0.374)	0.30 (0.476)
Pre CPSA/quantity mean = 7.96 std. dev. = 3.78 span = 4–15	0.589 (0.125)	0.87** (0.005)	0.60 (0.115)	0.54 (0.164)
Pre CPSA/quality mean = 22.0 std. dev. = 9.78 span = 8 — 36	0.363 (0.377)	0.81* (0.014)	0.75* (0.032)	0.75* (0.034)
Usage quantity				
Usage information-retrieval	0.81* (0.015)	0.74* (0.035)	0.47 (0.24)	0.32 (044)
Usage creation	0.67 (0.069)	0.82* (0.014)	0.65 (0.080)	0.56 (0.146)
Usage communication	0.77* (0.024)	0.66 (0.078)	0.38 (0.350)	0.285 (0.493)
Usage quality				
Number of relevant commented links in link list	0.21 (0.613)	0.82* (0.012)	0.72* (0.044)	0.68 (0.062)
Presentation grade	0.06 (0.884)	0.90** (0.006)	0.69 (0.085)	0.90** (0.002)
Representation grade	0.43 (0.335)	0.789* (0.035)	0.71 (0.075)	0.88** (0.009)

Learners as Authors: Innovative Features to Solve New Problems

As shown above, the opportunity to create and share documents helps students to learn. Nevertheless, the above described learning environment allows learners to become authors inserting nodes and links without an editorial filter. This specific approach can lead to four problems:

1) Some users participate more actively in the creation and construction of the hypertext, therefore enlarging their knowledge in a faster way than their co-learners (need for *process feedback*).
2) Not all of the contributions (new nodes) are of high quality (great possible variance of contributions' *quality*).
3) The entropy of the system (the number of links) becomes larger.
4) Not all of the links make sense to the different users because of their different usage contexts (*out-of-context linking*).

EduSerf introduces four different new mechanisms to deal with these difficulties, which will be described in this section

Process Feedback: Experience Points

In constructivist learning settings we focus on de-central, group-based work over a rather long period of time with some presentations and milestones scattered along. But how can learners get some feedback about their learning process? How can teachers look after the efforts of our students, if they work independently and highly parallel? The concept followed in EduSerf is that the learning process of the students should be made explicit, and to "force" them to externalize their steps and results. This is accomplished by asking the students to define their goals, create protocols of their work, create presentations, content representations, and give each other feedback. All of this information is put into a shared knowledge space accessible for each member of the system.

Therefore the general idea is to create some learning process feedback to the students.[3] This is done by awarding students so called *experience points*, based on actions relevant to learning. The idea of experience points (EP) is derived from role playing games, where "characters" (the players in the game) earn experience points for solving riddles or finding treasures. The EP therefore tries to symbolize the learning of the character in the game. The more EP a character has, the more powerful he or she is.

EduSerf extends this idea by introducing different kinds of EP. Users of the system gain EP for being active members of the learning community (see Figure 6.4 for some examples). If users don't log in once a week, they lose some EP. The different

---

[3] For a detailed discussion about quantitative versus qualitative measurement of experience points see Wolf (1999).

General	Create	Communicate
Log into EduSerf	Create a chart in a presentation	Send an Email
	Create a personal protocol	Answer a discussion thread
	Edit a representation	

Cooperate	Construct	Collaborate
Answer a discussion thread marked as a question	Insert a link between two representations	Create a group protocol
Provide feedback to a chart in a presentation	Reorder the structure of a presentation	Edit a chart or a representation created by another group member

Figure 6.7: Categorizing actions in EduSerf.

activities are assigned to the 5 Cs (see Figure 6.7), so that every user has a general EP (the sum of the 5C-EP and some general activity) and EP for the 5 Cs. The students can see their own EP level and the relative ranking of all the other students. Teachers and students alike can use this information to see, where they excel or fall behind.

If more learning related actions could be identified in following studies, the EP system would allow some kind of *process assessment* to be created instead of traditional tests. The evaluation has shown that not only quantity but also quality of actions must be taken into account.

Besides giving the users some feedback about the amount of their efforts, there is another important reason to introduce EP. It can be used to estimate the expertise of a user in a domain. When a user with a high EP level creates feedback information (e.g. by grading a document or using a link) his or her input should be weighted more so, than the feedback from a novice user with a low EP level.[4]

As the evaluation has shown, at least the categories *creation* and *communication* have a high correlation with learning success.[5] The EP system was very popular especially for students with high intrinsic motivation. They liked the fact that they could earn some "objective" recognition for their enormous amount of work. Students

---

[4] When expert users newly join EduSerf, their expertise will be under-represented until they start to actively contribute to the learning community.
[5] In the pilot study the amount of construction, cooperation and collaboration did not suffice for a detailed analysis.

following a work minimization strategy didn't like the EP system because it made their low involvement visible. However they reported that they didn't work harder despite their low EP level. Therefore the EP system wasn't perceived as extrinsic in the study (Wolf, 2002).

A problem of the current EP implementation in EduSerf is that it is solely a quantitative measurement. The system does not take into account, if a contribution is of high quality or not. This information could possibly be derived from the teachers and the other students. The categorization of experience points (following the 5 Cs), the validation in classroom and other settings as well as the fine-tuning of the system is the focus of the author's current research.

Collaborative Grading and the Problem of Varying Quality of Contributions

EduSerf allows all users to create their own presentations (linear sequences of charts) and hypermedia documents (see Figures 6.8 and 6.9) without an editorial filter.

The documents undoubtedly have a great variance in their quality. Submissions may have omissions, can be poorly written or even be downright wrong. The author implemented a system, which asks students to grade the documents in five categories (see Figure 6.10).

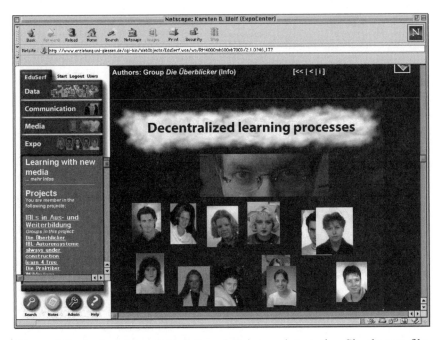

Figure 6.8: A chart in a presentation showing an interactive Shockwave file.

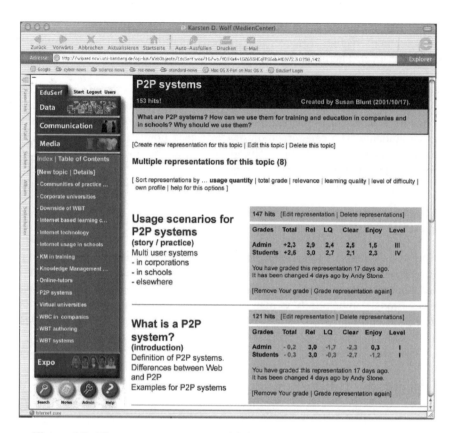

Figure 6.9: The users can create multiple representations for a content.

- *Relevance of content.* Do you think that everyone who wants to learn something about this topic, should read/view this document?
- *Learning quality.* Did this document help you to shape a deeper understanding of the topic it covered?
- *Clearness of presentation.* Did you understand this document? Did the authors manage to present the information in a clearly structured way?
- *Enjoyment value.* Did you enjoy reading this document? Was it interesting? Did it spur your interest in the subject?
- *Level of content.* Do you think that this is rather advanced or more basic stuff?

This concept of grading documents by the readers is known as "collaborative filtering" (Goldberg, Oki, Nichols, & Terry, 1992). In EduSerf, this information is used to create the hyperspace for a specific user dynamically on the fly. For example, if the users look at the list of representations for a specific content, they can sort them in the following ways:

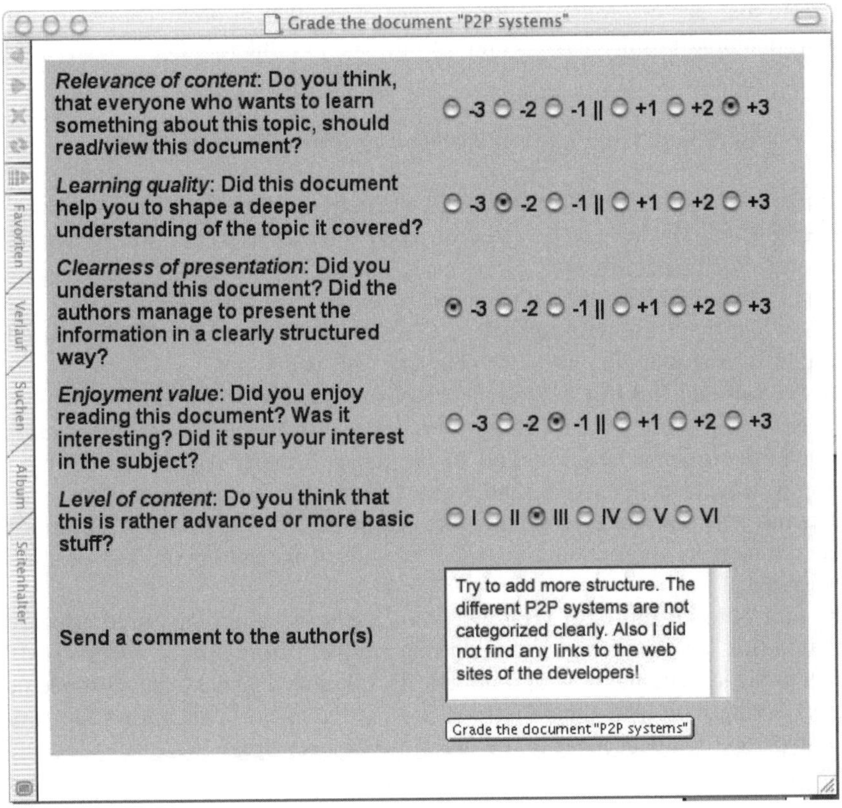

Figure 6.10: Grading a document.

- most often used representation;
- most relevant representation;
- clearest presentation;
- best learning quality;
- best enjoyment value;
- advanced or introductory information.

As a result, often used representations with good grades will flourish in the system. Poor representations are sorted, and moved further down the list. If an author changes a document, he or she can choose to notify all of the users who have graded the document so that they can eventually change their former evaluation. The grades of the students and teachers are kept separate from one another.

There are two side effects of grading. The first is that grading itself is a learning process. To grade the representation, the user has to think about the content in several different ways (see the grading categories above). The second effect is that the system can create matches of profiles between other users. It then promotes representations users with similar profiles have found useful, clear, or entertaining.

Sleepy Links, Mouse Votes and the Problem of Entropy in Hypertexts

In EduSerf the users are allowed to create as many links as they like from one node to another. The links have to be categorized by the user as a first hint of what others can expect. The categories are: (1) get some details; (2) see also; (3) there is another solution for this problem; (4) get some background; (5) I had the experience . . . ; (6) what is wrong with this representation; (7) problems; (8) other opinion; (9) contradiction; (10) example; (11) try it for yourself; (12) watch out.

If users can add links to a hypertext, this can quickly result in a structure where each node links to one other. One obvious reason for this is that different users can have quite dissimilar internal models of the topic. Another reason can be that users develop a deeper understanding and focus on other, more advanced structures. But often is the case that a user creates a link because he or she thinks it's a good idea, but later on forgets about it, and the link just adds to the entropy (= loss of structure) of the system.

The idea is to let links not seeing a lot of traffic first become "tired" (push them down in a link list) and later to entirely remove them from a node. Often used links flourish in the system and flow up into link list hierarchy. This system is implemented by users voting with their "mice" which links are valuable. This allows the structure of the hypertext to adapt itself to the users' needs over time.

More research has to show if sleepy links really lead to a better hypertext structure adapted to all possible users. Maybe the use of such a system only works with highly motivated and experienced hypertext readers, who are willing to dig deeper into the link lists. Other users may only use the first two or three links, so that the structure gets very rigid and a shallow style of reading prevails.

Paths and the Problem with Out of Context Links

The above-mentioned mouse vote approach is effective for small hypertexts, but it ignores the context of the hypertext usage. A system should take into account the path of the user, realizing *context sensitive hyperlinking*.

This idea is illustrated in Figure 6.11. The thickness of the arrows represents the number of users following a link. If we focus on node 3, a lot of users are coming from node 1 and most of them go to node 6 afterwards, some of them to node 5. If the links on node 3 would be sorted by total hits, the node 6 link would be at the top, followed by node 5 and node 4. But this wouldn't be right for users coming from node 2 to node 3. Most of them head on to node 4, and none of them to node 6! Therefore the link list should look different depending on the previously visited representation.

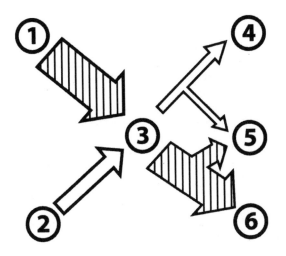

Figure 6.11: Context sensitive hyperlinking in EduSerf.

The solution to this problem is that the system creates link lists for each referer node by analyzing the paths of the users. Readers coming from node 1 in the example above see and contribute to the *node 3 (coming from node 1)* — sorting of hyperlinks. In this example node 6 will be at the top of the link list. Users coming from node 2 will see *node 3 (coming from node 2)* — hyperlink sorting. Here the link list is topped by node 4.

Conclusion

While a first study has indicated that the creation of hypertexts can enhance learning, it has also become apparent that this approach also creates new problems and asks for new solutions. Some of these have been presented in the previous section. From a research point of view, further work has to be done to look into the effects of individual versus collaborative creation and construction of large hypertexts. Also the learning effects of collaborative (or peer) grading, cooperation (asking and answering questions), and collaborative writing have to be investigated more deeply. Another point of interest is the gain in usability and semantic structure by usage shaping of hypertexts.

Internet-based learning environments can be very useful for future research, simply because of their ability to combine a more controlled situation with the complexity and duration of a field study. Overall becoming *learning* support tool, *evaluation* environment and (process) *assessment* instrument at once (LEA-model, see Wolf, 2001). Let's build on that!

References

Bransford, J. D., Sherwood, R. D., Hasselbring, T. S., Kinzer, C. K., & Williams, S. M. (1990). Anchored instruction: Why we need it and how technology can help. In: D. Nix, and R. Spiro (eds), *Cognition, Education, and Multimedia: Exploring Ideas in High Technology* (pp. 115–139). Hillsdale, NJ: Lawrence Erlbaum.

Brown, J. S., & Duguid, P. (1991). Organizational learning and communities-of-practice: Toward a unified view of working, learning, and innovation. *Organization Science, 2*(1), 40–57.

Cunningham, D. J., Duffy, T., & Knuth, R. (1993). The textbook of the future. In: C. McKnight, A. Dillon, and J. Richardson (eds), *Hypertext — A Psychological Perspective* (pp. 19–50). Chichester: Ellis Horwood.

Dochy, F. J. R. C. (1992). *Assessment of Prior Knowledge as a Determinant for Future Learning.* Utrecht: Lemma.

Goldberg, D., Oki, B., Nichols, D., & Terry, D. B. (1992). Using collaborative filtering to weave an information tapestry. *Communications of the ACM, December 1992, 35*(12), 61–70.

Harel, I. (1993). *Children Designers.* Norwood, NJ: Ablex Publishing.

Honebein, P. (1996). Seven goals for the design of constructivist learning environments. In: B. Wilson (ed.), *Constructivist Learning Environments: Case Studies in Instructional Design* (pp.11–24). New Jersey: Educational Technology Publications.

Jonassen, D. H., & Carr, C. S. (1998). Mindtools: Affording multiple knowledge representations for learning. In: S. P. LaJoie (ed.), *Computers as Cognitive Tools: The Next Generation.* Mahwah, NJ: Lawrence Erlbaum.

Kommers, P., Jonassen, D. H., & Mayes T. (eds). (1992). *Cognitive Tools for Learning.* Heidelberg, FRG: Springer-Verlag.

Papert, S. (1991). Situating constructionism. In: I. Harel, and S. Papert (eds), *Constructionism* (pp. 1–12). Norwood, NJ: Ablex.

Scardamalia, M., Bereiter, C., & Lamon, M. (1994). The CSILE project: Trying to bring the classroom into world 3. In: K. McGilly (ed.), *Classroom Lessons: Integrating Cognitive Theory and Classroom Practice* (pp. 201–228). Cambridge, MA: MIT Press.

Sembill, D. (1992). *Problemlösefähigkeit, Handlungskompetenz und Emotionale Befindlichkeit. Zielgrößen forschenden Lernens.* [Problem solving ability, action competence, and emotional state. Objectives of research learning]. Göttingen, FRG: Hogrefe.

Spiro, R. J., Feltovitch, P. J., Jacobson, M. J., & Coulson, R. L. (1992). Cognitive flexibility, constructivism, and hypertext: Random access instruction for advanced knowledge acquisition in ill-structured domains. In: T. M. Duffy, and D. H. Jonassen (eds), *Constructivism and the Technology of Instruction: A Conversation* (pp. 57–76). Hillsdale, NJ: Lawrence Erlbaum.

Vosniadou, S. (1992). Knowledge acquisition and conceptual change. *Applied Psychology: An International Journal, 41,* 347–357.

Wilson, B. (ed.). (1996). *Constructivist Learning Environments: Case Studies in Instructional Design.* New Jersey: Educational Technology Publications.

Wolf, K. D. (1995). The implementation of an open learning environment under World Wide Web. In: H. Maurer (ed.), *Multimedia and Hypermedia, 1995. Proceedings of ED-MEDIA 1995, Graz* (pp. 689–694). Charlottesville: AACE.

Wolf, K. D. (1998). *Komplexe Problemstellung Internetbasiertes Lernen I* [Complex problem internet-based learning I]. Unpublished manuscript.

Wolf, K. D. (1999). Erfahrungspunkte — Prozessfeedback in einer WWW-basierten Lernumgebung [Experience points — process feedback in a web-based learning environment]. In: Zentralstelle für Weiterbildung TU Braunschweig (ed.), *Elektronische Medien in der wissen-*

schaftlichen Weiterbildung [Electronic media in scientific further education]. Braunschweig: TU Braunschweig.

Wolf, K. D. (2001). Internet based learning communities — moving from patchwork environments to ubiquitous learning infrastructures. In: S. Dijkstra, D. Jonassen, and D. Sembill (eds), *Multimedia Learning. Results and Perspectives* (pp. 189–223). Frankfurt/M.: Peter Lang.

Wolf, K. D. (2002). *Gestaltung und Einsatz einer internetbasierten Lernumgebung zur Unterstützung selbstorganisierten Lernens* [Design and use of an internetbased learning environment to support self-organized learning]. Hamburg: Verlag Dr. Kovac (in press).

Chapter 7

Opening Windows in Each Other's Minds: Social Sharing of Hypertext Models

Alessandra Talamo and Alessandra Fasulo

This chapter explores the effects of the collaborative construction of a hypermedia on the collective reasoning skills of primary school children. The aim is to describe how small groups of children organize their work, make plans, create a product, and revise their work. Ten-year-old children who had worked on a three-year project at the production of a hypermedia presentation were compared with control classes in an experimental work-session which simulated a hypertext production. A qualitative analysis has been performed on the conversational data collected through recordings of group-work discussions, and the end-products (posters) analyzed in terms of internal logic and work practices. The results reveal a marked effect of the experimental condition: children involved in the hypermedia project deployed different skills in the social organization of work, in the management of information, and in the construction of the final product. Interactional features indicate that children trained on hypertext construction worked under a greater interdependence in the development of the task.

Constructing Hypermedia as a Didactic Practice

In recent years the analyses of how technologies sustain and enhance the development of learning processes showed that there is a mutual adaptation between users and possible uses of technologies in relation to the culture in which the usage of specific tools is embedded. Cornoldi and Caponi (1991) pointed out that the mediation carried out by technological tools on users' reasoning strategies is a core problem in education. Also Boechler (2001) notes that "promoting mental representation of spatial layouts of information is a good approach to improving the hypertext user's ability to access information" (p. 24). It is our belief that this is due to the fact that the spatial re-presentation of concept mapping in hypertexts is a culturally-based artifact, namely a dominant model whose characteristics are self-evident, concise, and widely shared;

thus this model fosters correspondence between how designers and users represent the storage, organization, and retrieval of information.

Of course this does not seem a sufficient basis for the introduction of hypertext production as a didactic activity within the classroom curriculum. What is the relevance of planning hyperspace for education? What are the main benefits that hypertext production can bring to school education? The value of studying situations in which students engage in the construction of hypermedia relies upon the activation of a *metacognitive habit*, that is shown in self-reflection on one's own cognitive activity and on the possibility of using it in different ways (Cornoldi & Caponi, 1991).

The use of technological aids for constructive learning experience affects the learning environment in many ways, first of all by shaping the information processing through particular forms of symbolic representation linked to the media (Olson, 1979). The study of constructive processes of a hypermedia product seems to be an adequate means to test the hypothesis that the exposure to non-linear information can produce an isomorphic conceptual organization (Salomon, 1992).

Technology and Collective Reasoning

What is called the "third generation distance education" (Kaye, 1994) supports computer-assisted education by offering students the tools to participate in a real communication network, thereby embedding classroom work in a wider context of interaction. The relevance of introducing technological resources in the school for the enhancement of communication practices lies on the potential of communication systems (e.g. *email, videoconferencing*) and sharing systems (e.g. *electronic blackboard, file exchange systems*). Teachers and students can now meet other colleagues as well as exchange documents, images and files, and discuss them. Furthermore they can directly communicate with the outside on classroom activity.

The creation of an authentic context of communication enhances the experience of meaningful educational activities (Brown, Collins, & Duguid, 1989; Vosniadou, 1994): school tasks have remarkable communicative effects and derive from real communicative intents (Pontecorvo, Ajello, & Zucchermaglio, 1995; Resnick, Pontecorvo, & Säljö, 1997). When hypertext construction is accomplished in a communicative context the existence of users as final addressees of the work is more explicit and evident. This situation facilitates the expression of children's communicative intentions (they have to articulate what they want to say, who the user is, how they can best express it). Moreover, the introduction of hypermedia technologies broadens children's knowledge of different communicative channels and of expressive languages. Like any real communicative act, hypertext construction is a process that posits hypotheses concerning what the user is seeking. Thus, due to the nature of the hypermedia structure itself, the planning of the links, nodes, paths should be organized in ideas networked on the basis of semantic relationships which rely on culturally shared premises within the specific content of the product (Jonassen & Grabinger, 1990). The choice of expressive forms and possible routes of navigation through the hypermedia needs a decision-making process that engages all the students in a collective reasoning on how to organize knowledge and communicate.

Furthermore, planning hyperspace and building hypertexts (or hypermedia) accords with many of the basic assumptions of constructivist educational theories (Resnick *et al.*, 1997).

The construction of a hypermedia enhances many aspects of communicative practices because it proceeds as live communication training. First, working on a project transforms the school context into a *"productive learning"* environment (De Corte, 1994). Second, the introduction of such an activity turns learning from a process of assimilation into an active construction (Salomon, 1992). The construction of a collective product amplifies communication inside the classroom in so far as it requires a habit to participate in collective discussion. Moreover, communicative capabilities develop within a network in which reciprocal understanding becomes essential (Crook, 1995). Cooperating on a hypermedia construction implies a joint understanding of the structural organization of information, of the selected communicative routes and of expressive languages used (King *et al.*, 1996). This enables every student to contribute to the productive process. Students are requested to share the design and the development of the product, so they have to agree upon the content and the shape of what they wish to express. Cooperation in planning of product plays an important role in cognitive development because it activates the communication of models for the organization of knowledge and it uses the group as a support for the activation of the proximal development zone (Pontecorvo, 1987).

Working on hypermedia construction involves not only discussion about organization of information, but also the management of working procedures: students have explicit references to rules of social organization, thereby achieving mutual social coordination (Crook, 1995). Our work was carried out within a Vygotskian theoretical framework on the social construction of higher functions. Such an approach has a great relevance both for research and practice on the topic under discussion; we argue that the great value of Information and Communication Technology (ICT) is a valuable educational resource as it amplifies the opportunities for communication, enhances collective reasoning and promotes cooperation. In our research, the effects of working on hypermedia are studied as group skills, thus we focused on group rather than on individual performance in the belief that the social changes which the contribution of hypertext presentations brings about are remarkable and consequential for social interaction both inside and outside the classrooms (Salomon, 1994).

The Interactive Nature of Hyperspace

According to Fisher and Mandl (1990), hypermedia can be distinguished from multimedia not only by the richness of its content, but because it allows the user to decide which parts of the hypermedia to examine and explore in greater depth. Thus hypermedia are conceived as *"virtual media* for the simple reason that their information value or outcome is the product of an interpretative act" (p. XIX). From a sociocultural view, writing is also conceived as a supra-individual activity: each writer is considered as a member of a community, where people contribute to the development and negotiation of shared meanings in written texts and usage contexts (Boscolo, 1999). Every form of communication involves all the participants in a collective, interpretative and situated process, that implies a co-construction of shared meanings (Orlikowski & Yates, 1994). Due to the potential flexibility in structuring the content of hypertexts, their production is, in this view, an interactive process that implies that users have in mind the planners and the planners have to preview the users' expectations. Since multiple paths are possible in a hypermedia, planners, in order to produce an effective tool, must anticipate the dynamic control of the user by constructing a metaphor that has to be concise, self-evident, culturally shared, and easily recognizable (Carrada, 2000). Which metaphors can more effectively help users retrieve information? This issue constitutes a core problem since a common model for structuring information would help match the reciprocal expectations between designers and users. This is always true, even in the case of books, but is especially true for the new tools for information organization whose structure is flexible and open. Awareness that different metaphors for navigating a hypermedia are available, is a resource that allows skilful designers to contact the end-users more effectively. Are children able to recognize the communicative value of culturally-shared metaphors? And how can the possible sharing been checked while planning hypermedia?

Which Metaphor for Planning Hyperspace?

Over the years the linear model of text-based literature represented, not only a way for conveying content, but also a pervasive model for dictating how information should be organized by learners on the basis of the flow of information that the books themselves presented. The development of the World Wide Web increased the consideration of the hyperspace as a new environment where information can be collected, retrieved, stored.

The increasing use of the Internet has contributed to the spread of both a more complex representation of the dynamic features and the complex relationships within information as well as the appreciation of the non-stable character of its organization and of the relevance of the way it is shown. Many scholars (Carrada, 2000) now argue that hypertexts and hyperspace are new environments for structuring information and that they necessitate the development of new rules for organizing and retrieving information. As opposed to books (but not in lieu of) these new "environments" for information storage and exchange are primarily conceived as a "space," or as a "place" where information resides. There are not specific terms for the new ways of organizing the information other than those related to the physical cues traditionally associated to information storage: Hyper*space*, Hyper*texts*, where information can be retrieved. The nature of the prefix "Hyper" just refers to something better, promising something *more than*, but is not expressed in any way that can lead to how the access to the information is concretely improved.

As one of the main features of hypertexts is the potential for a more flexible structuring of organization of information, both producers and users are faced with the problem of finding means of orienting themselves toward information, which cannot be always related to the conventional cues of reading documents (Gygi, 1990). The user is introduced to this experience by a physical reference that suggests a spatial representation of information organization. The spatial metaphor is also used to investigate the disfunctions of hyperspace: most cognitive researches on hypertext fruition evaluate the effectiveness of planning hypertexts on the basis of the cognitive overload which it demands of the user. This effect is often defined as "disorientation" (McAleese, 1989a, b).

When dealing with hyperspace the spatial metaphor is then already a cultural artifact. Moreover, it suggests a way of conceiving how hypertexts may effectively represent the content organization. Bromme and Stahl (1999) showed that the spatial metaphor also facilitates producers in directly linking hypertext with the structure of subject matter. Recent studies however show that the spatial metaphor does not adequately represent hypermedia in terms of information organization, rather it gives only a key for navigating through the information according to the producers' expectations and intentions. The spatial metaphor involves specific features that do not always accord with the possible models of hypertext organization. Boechler (2001), for example, identifies spatial cues that cannot be considered similar when applied to physical space as opposed to the metaphorical space of hypertexts. The main problems concern the consideration of *location*. Some of the most common assumptions based on the spatial metaphor for representing hypertext structure are:

- the relationship between *proximity* and semantic connection (hence conceptual "distance" is conceived of in relation to a specified location);
- the *direction* of information flow pre-defines a sequence and order in which information is presented;
- the *connections* and linkages spatially define the semantic relations between units of information.

Thus, according to Boechler, the main misconception in applying a spatial metaphor to hypertext planning and browsing is that, in such a space, navigation is a route between nodes or landmarks that have a not-arbitrary semantic-based sequence.

Nevertheless, it is evident that the spatial metaphor is still widely culturally shared and is a way of *re-presenting* a developed model for organizing topics and subjects as hypertexts. The question can be rephrased as follows: what are the spatial features of hypermedia that survive in their structure even if they are logical fallacies from a representational point of view? What kind of references can be conceived between space and semantic connections on the basis of communicative acts? Our work aims at detecting whether, once the co-construction of hypertexts is conceived as a communicative act, the cultural aspects of orientation are seen as useful even under their representative value.

The Telecomunicando Project

The project "Telecomunicando ti presento i miei tesori" ("I show you my treasures by telecommunicating") is a three-year-long project of a community engaged in the construction of hypermedia. The Telecomunicando project has been funded since 1993 as a pilot project by the Italian Ministry of Education and the STET Company (part of Telecom Italia Company).

The project is designed to test and evaluate both the didactic use of technological aids in the construction of hypermedia products and the introduction of new technologies for Computer Mediated Communication (CMC) into classroom activity.

The project started involving 15 schools, five elementary schools, five junior high schools, and five high schools, from five Italian towns (Milan, Genoa, Rome, Florence, Palermo). Actually about 150 schools in Italy are connected to the project. In this chapter we present only data regarding a sample of the primary grades in Rome, in the very beginning of the project.

Classes involved in the project work on the construction of a hypermedia presentation of a cultural artifact located near their schools. The experimental class whose activities we discuss here worked on a hypermedia of a square near the school. Children actively participated in the seeking and selection of materials to include, in the planning of the hypertext structure and in its implementation. Besides the computer work, the hypermedia production entailed a great effort in planning the final product and its parts, in the construction of a narrative which could help the user navigate the hypertext, in the creation and manipulation of images (icons, pictures, drawings) and sounds (narrations, voices, recorded noises, etc.), and finally through the choice of the expressive languages to be used in the different parts of the hypermedia.

In order to promote a CMC flow, schools have been supplied with the following technological supports: email addresses, internet access, a videoconferencing desktop, an ISDN connection, a shared blackboard.

Classrooms have also engaged in a reciprocal revision process: students of the same level can express their appraisal to work done by their peers from other towns.

Schools have been supported by teams of experts who assist in managing the introduction of technological resources (e.g., the familiarization of students with technological instruments) and in making pedagogical decisions (e.g. the social organization of the children, the introduction of project-oriented activities in the syllabus and the analysis of the processes that activate the social construction of knowledge).

The project emphasizes the constructive nature of knowledge acquisition (Caravita, Pontecorvo, & Talamo, 1996): children participate in an environment in which constructive activity becomes a collective process. Collaboration inside the classroom and outside of it represents a re-definition of learning context as an environment that extends beyond the classroom or the school in which the students work.

The exchanges at a distance promote cooperation between the schools in revising each other's work: the network of linkages between students makes it possible to test new forms of cooperation in which producers and users work together in refining hypermedia.

Studies on computer-aided collaborative writing have shown the positive effects of the telematic communication on the quality of writing (Allen & Thompson, 1995). Here hypertexts are produced for an audience which participates in the construction of the product: revision of the hypertexts includes suggestions concerning the choice of content (what could be desirable), expressive languages (how to express something better), and the projection of future work (how the work will continue). In the Telecomunicando project the end-user of the hypermedia is actively involved in its production and participate in the co-construction process of the representation of what the final product should be (Eco, 1979). The communication exchange and the revision chain between schools involved in the project are meant to help students in the development of their *"metaconceptual awareness"* (Vosniadou, 1994) through the public discussion of their representations.

Research Aims

Previous studies (Talamo & Pontecorvo, 1997; Talamo & Fasulo, 1999) on the same data corpus compared children from the Telecomunicando project with control groups (see p. 12) on the basis of the amount of time they spent in different activities and on the social modalities they showed during group work while planning a hypertext presentation (see below). Data showed that differences between the two groups mostly concerned:

- the great difference in the comparison of the total times of the two classes consists in the time dedicated to individual work, which is longer in the control class;
- control groups need also more time for reaching a common grounding, whereas experimental groups are mostly sharing practical activities (examining the material, planning the presentation, revising the work done) and less time to reach discursive agreement.

The present study is then an exploratory study aimed at understanding children's group processes during the collective planning of a hypertext presentation.

The main research question concerns the differences between experimental and control groups performances in terms of:

- expressive skills;
- metaconceptual awareness on the communicative aims of hypertext structure and contents;
- emerging intersubjectivity in the group process.

Some of the aspects of the collective construction of the product are investigated as "highlighters" of the quality of group process in the planning of the hyperspace. They are:

- a complex structure for the organization of information (planning several links and advance organizers, contextual frames);
- the management of communicative aspects of hypermedia planning (the efficacy of graphical solutions, the emerging of possible users' perspectives);
- the sharing of plans, the coordination of group work, the personal engagement by children in a collective action.

Methodology

Subjects   The subjects were students, nine to ten years old, from four classes of one primary school: two classes were under experimental condition (i.e. they participate in the Telecomunicando project) and two classes constituted the control groups (i.e. they were from equivalent classes but did not engage in any activity which required the use of technological implementation).

On the basis of the indications of the teachers, five homogeneous groups of four to five students were created in each class. Here we discuss data from two Experimental groups and two control groups.

Monitoring the Telecomunicando project   The most relevant dimensions touched upon the project are cognitive skills and relational competencies. As regards cognitive skills, the Telecomunicando project was designed to stimulate the complex organization of information, the identification of links between information units, the selection of relevant information skills, and the choice of different communicative codes in relation to the communication of content.

Furthermore, for the experimental classes involved in the project, the construction of the hypermedia also produced a new organization of students by increasing the number of groups over individual work. Thus, with respect to the relational dimension, the project entailed the intensification of collaborative work inside and outside the classroom.

We aimed at comparing the performance of the groups of students involved in the project with control groups on the basis of the ability to create a complex information structure and to self-manage a group situation by their own.

Both the classes participating in the project and the control classes were observed and video-taped during an experimental session in small work-group.

In order to monitor Telecomunicando, a test was designed to assess students' interpersonal and cognitive abilities as they related to the construction of hypertext products.

The "Test of the Castle"   The test (Talamo, 1998) requires each group of subjects to organize a hypertext on paper (no explicit words referring to hypermedia construction or a computer environment were included in the work assignment). The use of paper granted that also the control class could work with familiar material. The guideline in the selection of the material was to make possible divergent organizations of the given information, thereby permitting the students to create products which were

Aims of the work

You are kindly requested to organize a presentation on the topic "The Castle." The aim of this work is to show the different ways in which it is possible to talk about the castle and to establish some links between the information units.

How to use the material:

- you can use all the material or only some parts of it;
- you can cut from written texts and images some parts that you are interested in using;
- you can either write or draw something that you consider to be relevant on the empty stripes.

How to build the presentation

1) Place the material that you selected on the paperboards and, only when you are sure of its definite location, paste it.
2) Draw some lines in order to show the linkages that you intend to connect the different sections and write the reason of the linkage on the line.

15 minutes before the end of the second work session we gave to children a memo in order to help them in revising the products:

Now please check

- Did you draw all the linkages that you established among the sections of your board?
- In case you will discover more links you can add them now by tracing hatched lines.
- Did you write the explanation of each connection?

different in their nature and complexity.[1] The material, selected in accordance with the teachers who took part in the project, concerned the theme of "The Castle": this theme appeared to grant congruity with the experience carried out by the students during the

[1] The material provided to each group comprises: three paper boards (70 × 100 cm), scotch tape, a glue stick, coloured pencils, three empty paper strips, 11 short written texts, 11 images. The texts comprise descriptions of castles or of their inhabitants, medieval cooking recipes, song, rhymes on the castle theme, journal titles about wars in castles, small parts of poems, nursery rhymes. Images include ancient drawings of castles and their inhabitants, maps of fortified towns, multi-perspective images (i.e. Escher's ones), photos of existing castles, pictures of sand castles.

project (concerning elements linked to cultural heritage) and allowed a reference to past knowledge for the students and the management on different levels of complexity and abstraction.

In order to create a presentation on "the Castle" the groups could choose how to organize all the given elements (texts and pictures), either modified or untouched. Other elements considered as relevant could be also added to the presentation. The groups were then requested to trace the connections and to explain the links they wished to stress between the information units (cf. the assignment in the frame shown on p. 107). Two two-hour sessions were granted to each group.

Data Collection and Analysis

We video-recorded both work-sessions of one group for each of the four classes involved in the test. The discursive interactions (nearly 16 hours of conversation) have been entirely transcribed. We analyzed the content of talk in students' interaction in order to show qualitative differences between experimental and control groups in their collective reasoning, activity organization and sharing of metacognitive habits. Recursive readings of the transcripts allowed differences to be detected in the modalities of work between the experimental and the control groups, which could illustrate and also partially explain the striking difference in the end-products of the two work sessions. We have sampled the clearest and shortest examples out of a collection of interactional exchanges dealing with:

1) How to structure the available information (written and visual);
2) How to express contents and their relations by graphic and spatial means;
3) How to manage the interactional level and to divide tasks between themselves.

Finally, end-products are also analyzed as for the procedures they entailed and the final layout they presented, in order to show the intertwining between the conceptual model of hypertext, the patterns of social exchange and the nature of task.

Results

Starting Out: Work Design and Social Organization

The transcripts of the first minutes of work are very informative, in that the groups are sketching the general design of the work and set off with a division of labor. In so doing, they establish an inner normative setting which, though available to revision, represents a set of guidelines for the work to follow. Indeed, striking differences are evident between experimental and control groups in these moments.

Both groups in the experimental condition (E-groups from now on) engage in a long preliminary phase where they outline the frame of the project and figure out the connections between the different parts. This phase of the activity is characterized by the participation of the whole group, and the crucial points are object of collective scrutiny in search for unanimous agreement on the plan.

In Excerpt 1 we see that the project entails deciding the central "screen" from which all the links will be started. The "castle" is treated in this group as the synthesis of a series of activities and the spatial node whence to organize the whole representation.

Excerpt 1 E1 [43–50][2]

1	M	let's do a central screen
2	F	do we start with this?
3	M	°let's start with this, then ( )°
4	F	no, it's ugly
5	A	no::: Mattè we can write 'in the country of fairies' [°( )°]
6	F	[so let's do] Matteo let's start with one of these (1.0) there's a big castle, right

. . .

| 7 | M | This is the main situation |
| 8 | F | Then let's start with this (.) Mattè. I have an idea Mattè I have an idea let's start with this and above we write 'the castle' and then we add all things y'know? |

M's opening statement emphasizes the relevance of the first phases of the work for the development of the whole project. The turns which follow address the same concern: F's understanding check about "starting" with the photo of the castle; M's

---

[2] Transcription conventions

Excerpts are identified as for their sequential number in the paper, the group to whom the talk refers to and, in square brackets, the progressive number of the turns in the original transcript, to give an idea of the position of the interaction within the work session.

Transcription conventions have been reduced to a minimum; following is a list of the symbols used throughout.

(0.2)	numbers in parentheses indicate silence in tenths of a second;
(.)	a dot in parentheses indicates a silence gap briefer then two tenths of a second;
:	colons indicate that the sound of the last letter is stretched;
,	commas indicate suspended intonation;
.	periods indicate conclusive intonation;
?	question marks indicate marked ascending intonation;
!	exclamation marks indicate animated tone;
you	underlined parts are uttered with emphasis;
[ ]	words in square brackets in adjacent lines indicate that words contained in them are overlapped;
((*gets closer*))	descriptions in italics between double parentheses indicate non-verbal activity or voice quality;
( )	parentheses indicate inaudible talk or uncertain hearings;
°that's it°	degree signs indicate low volume of voice or whispering;
. . .	lines with only periods indicate omitted turns;
'the castle'	single inverted commas are used to indicate parts of talk referring to things written or proposed for writing.

repeated formulation of the castle as "the central screen" and the "main situation": and, finally, by F's to put a title above an image and make it the point of departure for all the other "things".

It was easy for us to recognize in this operative plan the inheritance of the Tele-comunicando project, which had offered a model in which a primary image functioned as both entrance and synthesis of various information paths. The connection between the hypertext activity and the poster construction was obvious for the children as they saw around them the same people — the researchers — in the two activities. However, it is noteworthy that from the very beginning they demonstrated the conceptual learning they had developed from the former experience. Without any explicit instruction, the group (in fact, all the experimental groups) applied this experience to a situation which presented quite different cues in terms of the task's operative aspects.

It is evident to the boys and girls of this group that ideational work was necessary in the initial phase (consider e.g. F. "I have an idea"). This reveals that they have developed metaprocedural competence on the phases in which intellectual effort is required. The project develops in a top down fashion, and is conceptually organized so that the castle is both a useful image to start with as a source screen and a meaningful historical entity, by virtue of its being the site of political and economical activities and characters.

The opening phase of the activity has quite different features in the control groups (hereafter, "C-groups"). In C1 for example, the first steps concern picking up a number of cuttings corresponding to the number of children and positioning them on the poster. The selection of the relevant pieces from the pictures and texts they have been given is carried out according to individual preferences: each of them choose a few items which are then organized spatially — but not conceptually — on the poster.

Excerpt 2 C1 [42–58]

1 V   First of all we have to lay out on the boards the material we have
       chosen ((*reading the instruction sheet*))
       and only when we have decided the definitive positions we have to
       glue it. (3.0) ((*listening to outgroup children*))
       wait let's see all the material that is needed ((*picks cuttings and
       examines them*))
2 A   This and this ((*gives V some cuttings*))
3 D   (   ) The castle
4 V   Sara which one do you like?
5 D   This one
6 V   Wait ((*A claps to D*))
7 D   I (like) this one
8 A   Well that one is nice in fact
9 V   So let's put this and not this
10 A   But do we need to draw it?
11 V   So we have to spread on the posters the material we have chosen
12 A   Wait ((*unrolling the poster on the table*))
13 V   So we have to also put in some writings

Following the written instruction which required them to select the paper cuttings before pasting them, the students express their preferences. In the same fashion, they divided the poster and each student started coloring the portion he/she had been allotted.

V points out in the end (line 13) that they must also add "some writings." It seems there is a model they are following which prescribes a one-to-one matching of image and text until they use up all the cuttings. The model is distributive and externally driven, bottom-up, in that they are heavily relying on the available material to get hints on what to do. In Excerpts 1 and 2 it is also possible to observe a different kind of interactional style: the students of the C-group proceed in a highly democratic manner (everybody chooses one thing) which, however, does not by itself ensure qualitatively good team work. The *conceptual* model is serial, namely the different items are juxtaposed, and consequently the resulting activity is rather simple: fair but not very productive. Despite the supportive atmosphere, at least at the beginning, (see turn 8, Excerpt 2) children do not engage in joint planning since the requirement of the interpreted task do not prompt them to do it.

On the contrary, E-group 2 understood that the project would have been best accomplished if they kept working together. Excerpt 3 shows that the group does not want to split into subgroups until the layout of the castle is finished:

Excerpt 3 E2 [105–109]

1	D	Let's each of us make a piece of the castle I'll make the bottom part of the castle
2	S	Me too (.) I want to do the bottom
3	A	Let's do it this way: Davide and Sara do the bottom part (.) or the top one
4	F	Let's all work together
5	D	He is right we don't need to split into groups

When D proposes to split into subgroups (turn 1) the other members initially accept and volunteer to attend to the different parts. When a subgroup is already formed according to individual preference, F counters the proposal by suggesting that they work collectively. D, who initially proposed the splitting option, agrees with F without discussion (turn 5). The ease with which the proposals are processed in the group, with no overt conflicts, led us to conclude that the nature of the activity motivates the different decisions, not the individual rights of the children. In other words, cooperation is a built-in feature of designing the castle. This organizational flexibility emerges also in a later segment of the activity when splitting becomes potentially fruitful. The group's rearrangement is negotiated and the same child (F) who had previously opposed forming subgroups now favors the idea.

Excerpt 4 E2 [818–821]

1	M	We have the ideas already so let's split in two groups (1.0) while one does the bot:: ((*M and D start coloring another poster*))
2	M	You do the part below we: Daniele and I will color the writings, ok?
3	F	Ok come on (.) that's (.) that's

Principles of Work Development

As we stated above the C-groups proceeded by matching images with texts: they created meaningful local units and assigned them a title before shifting to the next one. In Excerpt 5 we can see how this is practically achieved: students read the text and then they look for an appropriately matching picture.

Excerpt 5 C1 [235–241]

1	V	((*reads*)) "Then the next morning the three friends get ready for the adventure. They polished their armors and made sure that their swords were sharp and they carefully chose the lances, as victory and life depend on those things" (1.0) (1.0) so here (.) so here it talks about, well::
2	Ad	About soldiers
3	V	Yes
4	An	About a war
5	V	Yes (.) let's see if there is something ((*looks among the figures*))
6	An	So that entire soldier (.) that one that you can see:: that soldier that::::
7	A	Yes with the war ( )

They give a topic label to a text (a short narrative on soldiers getting ready for the battle) and look for a corresponding figure. As for the functional value attributed to the figurative material, the difference between experimental and control groups is striking. The control group adopts a very conventional strategy which gives absolute priority to the written text for setting up the topical domain, and uses pictures as mere illustrations of the text.

Attempts to generate a more autonomous and creative result sometimes emerge in the C-groups but these are not supported by the entire group. In the following excerpt, for example, a good idea is rejected in favor of a canonical solution.

Excerpt 6 C1 [310–312]

1	D	So I had thought let's make a big castle (.) inside we put rooms (0.5) look at this one ((*takes a sheet and lay it on the board*)) and then we paste other things on them
2	A	Listen instead we could paste the one about war and then we make a strip like this let's say (.) this is the way they did wars ((*points to the board*))
3	V	Wait let's just think a moment about the written pieces (5.0) wait ((*reads the various texts provided in the envelope*))

The proposal to dynamically use the basic image through the addition of windows and attachments, is contrasted with the pre-established juxtaposition of text and picture. The "one text-one figure" criterion is made explicit by the proposal to write an explanatory line above the text and figure unit: "this is the way they did wars".

V elaborates in the same vein with a focus on the written pieces, and D's suggestion is not taken into account.

The work in E1, on the other hand, unfolds by establishing the paths departing from the castle. A significant feature of the discussion is its level of abstractness: a schema is under construction and the children focus on how to render effectively the relationship between the castle and the various associated themes. The group initially discusses the location of some pictures (inside the castle or connected to it by an arrow) but the children quickly realize that the connections among the elements of the schema (i.e. what should they write on the arrows), are very important and have to be specified and that they must define the roles and figures historically associated with life in the castle.

Excerpt 7 E1 [659–693]

1	M	In the castle in the castle you do
2	A	All the armors, the . . .
3	M	No:: in the castle you make:: you a photograph there (.) there will be an image inside the castle
4	F	No:::: I say (.) I'll do something ok? we draw an arrow, we draw an arrow this way ok? and write the characters on it and then you do::
5	D	What do you mean the characters Federì
6	F	The inhabitants
7	M	Write it down here. 'In the castle'
8	F	No it's ugly you draw an arrow which is linked to this- 'the inhabitants' and then you make another arrow linked frontally to this which shows the other things
9	M	No because that one — the king (.) the king prince
10	F	No, the inhabitants
11	M	No, they aren't the inhabitants
12	A	They are the chiefs
13	M	No, they are those: the ways of life
14	D	No, they are the princes
15	M	One was the prince
16	F	But they were living in the castle
17	M	Yes there inside one was the prince (.)
18	F	[or a knight otherwise he was
19	A	[a commander no?
20	F	If we do an arrow
21	M	Not 'the characters'
22	F	without writing 'the characters' (.) let's draw an arrow and on top we write — I don't know, on the arrow:::
23	A	Enlargement
24	D	Enlargement what
25	F	Uh:: once again

In this long exchange it is possible to detect how the children conceived of their project: they are discussing what to write on the arrow which connects the castle with some of the cuttings they want to use. They are choosing the category which best fits such a link, and thus are reasoning concerning the degree of abstractness the category can have. They are also outlining a series of possibilities which concern the logical relationships between "characters," "inhabitants," "ways of life" and eventually the proposal of an "enlargement" (zooming in), which is viewed as a shortcut and quickly discarded. The significant presence of opposition and argument in this excerpt reveals the importance this group attributed to the internal logic of the product as a whole.

These children were also concerned with the historical accuracy of their placement of the images. "Who lives in the castle" is the underlying question which affected the decision of whether to consider peasants' and workers' characters within the castle (turn 17), or outside of, but connected to it in some other way. This process is top-down, and involves the use of historical knowledge to support decision making.

Products' Features

Before proceeding to the analysis of interactions, we will examine the end product. All the groups of the four classes, both experimental and control, created rather different products from one another. We will briefly sketch out the strategies adopted by those groups with experience in hypertext construction and which consequently enter the new activity with a common set of "anticipated organizers" (Ausubel, 1960) and those groups which were absolute novices

Logical Spaces

The importance E-groups assigned to the links among different zones of the poster emerges from the extended discussion devoted to the choice of their pictorial representation. E-group 1 is especially representative on this matter, since their text shows a wide variety of logical connectives. We find a combination of arrows plus an adverb or a verb ("then . . . ," "it happened"), the cloudlike arrangement of multi-content areas (i.e. several themes unified within a more inclusive category), different sizes and types of writing to indicate hierarchical position of themes (e.g. large and small print, different colors, bold letters, italics).

In the following excerpt we can observe the careful planning of one link's shape:

Excerpt 8 E1 [290–318]
```
1  F   We can draw an arrow this way (.) uh:: Mattè
2  M   [(  )]
3  F   [No because] we make it here::
        the arrow starts from here::
        like a cloud which passes through the arrow and then gets to 'What
        they eat'
```

4 M Oh:: (0.5) a cloud
((*sounds accompanying drawing gesture*))
z::::: [ta]

5 F [Ta] you got it? Is it ok with you? ((*addressing the other two children*))

6 A Yes

7 F I'll do (this) huh?

8 A So do it

9 M So do it

10 F I'll use a pencil first ((*draws*))

11 A Oh I see

12 F (0.5) ((*draws*)) Yeah, but now it's all crooked though. well.
. . .
Why don't we make a squared frame which comes out better? a square frame, ok? Otherwise, (to have) always these clouds looks bad
. . .
Come on, let's think of something more original

13 D No:: here she starts again

14 F Yeah za za za za the fractured coast

15 M Zig zag like

16 F No:: a zig zag shape is ugly

17 A Yeah zig zag is nice

18 F Yeah but you go crazy doing it

19 M Uh I got it

20 F You know we should do it like a blot, no? Like neouwo ((*sound of shape*)) (.)
do you have a piece of paper? anyway you know like a blot

21 M Oh well (0.5) but who can do it?

22 F I can do it (0.5) the blot

23 A Ah:: like blueprints going that way::

24 M No that kind of paint [which

25 F [yeah. did you see that thing:: wait. can I write on above here? (0.2) you see? something like this

Starting from the problem of how to shape the arrow shaft, the group focuses on the kind of enclosure they want for one of their subparts. It is clear here, as well as in other exchanges, that previous solutions are not preferred: they take each new task as a challenge to produce "something original." Thus, they engage in brainstorming and test different possible shapes within the group before actually drawing them in the poster. Consensus is consistently pursued. The children's previous experience in hypertext construction promotes and facilitates the search for creative solutions for the poster's construction.

This is evident in Excerpt 9 as well with regard to space. Space it is not taken literally as just the space afforded by the posters: children are able to freely add subparts or to work in the third dimension if their plan requires it.

Table 7.1: Features of the posters as constructed by E-groups and C-groups.

Experimental groups

The different parts of the product tend to be linked together and integrated, both logically and figuratively

Original situations and scenarios are created

Images are valued as sources of information

Images are manipulated in different ways (e.g. assembled, cut out)

Space is three-dimensional

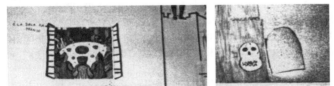

Products of different groups are rather different from one another

---

Table 7.1: (*continued*)

Control groups

The different parts of the product tend to be independent from one another, both logically and figuratively

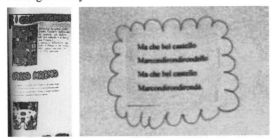

Themes are taken from available material with little invention

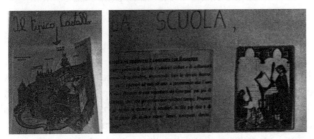

Images are subordinate to text and merely serve an illustrative function

Images are glued on the cardboard as they are found

Space is bidimensional

Products are comparatively similar to one another

Excerpt 9 E1 [704–716]

1 M   Listen though we could do three things ((*three areas*))
2 F   But we haven't enough [space to do it
3 M   [This one and this one ((*shows images for the three areas*))
4 F   But we haven't enough space to do it
5 D   We can take another poster
6 F   yeah
7 M   Federica::
8 F   but you have to paste it, right?
9 M   Federi look.
10 F   Where?
11 D   You paste it below
12 F   Uh
13 D   You see, with the scotch
14 M   Federica look (0.5) we'll do 'the castle' then we'll do 'in the castle' and further below 'outside the castle' ((*the three proposed content areas*))
15 D   Good
16 F   Good Matteo . . . so let's do it this way let's paste this one first

In this exchange the problem of limited space envisaged by Federica (turn 2) is overcome by two other members of the group who propose adding pieces of poster where needed. The supportive atmosphere of this group is remarkable: Federica's doubts (turns 2, 4, 8, 10) are regularly followed by explanations and practical demonstrations of how the pasting can be done in order to have the three content areas represented. Matteo's solution is eventually welcome by both Davide and Federica with warm approval. The questions arisen by one member and the persuasive efforts of the others have in fact helped the whole group to clarify and detail their plan.

Patterns of Intersubjectivity

The complex hypertext structure constructed by E-groups can also be characterized as a metatextual explicatory system of the text's logical organization. The primary site where children articulated and expressed the inner logic of their project was the group itself: as we have already observed, in their discussion the children tested the clarity and efficacy of their ideas and proposals. We have also discussed the need for establishing a shared general plan during the initial phase of the activity, and the decision making process the children undertook in defining structure and link of the products. In Excerpt 10 we observe that the same attitude is present when an interactive item, entirely figurative (a door opening into the tower), is to be added to the castle:

Excerpt 10 E2 [684–698]

1 A   You know what I say I got from Francesco that you want to do some stuff with the battlements, right?

2 F   Yeah ((*nods*))
3 A   You can make a column — a fat tower — and you draw a door into the column
4 F   Yeah
5 S   No
6 F   No:: look here at the battlements here
7 A   Look, like this. here there is the tower
8 S   Yeah this way
9 A   And here you draw the door
10 S   You can draw the other door there no?
11 A   Here, the other door.

Arianna publicly displays her understanding of F's plan and check its correctness: other members of the group join in reworking the project, triggered by Arianna's inquiry. The discourse takes the typical form of co-construction (Orsolini & Pontecorvo, 1992) with each turn addition building on the earlier ones and progressively adjusting the placement of the door.

Displays of each other's perspective can be found in both the E-groups analyzed: usually the overt nature of the activity minimized misunderstandings, whereas they could occur during the verbal planning, prior to handling the material. For this reason, members of the E- groups tended to use more understanding checks to coordinate their future activity.

Excerpt 11 E1 [235–240]
M and F are discussing whether to write "to the castle" or "in the castle" below the drawing, and it turns out F intended the writing as a general title, while M as the title of only one part.
1 M   You fancy it big
2 F   I mean *the title* of the poster
3 M   Oh:: this is how it must be::
4 F   You got what I meant?
5 A   This is the beginning Mattè
6 M   right. (1.0) 'in the castle'

The interdependency of product elements is mirrored in interdependency of groups' cognitive and practical operations. This is true for the C-groups as well, in the sense that the features of separateness and autonomy of the different blocks are replicated in the ideational and decisional processes. In C-group 1 responsibility for choosing a color is left entirely to the individual in charge of each of the three posters.

Excerpt 12 C1 [1125–6]
D and V are together in a subgroup, S is in another one
1 D   ((*to S*)) No, we already used this color
2 V   ((*to S*)) You do as you like if you want to do it yellow:: that poster is yours you got it (.) you have to color it

D is monitoring what the other subgroup is doing with their poster, and suggest they do not use the same color that had been used for a previous part of the poster. But another member comes in and states the independence of the subgroups and the freedom to do whatever they like on *their* poster. The final product is not understood, at least by some members, as a common accomplishment but as a divided property implying divided responsibilities.

There is yet another interactional aspect affecting the way E-groups work, and this has to do with their orientation to a rather concrete user or observer of the product. C-groups show a much higher preoccupation with the researchers' assessment: children often asked what could or could not be done, whereas E-group members asked the researchers what it will become of their work. Orientation to a non-institutional user, and to clarity rather than correctness can be detected in Excerpt 13:

Excerpt 13 E1 [210–217]
They are discussing what to write under the image of the castle, where they have drawn a path leading to the entrance door

```
1   F
2   M   What? ((getting closer))
3   F   Or shall I write 'the castle' here on top?
4   M   'Road to the castle'
5   F   No, you have to write ['the castle',
6   A                        ['the castle',
7   M   'Road',
8   F   No, otherwise how can they understand?
9   M   'At the castle'
```

The discussion focuses on the best caption to write in a certain position of the poster, and F's turn (b) clarifies for us that their criterion is the intelligibility of the poster layout for a potential reader: the E-group children construct the potential user, or observer of the poster, as similar to themselves. The experience of building up an interactive architecture such as the hypertext lingers in the clear perception of a recipient toward whom the work is directed. This is a noteworthy result in itself since typically school-work is addressed to school authorities: children are usually preoccupied with being correct and not with devising solutions which will be clear and appealing to a less institutional recipient. Probably one major accomplishment of the long experiment Telecomunicando is an increased sense of the usefulness and significance that the children attach to their activities. This surely affects the mood and the cohesion of the group as a social unit.

Summarizing, in the control group the activity unfolds in an associative way and does not appear to be hierarchically guided by a super-ordinate plan: the links are made on the spot on a semantic basis. Working in the spatial dimension (as necessary in building posters) does not evidently trigger by itself a different model of reasoning. From a social point of view, there are no traces of the "*lector in fabula*" (Eco, 1979) present in the work of the experimental group. The social organization of the group among its members and its connection (or not) with possible recipients and users is not an ancillary aspect but dramatically shape the layout and even the aesthetic of the product: one type of product shows a common space (the big castle) metaphorically and practically embracing the entire group, whereas the other type of product displays a loosely-related set of different foci.

Conclusions

In recent years, many studies have shown the potential of the introduction of techno-logical resources inside the classroom. Many scholars now agree that a successful implementation of computers at school can enhance all the basic dimensions of educa-tion and turn the class experience into a constructive way of educating. The introduction of the computers into the classroom is then closely connected with team-work, interdisciplinary curricula, learning by inquiry and intensive communication (Salomon, 1994). The advent of telematics and its introduction in the school has produced new opportunities for innovation in learning, especially as the introduction of new communication technologies is modifying the context in which teaching and learning develop. The complex relationships between all the innovative features of didactical projects involving computer-based activities, creates a context that distinc-tively affects the class work, so that the term "classroom" no longer adequately describes the reality of the environment in which learning takes place (Lawrence, 1996). As Salomon argues, computers, and particularly computer-mediated communi-cation systems, can act as "subversive instruments" for learning situations as they imply more complex cognitive activities and requires new forms of social organiza-tion of work (Salomon, 1992).

The qualitative analysis of the experience we proposed shows that there are rele-vant differences in the behavior of children that participated at the project. They spend more time and work discussing the plan on a metacognitive level. This comes out as a result of sharing not only some possible models for hypertext presentation, but also metacognitive assets. The central features of the hypertext model guiding children's work are of two kinds: one is the need for a logical and coherent organization of the different topics and subtopics; the second one is ensuring interconnections between different levels and across them.

Their involvement in an aesthetic research seems to overcome the traditional "curriculum requirement," i.e. the ordinary school tasks demands, in that aesthetics becomes part of the development of the project itself. The choice by Telecomunicando children of developing the task as a hypermedia (there was even an attempt by chil-dren to include sound in the presentation) triggers a process of attentive and creative exploration of all the expressive means related to different channels even if the actual medium provided (paperboard) could not allow their realistic use.

The habit of "working by project" seems to have fostered an analytic attitude so that children from the experimental classes put more care in the relationships and consis-tency between any part of the material put into the presentation and the overall structure they have planned. Indeed, both the experimental groups developed an over-arching conceptual frame within which each unit of information is embedded. In this way, information does not reside in each single unit but it can be found in the logical connection given by the complex structure of the project itself.

The spatial metaphor turns out especially useful for finding ways of expressing and sharing the practical features of the work, representing a widespread cultural code. Terms like exclusiveness/inclusiveness, or distance/proximity, are effective ways to index conceptual characteristics of topics and links. On the other hand, it must be taken into account that this kind of space does not consent arbitrary movements, especially from the point of view of hypertext producers. Navigation itself is not only possible but also interesting when the organization of the "isles" is planned, offering recognizable landmarks. The paths which can possibly be followed are various but each mirrors both vertical and horizontal knowledge-based connections.

As hypothesized, the structure of the project has a determining influence on the interactional asset of the group. We observed that children are driven from their model to plan together the general architecture and check at every step with each other the validity and the clarity of the different information units in their link structure.

The group is an ideal environment to give the model its full accomplishment: the search for the optimal structure is an intrinsic motivation for confronting versions, testing their applicability and robustness, and pushing for creative solutions. Observing the interactions of the children who interpreted the task as hypertext, we have noted a drive for intersubjectivity that made us think of the opening of windows in each other's cognitive space.

As Salomon (1994) argues, the real challenge for Technology-Intensive Learning Environments (TILEs) is "the radical change of instructional practices: From individual to team, from sterile, to authentic topics, from mono-disciplinary to multi-disciplinary topics, and from teacher-guided and dominated classroom life, to self-guided and communication intensive life" (p. 82).

References

Allen, G., & Thompson, A. (1995). Analysis of the effect of networking on computer-assisted collaborative writing in a fifth grade classroom. *Journal of Educational Computing Research, 12*(1), 65–75.

Ausubel, D. P. (1960). The use of advance organizers in the learning and retention of meaningful material. *Journal of Educational Psychology, 51*, 267–272.

Boechler, P. (2001). How spatial is hyperspace? Interacting with hypertext documents: Cognitive processes and concepts [Special Issue: Mind in the Web]. *Cyberpsychology and Behaviour, 4*(1), 23–46.

Boscolo, P. (1999). Scrivere testi [Writing texts]. In: C. Pontecorvo (ed.), *Manuale di Psicologia dell'Educazione,* [Handbook of Educational Psychology]. Bologna: Il Mulino.

Bromme, R., & Stahl, E. (1999). Spatial metaphors and writing hypertexts: Study within schools. *European Journal of Psychology of Education, 14*(2), 267–281.

Brown, G. S., Collins, A., & Duguid, P. (1989). Situated cognition and the culture of learning. *Educational Researcher, 18*, 32–24.

Caravita, S., Pontecorvo, C., & Talamo, A. (1996, September). *Exchange of Cultural Goods Among Schools.* Poster session presented at the congress The Growing Mind, Geneva.

Carrada, L. (2000). *Scrivere per Internet* [Writing for Internet]. Milan: Lupetti.

Cornoldi, C., & Caponi, B. (1991). *Metacognizione e apprendimento* [Metacognition and learning]. Bologna: Il Mulino.

Crook, C. (1995). On resourcing a concern for collaboration within peer interactions. *Cognition and Instruction, 13*(4), 541–547.

De Corte, E. (1994). Toward the integration of computers in powerful learning environment. In: S. Vosniadou, E. De Corte, and H. Mandl (eds), *Technology-Based Learning Environments* (pp. 19–25). Berlin: Springer-Verlag.

Eco, U. (1979). *Lector in fabula. La cooperazione interpretativa dei testi narrativi.* [Interpretive cooperation of narrative texts]. Milan: Bompiani.

Fisher, P.M., & Mandl, H. (1990). Towards a psychophysics of hypermedia. In: D. H. Jonassen, and H. Mandl (eds), *Designing Hypermedia for Learning* (pp. XIX-XXV). Berlin: Springer-Verlag.

Gygi, K. (1990). Recognising the symptoms of hypertext . . . and what to do about it. In: B. Laurel (ed.), *The Art of Human–Computer Interface Design* (pp. 279–288). New York: Addison Wesley.

Jonassen, D. H., & Grabinger, R. S. (1990). Problems and issues in designing hypertext/hypermedia for learning. In: D. H. Jonassen, and H. Mandl (eds), *Designing Hypermedia for Learning* (pp. 3–26). Berlin: Springer-Verlag.

Kaye, A.R. (1994). Foreword to: M. F Verdejo, & S. A. Cerri, *Collaborative Dialogue Technologies in Distance Learning.* Berlin: Springer-Verlag.

King, K. S., Boling, E., Annelli, J., Bray, M., Cardenas, D., & Frick, T. (1996). Relative perceptibility of hypercard buttons using pictorial symbols and text labels. *Journal of Educational Computing Research, 14*(1), 67–81.

Lawrence, B. H. (1996). Teaching and learning via videoconference: The benefits of cooperative learning, *Journal of Educational Technology Systems, 24*(2), 145–149.

McAleese, R. (1989a). Concepts as hypertext nodes: The ability to learn while navigating through hypertext nets. In: D. H. Jonassen, and H. Mandl (eds), *Designing Hypermedia for Learning* (pp. 97–116). Berlin: Springer-Verlag.

McAleese, R. (1989b). Navigation and browsing in hypertext. In: R. McAleese (ed.), *Hypertext: Theory into Practice* (pp. 6–44). Westport, CT: Ablex.

Olson, D. R. (1979). *Linguaggi, media e processi educativi* [Language, media and educational processes], edited by C. Pontecorvo, Torino, Loescher.

Orlikowski, W. J., & Yates, J. A. (1994). Genre repertoire: The structuring of communicative practices in organizations. *Administrative Science Quarterly, 39*, 541–574.

Orsolini, M., & Pontecorvo, P. (1992). Children's talk in classroom discussion. *Cognition and Instruction, 9*(2), 113–136.

Pontecorvo, C. (1987). Discussing for reasoning: The role of argument in knowledge construction. In: E. De Corte, J. G. Lodewijks, R. Parmentier, and P. Span (eds), *Learning and Instruction* (pp. 239–250). Oxford: Leuven Pergamon Press/ Leuven University Press.

Pontecorvo, C., Ajello, A. M., & Zucchermaglio, C. (eds) (1995). *I contesti sociali dell'apprendimento* [The Social Contexts of Learning]. Milan: LED.

Resnick, L., Pontecorvo, C., & Säljö, R. (1997). Discourse, tools and reasoning. In: L. Resnick, C. Pontecorvo, R. Säljö, and B. Burge (eds) *Discourse, Tools and Reasoning: Situated Cognition and Technologically Supported Environments* (pp. 1–20). Berlin: Springer-Verlag.

Salomon, G. (1992). What does the design of effective CSCL require and how do we study its effects? *SIGCUE Outlook, 21*(3), 62–68.

Salomon, G. (1994). Differences in patterns: Studying computer enhanced learning environments. In: S. Vosniadou, E. De Corte, and H. Mandl (eds), *Technology-Based Learning Environments* (pp. 79–85). Berlin: Springer-Verlag.

Talamo, A. (1998). Il monitoraggio dei processi e dei prodotti: La prova del castello. In: A. Talamo (ed.), *Apprendere con le tecnologie* (pp. 135–147). Florence: La Nuova Italia.

Talamo, A., & Fasulo, A. (1999, August). *Planning the hyperspace.* Paper presented at the VIII European Conference for Research on Learning and Instruction, Göteborg.

Talamo, A., & Pontecorvo, C. (1997, August). *Constructing Hypermedia: Skills and Processes in a Communication Context.* Poster session presented at the 7th European Conference for Research on Learning and Instruction, Athens.

Vosniadou, S. (1994). From cognitive theory to educational technology. In: S. Vosniadou, E. De Corte, and H. Mandl (eds), *Technology-Based Learning Environments* (pp. 11–18). Berlin: Springer-Verlag.

Chapter 8

Slicing Books — The Authors' Perspective

Ingo Dahn, Michael Armbruster, Ulrich Furbach, and Gerhard Schwabe

The next generation of hypertext documents will be based on richer semantics and have more potential for automation and personalization than is currently possible. One system that shows much promise is the "sliced book". Slicing Book Technology splits textbooks into small, self-coherent slices and then uses semantic links to make structural relationships such as "Slice A builds on Slice B" explicit. This approach allows the reader to create personalized textbooks. The creation of sliced books poses new challenges to authors and "slicing book re-engineers." New tools support them during the creation of those features of electronic documents (multiple links, personalization) that are also specific for hypertext documents and are particularly relevant for learning. We therefore envision that learners will actively participate in the creation of sliced books. As a first step in this direction, this chapter presents the technology and the experience of slicing book authors. The chapter first introduces the Slicing Book Technology. Then the process of slicing books is described, presenting several approaches on how to create a sliced book. The fourth section contains a description and analysis of the experiences gained so far in the creation of sliced books. The final section describes the new learning approach we are currently working on: collaborative slicing.

Introduction

While authors are still struggling to understand how to make best use of the potential offered by hypertext documents, computer science researchers are already developing the next generation of digital documents. This next generation will be based on richer semantics, more potential for automation and personalization and will pose new challenges to the authors. This chapter aims to give a first impression of these challenges. It is written by the developers of a new digital document type — called sliced books

Writing Hypertext and Learning: Conceptual and Empirical Approaches
Copyright © 2002 by Elsevier Science Ltd.
ISBN: 0-08-043987-X

— and reports on their experiences during the first trials. Sliced books require a comprehensive support for writing semantically-linked documents. New tools support authors and slicing book re-engineers during the creation of those features of electronic documents (multiple links, personalization) that are also specific for hypertext documents and are particularly relevant for learning. We therefore envision that learners will actively participate in the creation of sliced books.

Slicing Book Technology

Hypertexts offer readers new qualities of service. Links take readers instantly from one point to any other point which is referenced to at this spot. Thus the classical hierarchical document structure is augmented or even replaced by a network of pages. However, still, information that is needed for a specific purpose remains scattered within this network. Slicing Book Technology goes one step further by compiling this information into a new document. Thus it can be seen as a combination of hypertexts with the dynamic generation of documents.

A sliced book consists of

- a hierarchy of semantic units together with
- a set of meta-data.

Unlike web pages, semantic units need not be complete documents that are ready for delivery. Rather they can be pieces of information that have to be combined with other pieces and processed appropriately in order to obtain a deliverable document. For example, to obtain a deliverable HTML page a number of fragments of HTML code may be combined into a new file, augmented with HTML header and footer and with an appropriate style sheet. This process may be varied in many ways. It may depend on characteristics of the particular user who has requested that page whether a certain fragment is included or not. Also the particular style sheet may be chosen to suit the user's preferences.

This offers many possibilities for the production of personalized documents. In order to select among these possibilities, the aforementioned meta-data are used. These meta-data contain for each of the semantic units information about this unit and about its relation with other units. An intelligent system needs that information in order to decide whether this unit should be included in a requested document. For example the meta-data for unit *1/1/3* may state that *it* is an exercise on topic *set theory* that requires the prerequisite units *1/0/5* and *1/0/10* for its solution. A teacher looking for exercises for an exam on set theory may just get *1/1/3* delivered but learners may also get *1/0/5* and *1/0/10* in order to prepare for that exam (Figure 8.1).

From the point of view of the *reader*, the generation of a personalized book is done in two main steps.

1) Compose a table of contents that contains the selected slices.
2) Request the generation and online delivery of the final document.

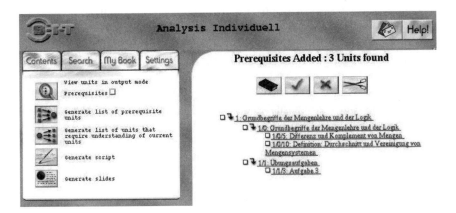

Figure 8.1: Example of a sliced book.

There are several tools available that assist the reader in the composition of a table of contents. The most familiar ones are the search functions. They yield a list of all slices that match the search criteria. Once on a screen, the reader may decide to put particular slices into his personal book. In this way, the reader can assemble any collection of slices in the table of contents of his personal book.

Similarly the button with the scissors on it may be used to remove slices from a given table. The buttons on the left of the screenshot in Figure 8.1 that generate the list of prerequisite units and the list of units that require understanding of the current units also produce appropriate content tables. These functions make use of the semantic links between the slices that are stored in the database on the server.

Currently, the most advanced function is the script function. It generates a table of contents of all slices that lead the reader from slices he or she has marked to slices that constitute the current learning objectives without detours. This is just a first implementation of a powerful general principle.

The knowledge of how to compose and format documents for teachers or learners is formulated in a general way, i.e. independent of the concrete units. Appropriate knowledge management procedures combine this general knowledge, the meta-data describing the content and the available information about the user and his current interest. They infer which slices should be presented to the user and how the document should be formatted. If possible, the knowledge management will resolve conflicts and select among possible alternatives.

When the reader wants to see the content, a click on the button with the magnifying glass in Figure 8.1 lets the server generate a new document consisting of the collected slices only. This document will be instantly delivered over the web in the same format in which the complete book would have been available for delivery, for example as a single pdf document. When new documents are combined from different sources, conflicting document styles may enforce the delivery of several separate documents that can be accessed through a common table of contents.

We note that the described architecture — consisting of a collection of meta-data annotated slices, a knowledge management system and a dynamic generation of personalized documents — coincides with the vision of the future World Wide Web as a semantic net. This vision was stated by Tim Berners-Lee — the inventor of the World Wide Web — at the conference XML 2000.

The first server using Slicing Book Technology has been online since May 2000. It can be accessed at http://www.slicing.de/books/ (Wolter & Dahn, 2000). The project "**T**ools for **R**eusable **I**ntegrated **A**daptable **L**earning — **S**ystems/standards for **O**pen **L**earning **U**sing **T**ested **I**nteroperable **O**bjects and **N**etworking" (Trial-Solution) started in February 2000 and investigates the possibilities of combining documents out of slices from various sources (see http://www.trial-solution.de). Six universities, two publishers and four other institutions cooperate in this project. It is funded in part by the European Commission within the 5th Framework program. In the project currently (December 2001) a repository of more than 25,000 slices from 3600 pages obtained from 11 books is handled.

In order to make Slicing Book Technology work, collections of interoperable annotated slices must be available. Such collections can either be created from scratch or they can be generated by the adaptation of existing documents. Subsequently we shall concentrate on these authoring processes. Our report is based on the experience we gained during the authoring of the sliced book (Wolter & Dahn, 2000), during the preparation of further pre-existing books within the Trial-Solution project and during the writing of another book specifically for the use with Slicing Book Technology.

The Process of Slicing Books

Production of Sliced Books

The demand for high quality content, available online, is continuously increasing. This is an urgent issue, especially in the fields of online supported education and distant education. However, designing materials specifically for electronic media is currently rather expensive and it requires a combination of competencies that hardly any author can provide. On the other hand there is a large number of approved and appreciated documents available in print. In this section we will describe the process that makes these documents appropriate for online delivery, personalization and added value electronic services. A description of the benefits that can be obtained in this way can be found in the reference (Dahn, 2000).

For using Slicing Book Technology, an existing document must be disaggregated into a set of slices and these slices must be augmented with meta-data. Since slices are intended for reuse, the content should be organized in a well-structured way so that the isolation of reusable units is possible. Well-written textbooks and legal and technical documents are good examples. The personalized documents that are generated will be composed of different sized slices. The formatting may also be adapted to the users needs. Therefore, documents in a data format that intimately link their contents with their layout are hardly appropriate. We mention QuarkXPress and Postscript here. XML-based documents are ideal candidates since they are clearly structured according to a Document Type Definition and have the layout separated in their corresponding style sheets. LaTeX documents are also appropriate and Microsoft Word documents can be used.

The preparation of a document is performed in two large steps. In the first step, the document is automatically disaggregated and meta-data are automatically assigned. The second step consists of a manual revision of this automatically generated sliced document. Before a document can be sliced, the required granularity has to be decided upon. The size of a slice may vary between a chapter and a single line. The more finely grained the structure is, the more flexible possibilities for the generation of documents are obtained.

However a more fine-grained structure also results in a larger set of slices and requires more meta-data to be added for the description of these slices. Therefore the intended quality of service and also economic considerations determine which parts of a document are stored as separate slices. The following definition may help to determine appropriate parts (see Dahn, 2001).

Definition
A potential slice is a connected part of a document that can be reused under well-defined conditions.

Splitting up a book into slices can be done by an automated tool, called the splitter, from the vendor Slicing Information Technology, Berlin (SIT) (for the system architecture ref (Dahn & Schwabe, 2001), for the tools see Figure 8.2.

Chapter and section headings are most easy to recognize automatically as borders of slices. However, figures, tables, exercises, and examples are also often clearly marked and can be extracted as slices. The way in which these elements are annotated varies from author to author. Therefore the existing automated slicing tools must be specifically configured for each author. A single configuration may serve them all only if a group of authors uses the same style.

The result of this slicing process can be conceptually interpreted as a tree of files. Leaves on this tree are atomic slices while inner nodes represent aggregations of slices.

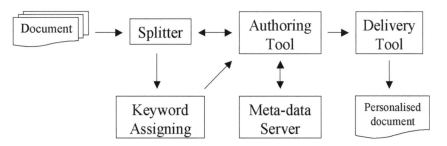

Figure 8.2: Tools used in the process of slicing.

Each node may have a file with its specific content and two more files, named start file and end file. The purpose of these files is to ensure that generated documents are technically well formed. To achieve this, whenever the content of a node is to be included into a personalized document, this content will be enclosed between the start and end files of all parent nodes of the given node. For example, if the list

"A sliced book consists of

- a hierarchy of semantic units together with
- a set of meta-data."

is to be disaggregated, the list may be represented by a node that has a descendant for each item of the list and eventually the start and end tags of the list (<ul> and </ul> in case of an HTML document) in its respective start and end files. Furthermore the start file of the list will contain the introductory phrase "A sliced book consists of", which is valid for each item of the list. In this way, whenever the second item is to be presented, it will be enclosed between the appropriate list tags and the introductory phrase will always be presented, too:

"A sliced book consists of

- a set of meta-data."

The next step is the automated assignment of meta-data. Meta-data are all information that describe slices. Meta-data have to fulfill several needs. In order to retrieve the slices that satisfy a user's need, the content of the slices must be described in an appropriate form. The simplest way to do this is to use keywords. Perhaps keywords have already been assigned by the authors. Such keywords can easily be extracted automatically. In electronic publishing, keywords can be used much more flexibly than in printed books. They can be embedded into a thesaurus that also indicates relationships between keywords like synonyms or related concepts. These relationships can be taken into account when a reader starts a keyword search.

Unfortunately, authors do not define keywords in a standardized way. Therefore — in order to enable a uniform search for a library of sliced books — their keywords must be mapped into already existing thesauri. It is normal that authors define keywords that cannot be found in any available thesaurus. In these cases the new keywords must be standardized and incorporated using appropriate tools. A central meta-data server will be developed for this purpose within the Trial-Solution project.

More keywords can be assigned by using automated indexing techniques. A number of such techniques have been developed, especially for the indexing of large sets of web pages. These techniques are based on statistical or on linguistic considerations. For fine-grained sliced books, the atomic slices may contain too few data to apply automated indexing techniques. In these cases the indexing must be applied to larger aggregations of slices so that the slices can inherit the assigned keywords from these aggregations. The automatically assigned keywords must also be integrated into an existing keyword system.

Another type of meta-data describes the types of information that is contained in a slice. For example, a slice can contain an example or an exercise. These types can frequently be determined automatically either from the way in which these slices are formatted or from the position of the slice in the structure of the document.

More complex meta-data describe how slices are related to each other. It is most important to define which slices are pre-requisites for understanding a given slice. The automated extraction of hyperlinks from the source document can serve as a first draft. The analysis of phrases like "see also" or "using formula . . ." can also provide hints. Usually this information is only in part explicitly available, but whenever it is found in the document it is used to add links between slices automatically. Of course these phrases also help the re-engineer of the automatically sliced document to understand the context better and manually add more meta-data later. But for the time being the splitter itself cannot "understand" the actual meaning of the document, so it is not able to extract all meta-data which relate slices to each other.

The meta-data described so far are the basis for determining which slices are to be presented to a reader in a concrete situation. Other meta-data can give the author and the publisher the opportunity to control how this is done. Most important is the inclusion of information that describes intellectual property rights. It must be possible to trace the authors, source and original location of each slice included in a personalized document. This kind of meta-data is usually inherited from the description of the complete document. The author or publisher may also wish to restrict the re-use of a set of slices. For example, he or she may not allow the rearrangement of slices or the combination with material of a competitor. This information is not contained in printed books and hence cannot be extracted automatically.

The meta-data system described here can be extended in various ways in order to provide additional services if this is useful. Some international consortia, for example IEEE, Dublin Core and IMS, have specified their own meta-data systems. None of these extensions is well suited for automated meta-data assignment.

The Evolution of Re-engineering and Authoring Approaches

During the development and tests of sliced books, we discovered the following approaches in the creation process: slicing as re-engineering, slicing as authoring and slicing as iterative re-engineering and authoring.

Slicing as re-engineering Initially, we took a straightforward approach to the process of creating a sliced book: A slicing book re-engineer was given the digital version of a book. First, the book was cut into slices and a second step defined the logical connection between those slices. The resulting sliced book could then be used to create personalized documents (Figure 8.3, left side).

We call the person a re-engineer because he or she does not add any content (as an author does), but his or her task is more sophisticated than the work of a conventional book editor (who can abstract much more from the content he has to edit). The first

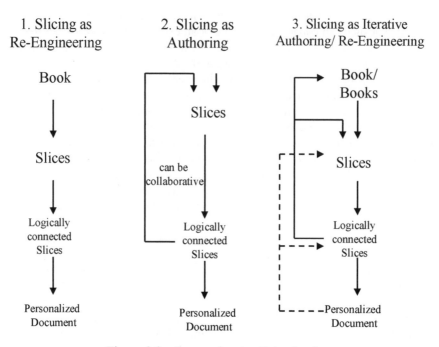

Figure 8.3: Approaches to slicing books.

part of the next section (Experiences) will reflect on the work of one slicing book re-engineer.

This re-engineering approach works well if

1) there is a complete book as a starting point;
2) the objective is to produce a high-quality sliced version for a large number of consuming readers;
3) the slices can easily be identified by the re-engineer.

If the author is the re-engineer and is doing the slicing him- or herself after the manuscript has been finished, he or she will have clear ideas about the constituents (slices) of his work and of their relationships. This was the case in the preparation of (Wolter & Dahn, 2000).[1] If the re-engineer is a different person with competence in the respective domain, slicing becomes more of an iterative nature: the re-engineer proposes a set of slices to the author, discusses the proposal and problems with the author and then revises the slices. This is the typical situation found in the Trial-

---

[1] The author may even mark up his or her manuscript before the automatic slicing to make sure that it will be successful. Then relatively little manual restructuring will be required during the re-engineering phase.

Solution project. The authors here have agreed to the re-engineering of their work and are ready to give advice, but they want to invest a rather limited effort.

Not only the collaboration between the author and the re-engineer turned from a sequential to an iterative process, but also the use of the automatic splitter tool and the manual re-engineering, bringing in another person which we call the slicing expert.

In our first attempts, the automated decomposition of the document was done as the first processing step as soon as the source was received from the author. The splitter slicing tool was used with default settings. It turned out that the slicing obtained in this way was often too fine-grained. The splitter, however, is adaptable to various levels of granularity and to a large variety of writing styles. We found it most convenient that the re-engineer, who is a domain expert, had a first look at the unsliced document from an end user's point of view and determined how it should be sliced. Then the slicing expert analyzed the document from a technical point of view and configured the splitter in an appropriate way. The resulting sliced document was imported into the authoring tool and inspected by the re-engineer and eventually by the author.

This process may have to be iterated several times. In this phase there are four ways to solve problems.

1) The slicing expert reconfigures the splitter.
2) The re-engineer or the author adds information (invisible in print) to the document to assist the automatic slicing process.
3) The slicing expert provides a special tool to add this information automatically.
4) The problem is deferred to the manual re-engineering phase.

In most cases the first of these variations is feasible. The others are required only in case of major irregularities in the document. The manual re-engineering starts only when the granularity, structure and meta-data are established.

Even then the slicing of some parts may have to be revised automatically during the re-engineering process. Then the re-engineering tool will export the current sliced document and the splitter will re-process parts, maintaining the results of the previous re-engineering work as much as possible.

Collaboration becomes more complicated when several re-engineers work concurrently on related parts of the same book or on related books. The main problem here is that one re-engineer has to set references into a structure that may be changed by a second re-engineer. Currently this requires considerate cooperation between the re-engineers. This can be supported if the related documents are considered as parts of a common super-document. For example, if a re-engineer sets a reference to a slice already handled by his or her partner, he or she will see the proposed key phrases that the partner had already assigned.

Slicing as authoring   In the In2Math project, we are faced with the situation that a sliced document is produced from scratch, i.e. there is no book as input. In this situation, slicing has to be integrated with authoring. Slicing can become an integral part of the authoring process in a similar manner as the usage of the outlining tool of an editor can become an integral part of the writing process for a conventional electronic document. Slicing becomes authoring (Figure 8.3, center). The author first creates the slices and then incorporates them into the network of existing slices and relationships. The second part of the section on Experiences will reflect on the work of a slicing book author. The work is currently still seriously hampered by the lack of appropriate tools. While the role of the automatic splitter is reduced, the author needs integrated slicing and relationship-building features in the writing environment. The product of slicing as authoring is again a sliced book that can be used to generate personalized books.

This authoring approach works well if

1) there is little or no material as a starting point;
2) the objective is to produce a high-quality sliced version for a large number of consuming (!) readers;
3) the slicing process can easily be embedded into the writing process.

The section on Collaborative Slicing will describe scenarios and first experiences and how several actors can organize their collaboration in slicing books. If some of the collaborating actors are students, it may even turn out to be economically feasible to produce slicing books for a smaller number of active (!) readers.

Slicing as iterative re-engineering and authoring   The benefits of the sliced books should lead to improved traditional books, too (Figure 8.3, right side). The basic idea is to combine slices from several books into a slicing pool.[2] From this slicing pool, all authorized users can then generate personalized books across book boundaries. If a certain selection is very popular, the publisher can then use the selection as the basis for a new (conventional) book. We now envisage even more complex feedback mechanisms.

Reader feedback as well as new developments in the respective field may suggest a revision of the sliced documents (right part of Figure 8.3). This may affect the content of slices but also the assigned meta-data or rules for document generation. We have experienced cases where the suggestions of the intelligent advisory engine for the reader could be improved by correcting relationships between the key phrases following an analysis of user feedback. Note that this is very efficient since it will immediately improve recommendations for all books using this thesaurus.

For the future we envisage even more complex collaborative scenarios. Readers can compose their personal book from slices from different authors. This may put the work of the individual authors in a valuable new context. The resulting composed document will naturally be a new sliced book which can then be re-used by others. In this scenario a new role is created for the person who composes the document — not only as a reader but as an editor of a new sliced book. When this process is iterated, the editor will not only eventually collaborate with the authors but also with other editors.

---

[2] This approach is currently being tested in the In2Math project.

This iterated process poses new questions concerning the author's rights. These questions have been discussed in the Trial-Solution project. We suggest that a reader can only forward the structure of a composed book for re-use; other readers will have to refer to the original sites of the copyright owners in order to retrieve the content. Every composed book will contain meta-data that allow the reader to trace each part of the document back to its very first source and author, also stating the person(s) who provided the compilation. The Trial-Solution meta-data-system takes care of this in very much the same way as in conventional collections of articles.

Experiences

After introducing the different approaches to the creation of sliced books in the previous section, this section will report on the experiences of a slicing book re-engineer and of a slicing book author. Both are co-authors of this chapter.

Experiences as a Slicing Book Re-engineer

In this part of the chapter we would like to reflect on experiences gained with the manual revision of sliced books by the slicing book re-engineers at the Chemnitz University of Technology. The manual revision of sliced books includes the following operations which will be individually described below:

1) checking of the slicing structure;
2) assignment of titles, keywords and types to single slices;
3) assignment of references between slices.

The work on the sliced version of "Mathematik — ein Lehr- und Übungsbuch" by Regina and Carsten Gellrich (Gellrich & Gellrich, 2001) took several months. It is a textbook on mathematics for students of technical and economic sciences at technical high schools and colleges. The authors assumed that their readers do not want to deal with mathematics as a science but to use it for solving problems in their special fields. Consequently, no proofs and theoretical research are presented, but many examples, exercises and solutions were included. The book consists of 479 pages divided into eight chapters on the following topics: set theory, basic arithmetic operations, equation-solving, simple equations of higher degrees, linear and quadratic functions, proportions, powers, radicals and logarithms, trigonometry, functions, complex numbers, inequalities, and mathematical basics of computer science.

The process of manual revision started on the sliced version of the book delivered by the splitter slicing software from Slicing Information Technology, Berlin. The re-engineering tool used was developed with the first author at the AI-research group at the University of Koblenz-Landau. It presents itself in a conventional Web-Browser like Netscape or the Internet Explorer. With the re-engineering tool the slicing book re-engineer gets access to the file system consisting of several thousand files which

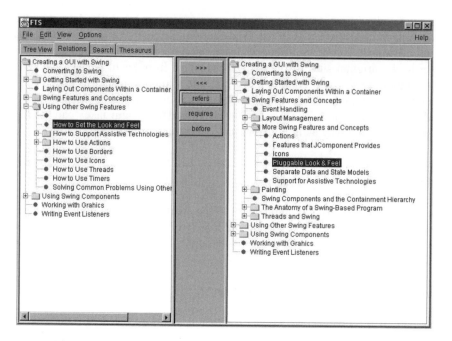

Figure 8.4: Screenshot of the trial-solution re-engineering tool.

make up the whole book. No other software is needed. Each file, i.e. each slice, of the book can be manipulated on its own.

Now, what had to be done with the slices? First of all the structure of the slices created by the splitter had to be checked. The main question to answer for every single slice is: "Is the slice the correct size?"

A slice is considered to be a (basic) learning object, i.e. a bit of text which makes sense on its own and should not be split into smaller objects. In this context, for instance, a definition or a theorem, but also a single paragraph in an explanatory text, can be a (basic) learning object. In the cases of theorems and definitions, which usually use special environments in LaTeX, it is easy for both man and machine to extract them from the text and put them in slices of their own. It is hard to deal automatically with epic text, although the use of paragraphs by the original author might help the machine. So, bigger slices had to be split into smaller ones by reading and understanding the text and finding the points where the original authors changed from one learning object to another.

There were also slices which did not make sense on their own, for instance a split enumeration of the steps of solving a quadratic equation. One could argue that this could have been avoided by correctly slicing in the first place, but it is difficult to decide in advance where to split the text just by looking at the structures and environments of LaTeX and not at the actual occasions where these are used. Sometimes an enumeration cannot be split, on other occasions every item in an enumeration is a learning object of its own and should be separated from the other items.

An easier task to solve was the creation of titles for every small slice, although language consistency was an issue. Assigning keywords to every slice was more complicated. Keywords had already been assigned by the original authors, but it was obvious that the prospective user could ask for more which were not yet assigned and sometimes were even not yet included in the used library of keywords. This means the slicing book re-engineer had to "make them up" using his knowledge of the subject. Still it was not easy to decide where to assign a keyword. Until now only human users of the sliced books and their demands were considered. It is well-known that a human looking for a special term with a search engine in the web can deal with a handful of found pages, but when the search results are several hundreds of pages he or she just cannot have a look at every single one of them. The same is true for a human searching in a book for a keyword which is assigned to too many pages or slices. On the other hand a computer can use thousands of these search results and deal with them in a sensible way. For the slicing book re-engineer it is difficult not to overshoot the limits of assignment of keywords usable by human readers and assigning the same keyword to too many slices although it makes sense at every single occasion. But on the other hand this might enable the user to a more specified search for several keywords in a slice.

Another problem is the assignment of types like definition, theorem, remark and exercise to every single slice. Often it is not easy to decide what the type of the slice in question is. Sometimes the original authors abused LaTeX environments defined for a semantic construct like a definition, to achieve a certain layout of the text though — from a semantic point of view — the content of the environment is no definition at all.

The main manual work on the sliced book is assigning references between slices. There are two different kinds of references. First of all there are references of the kind "The reader has to understand slice A in order to be able to understand slice B". For instance to understand a proof of a theorem the reader has to understand the theorem itself and all other theory needed in the proof like definitions, other theorems and so on. This kind of relationship between slice A and slice B is called a "refers" relationship. In slice B a reference to slice A has to be recorded. Once all references of this kind are set in all slices of the book the user can seek answers to questions like

- "What theory do I need to solve Exercise 135?"
- "What is the definition of a function used for?"

The other kind of relation between slices is the so-called "requires" relation between two slices. If slice B has a "requires" relation set to slice A, then whenever slice B is presented to the reader so should slice A. This kind of relation can for instance be used when the text of a certain slice refers to a picture or table situated somewhere else in the book and therefore in a different slice.

To assign references to slices, and especially references of the first kind, it is vital that the slicing book re-engineer has a thorough understanding of the book's subject.

Although he or she still has to read the book (and could thus learn the subject), this would prolong the time needed for the manual revision extensively. This is especially the case when the book is large, deals with different subjects which are related or when a whole library of books with links between books shall be created. A slicing book re-engineer who is not experienced in the subject could easily forget important references.

Most of the time needed for the manual revision of "Mathematik — ein Lehr- und Übungsbuch" was used to assign references to the hundreds of exercises in the book. There were similar exercises which basically needed the same theory to solve them, but the slicing of the theory in question was and should have been so detailed, that no single exercise could get assigned the same references as a similar exercise without solving both of them beforehand and comparing the solutions. For instance, there were exercises dealing with calculations of angles and sides of triangles. The theory includes the Sine-Theorem and the Cosine-Theorem. Which one can be used depends on the given values in the exercise. Of course one could refer to both or to the whole theory before, just to be on the safe side, but this would not be satisfying for the potential reader of the book. Often several ways to a solution are possible, so all the theory needed for these different solution approaches should be referenced. In this context the original author of the book can make life for the slicing book re-engineers much easier if he or she includes remarks (for instance on the necessary theory for solving exercises) in the source of the book when the author writes it in the first place. Of course this is difficult if he or she also only takes some exercises from other material.

To conclude and look ahead to further developments, let us state the following: to the later user of the sliced book it might look like magic done by the computer, if he or she just has to press a button and the computer "explains" the relationships between different learning objects to him or her. But until now computers are not able to extract the needed references between learning objects unless the author has placed them explicitly in the text. So we still need manual revision and the search for techniques which help the slicing book re-engineers continues.

The activities of a slicing book re-engineer are highly relevant for learning: by making "builds-on" relationships between slices explicit, the re-engineer actively creates the overview knowledge so often lacking in conventional learning. Similarly, making relationships between descriptions and examples explicit gives the learner a deeper understanding of the text's rationale. Thus, fragments of knowledge do not only become connected in sliced books but also in the learner's mind. The networked knowledge structure of sliced books is not only more flexible than the sequential texts of textbooks, but gives also more structural clues than the usual links of traditional hypertexts. We will further elaborate on these opportunities in the section on collaborative slicing.

Experiences as a Slicing Book Author

One of the authors (Furbach) is currently working on a book on "Logics for Computer Scientists", which is intended to cover the material for a second year course in computer science. A LaTeX-document[3] is the basis for the book which was originally developed for transformation in HTML, so that the text could be used directly in the classroom. This text does not include proofs of mathematical theorems (because these were presented in class on the blackboard) and it does not include motivational material (which instead was presented during the lectures). For the ongoing preparation of the book, all this has to be added to the already existing material. Altogether such a starting point appears to be very typical for book authors in an academic environment: there is material which was used during some courses and which has to be modified and extended toward a book. Typically an author wants to extend the material for the book in order to cover some more detailed and specialized aspects, which can be skipped during use in an introductory course. In our case the material now includes 60 pages together with links to interactive systems which are used in this course. It is currently extended and there are plans to connect it with other course material on similar topics.

Until now, the slicing book project has gathered experience from authors who delivered a finished text, which then was sliced automatically by the splitter. The author had to check and update the slices (see the report given above); although this may have caused a lot of work, this method had the advantage of allowing the author to select an editing or desktop publishing system, as long as the result was a LaTeX-document. Hence, the author worked within his or her well-known environment.

The author has to use a special tool when the book has to be developed together with the slicing structure and the meta-data. A prototype of an authoring tool developed by Ingo Dahn is available.

For authoring tools there are, in principle, two possible kinds of architectures:

1) The authoring tool is responsible for bookkeeping and navigating through the slice structure of the material. The author has to use this navigation tool to visit previously written slices and to restructure it. Whenever the author wants to modify or to add text, he or she browses through the structure to the location of interest. Then the authoring tool invokes a text editor which allows the input of LaTeX code for this particular unit.
2) The author uses a text editor to browse through the LaTeX source code of the document, i.e. he or she can basically use his or her usual preferred method to write and manipulate the manuscript. The author has to understand and modify the structuring commands which are included into the LaTeX source if he or she wants to introduce new slices or to modify the slice structure of the material.[4]

For the second method the author must be well aware of the data structures which are used by the Slicing Book Technology. Of course, this can be hidden by

---

[3] LaTeX-Documents make the formatting of documents explicit by embedding formatting instructions into an ASCII text. On the one hand this approach makes it impossible to create pure WYSIWYG-Editors. On the other hand, these formatting instructions allow much more sophisticated formatting than with editors like Microsoft work, e.g. the formatting of mathematical expressions. We used LaTeX documents for sliced books because most mathematical texts are edited in LaTeX and because the explicit formatting simplifies the re-engineering process.

[4] Other similar approaches are possible once XML-editors become common.

incorporating these structure-browsing capabilities into the text editor, by modifying its implementation. Taking into account the fact that authors who produce LaTeX code usually are not using the de facto "industrial standard" offered by Microsoft, we felt that it would not be a good idea to force an author to use a specific editor. Hence we decided to focus on the first method, where it is no problem to invoke arbitrary text editors from the authoring tool.

Until now, the authoring tool was used more or less for the following tasks:

Browsing and inspecting the structure of the document developed so far   This is like reading the book on a meta-level, which usually authors do not explicitly do. Suddenly the author finds him- or herself in a situation where he or she is thinking how a future reader might access the document. There is a section in the introduction of most textbooks, which tells the reader what he or she is supposed to read in which sequence and which material he might skip through upon first reading. Usually this is depicted by a kind of dependency graph for sections. In our case this dependency graph is much more fine grained, its nodes are slices or units and, even more important, the graph cannot be defined a posterior, it has to be incrementally constructed during the writing process of the book. This structure definition has to be done by the author.

Inspecting the content and the layout of the document or at least parts of the document   This task is even difficult in traditional writing because it forces the author to permanently switch between two different aspects: the layout of the document and the contents. Inspecting the contents without a minimal attention to layout and typesetting is impossible because the LaTeX text formatting system will not produce readable output if the text contains typesetting and layout errors. In our case there is now a third aspect, namely the focus on a unit-based view, which forces the author to navigate through the text and to decide which units he or she wants to preview as a document. The author has to navigate through the structure in order to read the contents.

Preview of the entire or, at least, large parts of the document   For this task the authoring-tool was used to specify which units the author wants to preview, which then results in a display of the postscript file of the corresponding part. In this preview the units of the document are marked at the margins; these marks can be used to identify those parts of the documents which the author wants to work on.

Altogether we have three different aspects of a document — the contents, the layout and the slicing structure (including the meta-data). The author has to pay attention to all three aspects while developing the material. For each of these aspects we have tools to works with: the editor to produce the text, the LaTeX system for typesetting and the authoring tool for navigating. The more these systems are separated from each other, the more difficult the task is for the author. He or she has to do three jobs at a time: writer, designer and knowledge engineer.

Let's take, e.g., the task of extending a subsection within the text. The author first has to localize the appropriate unit: for this he or she browses with the re-engineering tool (Figure 8.4) through the slicing structure. In order to check the contents of a unit, the author invokes the preview-option of the tool and reads the content of a unit and its immediate context. When he or she finds the appropriate unit for the planned extension, he or she invokes the text editor for this unit and is now able to introduce new text. However, the editor only contains the unit the author is working on together with some immediate context; in order to check some cross-dependencies the author has to again enter the unit-browser, navigate to the unit in question and again invoke the preview-options. During all this, the usual layout-tasks have to be solved by including LaTeX commands in the text. Finally the meta-data for the extended unit, like keywords and dependency descriptions, have to be inserted. Altogether, the author has to change the tools and the view to the book several times throughout this sample-task; he or she constantly has to switch between the different views of his document.

One possibility for facilitating the above task, would be to integrate the browsing tools for navigating through the slicing-unit structure into the text editor or the layout-preview tool.

An integration into the text editor would certainly reduce the author's workload. He or she is used to producing text together with layout LaTeX commands by means of the editor; the additional work in taking care of the slicing structure seems to be manageable. As mentioned before, the disadvantage of this solution might be that the editor is fixed. The alternative solution, namely to present the structure together with the preview of the documents, would certainly be appropriate if the preview allows interaction. In this way, the author could use the layout-preview to browse through the document and to invoke an editor from there.

Figure 8.5 shows an example of such a combined previewing–browsing approach in the recently introduced version of the German newspaper *Rheinzeitung* (see http://epaper.rheinzeitung.de/01/05/30/). The user gets a preview of the newspaper and this graphical presentation can be used to browse through the newspaper, very much like the paper version.

Parts of the presented pages are links which connect readers to the respective articles. If the user activates a link he or she gets the contents plus the graphical browsing possibility that is maintained via thumbnails of the pages.

Analysis of Experiences

The experiences we have collected permit us to derive some conclusions on the creation of sliced books. Note that we do not consider the cases where authors program complex multimedia applications. Please also note that we report on work in progress.

The process of creating sliced books is knowledge work It can therefore not only be applied to the production of electronic books by professional slicing book re-engineers and authors, but also as a means for learning. One of the more interesting uses involves the collaborative creation of sliced books by teachers and their students (we will elaborate on this scenario in the next section). A general observation appears to be that the slicing book knowledge representation can be created and used in diverse contexts without changes. But each context needs special functionality and often even

Figure 8.5: Previewing–browsing the *Rheinzeitung*.

Figure 8.5: (*continued*)

a special tool to access and manipulate the knowledge structure. The reported experiences of the first slicing book author shows that the cognitive load is much too high if tools developed for one context are applied in another context.

Knowledge work can rarely be done in isolation, but builds on other information. For example, the document should have numerous key phrases assigned and each key phrase should be assigned to all parts that consider the corresponding topic as a major concept, not only to the first place where this concept is introduced. It is recommended that authors re-use key phrases that have already been assigned in related books. This facilitates the development of unified access tools. A detailed thesaurus of recommended key phrases maintained by competent personnel and available over the Internet would be a great help. It is intended that the thesaurus developed in the Trial-Solution project will be made accessible to the public through Fachinformationszentrum Mathematik/Informatik Karlsruhe, Germany.

Sliced books are constructed   There are different approaches to writing texts or hypertext documents. The slicing book approach has a bias toward viewing document creation as a construction activity. The definition of modules and their relationship, typical for engineering, is an important part of the creation process. Much like an engineer, the creators of sliced books can build libraries of components and reuse them in different contexts. If compared to software construction, the creation of a sliced book bears the closest resemblance to declarative programming (e.g. with Prolog).

A particular future challenge will be to support the early phases of the creation of sliced books. Much as an architect needs a manual sketch before he plans a house in detail, the sliced book authors need semiformal representations of slices and their relationships before they define them in detail. A candidate for supporting early phases will be Mind Maps.

The creation of sliced books is not the same as the creation of classical hypertext documents, but there are some important similarities

Sliced books and guided tours   Slicing Book Technology enables the adaptation of documents for specific purposes. One of these is to serve as an introduction to a book or topic similar to a guided tour in hypertext documents. Software prefabricated books play this role in the existing SIT-Reader. These are recommended first readings for certain user groups (stereotypes, cf. (Rich, 1989)). Unlike a guided tour, a prefabricated book is copied to the reader's personal book on the server. He may read it, but more importantly, he can at any point augment it automatically with more information he is interested in. Therefore it is important to select such slices for prefabricated books that have numerous links to various parts.

Prefabricated books can be considered as initial user profiles recommended for certain groups of readers. Thus they can also recommend settings for electronic search procedures. For example the possibility to search for detailed proofs will not be selected in a prefabricated mathematical book that is designed for people who want to get a brief overview only. Prefabricated books are mainly intended for first time readers. They draw the attention of these readers to the parts of the book that are of special interest to them.

Hyperlinks and relations   Hyperlinks take readers of a hypertext from one place of the text to another or to another document. Similarly, the *refers* and *requires* relation relate different parts of a document. However there are a number of important differences too.

- A hyperlink has no specific semantic; the relationship between slices typically has a semantic. This semantic richness changes the process of creating a sliced book (we would argue that it makes it easier for authors and slicing book re-engineers) and is the basis for automated support. The lack of semantic richness of hyperlinks is the basic argument for Tim Berners-Lee to propose a new Semantic Web architecture (Berners-Lee, Hendler, & Lassila, 2001). The slicing book architecture contains a few predefined relationships, but the tools we currently use are flexible enough to support new types of binary relations between slices when they are needed by authors.

- Not all required relationships have to be explicitly represented. It is possible to introduce derived relationships by defining them formally on the basis of previously introduced relations and attributes. The automated inference systems that are used to compose personalized documents can resolve these definitions at runtime. This significantly reduces the work for the creators of sliced books: the numbers of manually defined relationships is typically lower than the number of hypertext links. The author can rely on a few general definitions instead of defining many specific relationships.
- Relationships connect (groups of) slices. Unlike positions connected by hyperlinks, these slices carry specific content. Thus relationships between slices can much better reflect relationships between contents.

Of course, ordinary hyperlinks can be used in addition to meta-data. Even if the text to be sliced was a hypertext, they can automatically be analyzed in order to derive useful meta-data.

Formatting   Hyperlinks are visible in the hypertext. They are intended for use by humans and need an explanatory text or image. In contrast, the reader of a sliced book will not see the meta-data. These are only intended for use by the advisory engine that helps the reader to collect the slices he or she is interested in. On the one hand this means more freedom to the author: he or she is free to add as much meta-data as necessary in order re-use the material. On the other hand the author has more responsibilities to ensure quality; while a hypertext reader may discover meaningless or faulty links by him- or herself, and will quickly get lost if there are faults in the knowledge structure underlying a sliced book. If, however, slices are created and linked carefully, the reader will not as easily "get lost in Hyperspace" as with hypertext documents.

The author of a hypertext has much more control of the formatting than the author of a sliced book. In practice, the final layout of an HTML document will be not determined by the author but by the reader's Web browser. The author of a sliced book, however, cannot even be sure about the context in which the text will be re-used. The slicing book author will also design a presentation, but just as a kind of "master document." The author should strictly separate the presentation from the content. The tools that produce the final personalized documents will try to respect the design of the author as much as they can but they will also change it where necessary — either to meet the requirements of the reader or to support the combination with content that had been formatted in another way. In cases where automated re-formatting is problematic, the author may additionally decide to provide alternative versions of some slices. The author can determine the conditions of re-use for each of these versions by using appropriate meta-data.

The creation of sliced books iterates between automated phases and manual phases   It is neither advisable nor feasible to automate the creation process (even if a completed book serves as an input), nor is it advisable or feasible to create a sliced book completely manually. This observation is interesting because the explicit representation of content knowledge significantly enhances the potential for automation in comparison to traditional hypertext documents. Still we find that all automated phases need some manual preparation or rework.

Given the sheer number of slices (1500–3000 in a finely sliced average book) it is essential to automate the slicing and meta-data assignment as much as possible, knowing that perfection cannot be achieved automatically. In many cases meta-data are present in the documents, though they are not explicitly annotated. For example, we have sliced a collection of legal documents which contained laws, cases, addresses and comments. These different types of slices had not been mentioned in the text but they could be extracted automatically from the table of contents and inherited by the individual slices. The way in which meta-data are encoded varies greatly from author to author, which means the tuning of the splitting and meta-data assignment tools is essential. The invention of meta-data pattern by which meta-data can be automatically assigned to groups of slices has considerably simplified the work of the re-engineer. These patterns are defined by the re-engineer himself. It is possible to propose pattern automatically using machine learning techniques.

Automated key phrase assignment is inherently difficult. Better linguistic tools could be an important help here but even then the linguistic material in a slice is frequently too small for a reliable semantic analysis. In these cases key phrase assignment must recur to the analysis of groups of slices. When the analysis has identified key phrases that describe concepts handled in a slice, it is necessary to distinguish between concepts that are indeed discussed in that part and those that are only used as auxiliary concepts. The current limited experience suggests that automatically assigned key phrases must be critically inspected by the re-engineer. Nevertheless automated key phrase assignment is very important since it suggests key phrases from a controlled vocabulary to the re-engineer. This helps maintain a coherent pool of key phrases.

Automation of the slicing process can be considerably improved by following some simple rules during the writing of the document. Above all, the document should be clearly structured. Start and end of re-usable parts should be clearly mentioned. This can be done in different ways for parts of different characters; e.g. examples can be annotated differently than exercises. This should be done in the same way for each type throughout the document. Style templates should be used instead of manual formatting whenever possible. In general, manual formatting should be avoided. Electronic re-use is not tied to the size of a print page and necessary re-formatting cannot be foreseen in advance. Therefore this is best left to the electronic formatting systems, web browsers, etc.

Seamless integration into standard tools and the reliance on open document standards is paramount   However different the creation of sliced books may be, many individual steps are derived from current work practices. We are already used to creating paragraphs of text documents and to format documents with standard word processors (such as LaTeX or Microsoft Word). Standard tools support even more sophisticated editorial activities such as the creation of keyword lists. The learning load is acceptable only if the user can apply his conventional tools to these slicing book activities. Standardization also applies to the document formats. Currently there are numerous discussions on open standards for the description of meta-data for documents and learning objects. Choosing between these proposed standards is a hard task for an author. In our view this is a secondary question that should not concern the author too much. It is, however, important that the document contains a maximum amount of information that can be used to recommend parts to an interested reader. This information should be included in the document in a uniform way. Then it can be later automatically extracted when needed. The upcoming XML-Standard encourages the production of structured documents and thus reduces the re-engineering work.

There is still considerable work to be done on developing better support for authors. Document structuring and the addition of meta-data should be supported by popular editors. Their conversion into DTD-based comfortable XML editors would be a great step forward in this direction. Separate tools for slicing and re-engineering are still required if other editors are used.

Sliced books offer authors the opportunity for new business models The online component of a sliced book can be easily changed. Outdated material can be replaced or augmented. Thus the author can modify his work based on feedback from the reader. When building prefabricated books, the author may realize that some parts are missing to make the content intelligible for certain outside readers. Then such parts may be augmented later or they may be pulled in from other sliced books. Alternatively, other authors may provide just the small parts that are missing in order to provide a link with their own material. As with conventional citations, authors will have the right to set references to any slice from another author but they cannot be sure that links to their work are included in other works. When the author of a book sets a link to a book from another author, this does not imply that the readers of the first book have the right to access content from the second. For such situations, authors should prepare attractive information that they are willing to deliver for free instead of the content (for example an abstract of the content).

Collaborative Slicing

Up to now this text focused on the creation of sliced books by individuals. The complexity of the creation of sliced books suggests making the creation of sliced books a collaborative effort. As we are currently only exploring how to proceed in this area, this chapter will only introduce scenarios for collaborative slicing.

There are at least three scenarios for collaborative authoring:

1) Author–author collaboration: A group of authors and editors prepare a sliced book that will later be used by the reader.
2) Author–reader collaboration: Authors and readers collectively develop a sliced book starting from a base manuscript. For example, a university lecturer and his or her student jointly develop a sliced book starting with the traditional lecture notes. Slicing a book is regarded here as a learning methodology.
3) Author–others collaboration: After preparing the content of a book authors collaborate with other persons such as publishers, meta-data authorities and re-engineering staff in order to fine-tune and manage the content.

Author–Author Collaboration

Collaborative slicing can be seen as a special case of collaborative writing. Collaborative writing is difficult because authors on the one hand need to be aware of what the others are doing, in order to produce a coherent result (Schwabe, 1995). On the other hand, they need times of undisturbed work in order to formulate their own thoughts. Typical tools for collaborative writing therefore distinguish between divergent (loosely coupled, often asynchronous) modes, where each author works on his own section of work, convergent (closely coupled and synchronous) modes, where all authors see the same content, and mixed modes where some authors work in a convergent mode and others in a divergent mode. Divergent phases further the deliberation of the content and ensure that all needed information is included in the product; convergent phases ensure that the product becomes a coherent whole (for a general introduction to collaborative tools, see Holmer, Haake, & Streitz, 2001; for collaborative hypertext, see Mark, Haake, & Streitz, 1997; for a theoretical discussion on convergent and divergent phases see Dennis & Valacich, 1999; Schwabe, 2001).

Collaborative slicing needs both convergent and divergent modes, too, but the activities in these modes differ from conventional tools. Although tools have been developed to reserve sections of any granularity for personal work, experiences show, that for divergent phases authors mostly reserve paragraphs or sections for their own work. In sliced books, individual authors will be inclined to reserve individual slices for their personal work; these may be, but do not have to be, equivalent to paragraphs or sections. Furthermore, sections can be recursively aggregated, slices cannot be.

The interesting activities, however, happen through the convergent phases. Here, the authors jointly prepare the meta-data. An easy approach could be to let one author do the physical editing and others just participate orally. This may not be very productive, so at a minimum, the passive authors need a pointing device to contribute or there needs to be support for taking turns in active editing. A much more interesting approach might be a structured division of labor: slices have (by definition) a module-like character. Thus, in a first step, each author may define pre-conditions and post-conditions for his slices. In a second step, the author searches for other slices that have post-conditions that fulfill the preconditions of his slices. Here, both — a shared framework of reference and intelligent tool support — may be needed to make this feasible. If there is a slice that at least partially fulfills his requirements, he negotiates the interface with the other author as a third step. On the basis of this negotiation, both authors may also agree that it is necessary to rewrite the slice. If no existing slices fulfill his requirements, the precondition is noted on a list that is the basis for further writing. In a fourth step, the total structure of the document is discussed and settled in a group session with all authors.

These four steps can be iterated several times. Besides sufficient tool support, it requires good moderation skills within the group of authors. We have not yet tested this approach, but it is useful to demonstrate how the modular and logical structure of sliced books can lead to new collaborative authoring approaches. Other approaches can be based on the similarity of slicing authorship to programming. Here one could try to transfer collaborative programming approaches (e.g. pair programming or approaches for shared program repositories) to collaborative slicing book authorship.

Author–Reader Collaboration

In learning contexts, authors and readers can together construct their shared understanding in a collaborative writing scenario. Here computer supported scenarios can be particularly useful (Bromme & Stahl, 1998; Briggs & Brown, 1997). First evidence from usage of our sliced book in University contexts indicates that authoring slicing text can be an even better learning instrument, because the relationship of knowledge pieces (= slices) is made explicit. Students switch between content understanding/preparation and reflections on the content. What could be a suitable scenario for such an author–reader collaboration?

The scenario can again be based on divergent and convergent modes: the teacher–author could prepare and present the content as unconnected slices in a divergent mode to a class of students. The students then split in subgroups of two or three persons and try to build the slicing relationships and thus explore the deeper structure of the content presented. In a third convergent phase the whole class tries to arrive at a shared understanding of the slicing structure. There can be several variations of this approach: (a) the students prepare the slicing relationships at home and only the subsequent third phase is done in class; (b) the author and the readers discuss the slicing relationships in an oral discussion. Here content discussion and meta-discussion can be interwoven. (c) the author presents only parts of the necessary information. The readers then have to collect the other data and prepare the slicing hierarchy. This approach can be useful for case studies or experiments; (d) besides the shared representation of slicing book content and slicing relationships exist individual annotations and individual slicing relationships. This approach would take individual preferences on knowledge representation into account. Current tools do not sufficiently support author–reader collaboration yet. Requirements for a future collaborative tool include

1) an easy to use interface for ad-hoc in-class slicing;
2) shared access to a shared slicing representation (including concurrent access, locking, view linking, tele-pointing, etc.);
3) personal annotations to a slicing representation;

4   author-control of the collaborative process;
5   functionalities to test the slicing representation.

Currently we are working on building special tool for these purposes and have been involved in first exploratory experiments (Valerius, Dahn, & Schwabe, 2001).

Author–Others Collaboration

Sliced books gain considerable added value if their slices can be reused in combination with slices from other documents. In order to support this, the meta-data used for the description of the slices of a book must be integrated with the meta-data used for other books. This integration should be taken into account at an early stage of the authoring work. We envisage a central meta-data server from which authors can download already existing meta-data. This is necessary in order to encourage the author to use keywords that are also used in other books. Nevertheless, it cannot be expected that already existing meta-data are sufficiently detailed to describe specific finely grained sliced books. Therefore, authors must have the possibility to define their own meta-data assignments.

Authors are domain experts. It cannot be expected that they will define their new meta-data according to some general standards. Therefore, they will have to cooperate with meta-data experts that can integrate the new meta-data consistently into existing systems. The author may also have to cooperate with experts that develop specific styles for the presentation of his or her book. Since slices can be easily linked to slices in other books or to other resources on the Internet, cooperation with authors of other books in order to settle issues of combination of slices is relevant. These issues also concern respecting intellectual property rights — an item that is also of importance for publishers.

References

Berners-Lee, T., Hendler, J. & Lassila, O. (2001). The Semantic Web. *Scientific American*, May.

Briggs, R., & Brown, H. (1997). *From the Sage-on-the-Stage to the Guide-on-the-Side: Re-engaging the Disengaged Learner with Collaborative Technology*. Retrieved January 17, 2002, from University of Arizona, Tucson. http://www.cmi.arizona.edu/personal/bbriggs/ Downloads/aincost1.doc

Bromme, R., & Stahl, E. (1998). Räumliche Metaphern und das Schreiben von Hypertext — Eine Studie im Schulunterricht [Space metaphors and the writing of hypertext — A study within schools]. *Zeitschrift für Pädagogische Psychologie, 12*, 156–166.

Dahn, I. (2000). Symbiose von Buch und Internet [Symbiosis of book and Internet]. In: U. Becker, and W. Sommer (eds), *Learntec 2000*, (pp. 551–558). Karlsruhe: Karlsruher Kongreß- und Ausstellungs-GmbH.

Dahn, I. (2001). Slicing book technology — providing online support for textbooks. In: *Proc. 20th World Conference on Open Learning and Distance Education*. Düsseldorf: Proceedings on CD-ROM.

Dahn, I., & Schwabe, G. (2001). Personalizing textbooks with slicing technologies — concept, tools, architecture, collaborative use. In: *Proc. 35th Annual Hawaii International Conference on System Sciences*. Retrieved January 17, 2002, from IEEE Computer Society: http://www.hicss.hawaii.edu/diglib.htm

Dennis, A., & Valacich, J. (1999). Rethinking media richness: Towards a theory of media synchronicity. In: *Proc. 32nd Annual Hawaii International Conference on System Sciences*. Retrieved January 17, 2002, from http://www.hicss.hawaii.edu/diglib.htm

Gellrich, R., & Gellrich, C. (2001). *Lehr- und Übungsbuch für Fachhochschulen* (Bd. 1) [Textbook and Exercises for Universities of Applied Sciences (Vol. 1)]. Frankfurt/Main: Verlag Harri Deutsch.

Holmer, T., Haake, J., & Streitz, N. (2001). Kollaborationsorientierte synchrone Werkzeuge [Collaboration oriented synchronous tools]. In: G. Schwabe, N. Streitz, and R. Unland (eds), *CSCW-Kompendium — Lehr- und Handbuch zur computerunterstützten Gruppenarbeit* (pp. 180–193). Heidelberg: Springer-Verlag.

Mark, G., Haake, J., & Streitz, N. (1997). Hypermedia use in group work: Changing the product, process, and strategy. *Computer-Supported Cooperative Work: The Journal of Collaborative Computing*, 6, 327–368.

Rich, E. (1989). Stereotypes and user modeling. In: A. Kobsa, and W. Wahlster (eds), *Usermodels in Dialog Systems* (pp. 35–51). Berlin: Springer-Verlag.

Schwabe, G. (1995). *Objekte der Gruppenarbeit — ein Konzept für das Computer Aided Team* [Objects of Group Work]. Wiesbaden: Gabler.

Schwabe, G. (2001). Mediensynchronizität — Theorie und Anwendung bei Gruppenarbeit und Lernen [Media synchronicity]. In: F. Hesse, and H. Friedrich (eds), *Partizipation und Interaktion im virtuellen Seminar* (pp. 111–134). Münster: Waxmann.

Valerius, M., Dahn, I., & Schwabe, G. (2001). Adaptive Bücher für das kooperative Lernen, Anwendungen — Konzepte — Erfahrungen [Adaptive books for cooperative learning]. In: M. Engelien, and J. Homann (eds), *Virtuelle Organisationen und Neue Medien 2001* (pp. 391–413). Lohmar: Josef-Eul-Verlag.

Wolter, H., & Dahn, I. (2000). *Analysis Individuell* [Personalized calculus]. Heidelberg: Springer-Verlag.

Chapter 9

Authoring Hypervideos: Design for Learning and Learning by Design

Carmen Zahn, Stephan Schwan, and Beatriz Barquero

Non-linear information structures are not only confined to texts, but can also be found in the realm of audio-visual information presentations. Accordingly, different kinds of non-linear and interactive video applications have emerged, which include hypervideos. The latter allow the users to interact with video information in discontinuous ways: for example, they are able to select video scenes and rearrange them in different sequences or activate links for obtaining additional information on specific topics, concepts, or objects. Thus, from the viewpoint of constructivism, hypervideos seem no less suited as a tool for learning than hypertexts. The present chapter addresses the issue of acquiring knowledge through hypervideos, in which two main perspectives are to be considered: (1) learning by working with a pre-existing hypervideo, and (2) learning by producing or designing a hypervideo. In the first section, the basic features of hypervideos are described and important similarities and differences between hypervideos and hypertexts are outlined. In the second section we present an agenda for research on "designing hypervideos for learning." In the third section we concentrate on an explorative study of the proposals for video-based hyperlinks made by participants with varying degrees of background knowledge and perspectives. Finally, in the fourth section we focus on the proposal "learning by designing hypervideos" and indicate some educational implications of the design activity.

What is a "Hypervideo"?

Although video scenes are an integral part of many hypermedia applications, not all of them qualify as "hypervideo." The main difference between video scenes found in traditional hypermedia software and hypervideo lies in the importance attached to the video material (that is, dynamic audio-visual information) in relation to other symbol systems. In the case of traditional hypermedia software, pages of written text constitute the core of the system to which additional non-textual information, including video scenes, is appended at different points. Thus, at bottom, the user has the impression of reading a text, which is illustrated by other types of information. By implication, because video clips are commonly used in an illustrative manner, typically the scenes themselves are viewed in a linear and non-interactive fashion. In contrast, in hypervideos, the video material plays a far more prominent role, as it forms the "backbone" of the system to which other materials may be appended. The user has the impression of watching a film, which may be supplemented by additional non-filmic information, e.g. texts or graphics (Guimarães, Chambel, & Bidarra, 2000). The video material may be interrupted to access additional information and can thus be viewed non-linearly and interactively. Acquiring knowledge through hypervideo tends to proceed in sequence from concrete to more abstract information, since hypervideo presentations start from visual images of concrete aspects of the represented topic, which are then integrated into a more general and abstract frame through links to diverse information.

With regard to the non-linear organization of hypervideos, at least three different types can be found (see Figure 9.1). The first type is exemplified in "HyperCafe", which was one of the earliest hypervideos (Sawhney, 1996; Sawhney, Balcom, & Smith, 1996). Here, a substantial number of short video scenes are linked together in a network-like form. This form of hypervideo comes close to the principles of classic hypertext. Secondly, an existing linear film can be divided into single scenes, which are indexed according to different criteria or "themes." Depending on the theme specified, different sequences of the film's scenes are then selected, rearranged and presented to the viewer. This type of hypervideo is exemplified in a well-known paper by Spiro and Jehng (1990), in which the authors describe a hypervideo tutorial for the interpretation of Orson Welles' film *Citizen Kane*. By using hypervideo technology, users may filter the scenes that pertain to a main topic of the film and then proceed to view them in immediate succession. By repeating this process several times over and from different thematic perspectives, the viewers are assumed to develop a more flexible mental representation of the structure and content of the film. These first two types of hypervideos may be considered homogeneous, insofar as they primarily consist of dynamic audio-visual information, giving the user the overall impression of a continuous stream of moving pictures. In contrast, the third type of hypervideo identified would be considered heterogeneous, because here, different symbol systems — texts, pictures, or graphics — are linked to a main video, giving the user the impression of watching a film supplemented by multimedial "footnotes." The concept of heterogeneous hypervideos addressed in the empirical study is described in the third section. In this study subjects were asked to propose links leading to supplementary in-depth information for three different linear videos.

Obviously, hypervideo shares with classical hypertext the characteristic of having a non-linear structure, which gives the user the opportunity of taking different "routes" through the learning material. Does this structural similarity imply that the well-known benefits and drawbacks of acquiring knowledge through hypertexts — e.g. the extended possibilities of self-guided learning as well as the dangers of experiencing feelings of cognitive overload and disorientation — may be generalized to hyper-

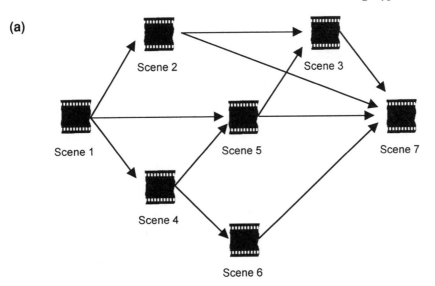

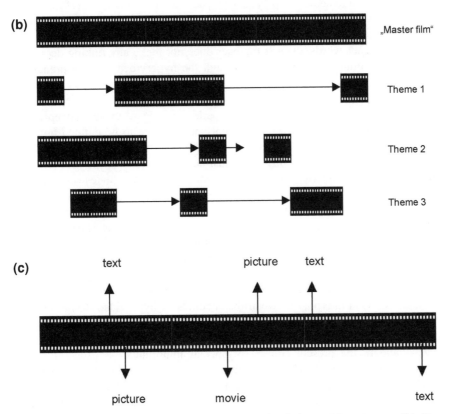

Figure 9.1: Types of hypervideos: (a) Network of short video scenes; (b) Decomposition of "master" film into multiple versions which correspond to different themes; (c) Main film is linked with multimedial "footnotes."

videos? This continues to be an open question, as empirical findings pertaining to hypervideos are rare (see below). Besides their similarities, hypervideos differ in at least three important aspects from classical hypertexts.

Firstly, hypervideos (like instructional video applications in general) are based on *audio-visual* information, whereas hypertexts, even if enriched by additional materials such as graphics or illustrations, are based on written language as the primary medium. Hence, the general differences between audio-visual media and texts do apply. In particular, audio-visual materials are specifically suited for concrete as opposed to more abstract topics, preserve more details, have a motivating impact on the learners, and yet may be processed less elaborately (Wetzel, Radtke, & Stern, 1994).

Secondly, hypervideos present their audio-visual information *dynamically*. Whereas hypertexts (as well as texts in general) consist of static pages, allowing the readers to process information at their own pace, in hypervideos the pace of information presentation is more or less determined by the video itself. This dynamism has some implications for the classical notion of both "nodes" and "links." The crucial difference between hypervideo nodes and their traditional counterparts lies in the self-terminating character of the former. Hypervideo nodes consist of short video scenes, which, once activated, are played from beginning to end. Therefore, if the user does not activate a link during the course of the scene, he or she is linked automatically to a subsequent node at the end, so as to avoid the hypervideo simply stopping short. In other words, even if the user does not make any linking decisions, he or she has to be guided automatically through the hypervideo along a predefined sequence of nodes, thus giving the impression of watching a continuous stream of information as opposed to exploring a network of distinguishable nodes. Similar time-related design considerations have to be made with regard to the conception of links. Hypervideo links (often identified as "hot spots") have to be defined not only by their spatial position within the picture frame, but also by their temporal position and extension within the hypervideo, which must be made salient to the user (Hodges & Sassnet, 1993). Additionally, the dynamic character of both nodes and links in hypervideos includes a number of consequences for the cognitive processes of the users. In general, due to their time constraints, dynamic audio-visual information presentations make greater demands on the cognitive system of the learner than do static information presentations, as numerous studies in the fields of television and multimedia have shown (e.g. Lang, 2000). This is especially true for non-linear audio-visual media: for instance, hot spots put far more time pressures on the navigational decisions of the user than the links in hypertexts, because they are accessible only for a certain duration. This interplay between the specifics of hypervideo design and the processes of knowledge acquisition is discussed in more detail in the second section of the chapter.

Thirdly — and in the present context of special importance — users of audio-visual media in general and of hypervideos in particular are considered as mere *recipients*. It is uncommon to consider them authors or designers. Creating scripts and storyboards, shooting and film-editing have not been considered key competencies in our educational systems so far, whereas writing and editing texts (skills needed to create own hypertexts) are skills promoted by instructional means. In short, with the exception of some basic experiences with home videos, skills for creating and designing video footage are lacking in our culture. Obviously, this has various implications for learning by designing hypervideos, which we will touch on in the fourth section.

Designing Hypervideo for Learning

At a first glance, the notion of hyperlinked videos opens up new vistas for instructional media as they present potentials somewhat different from those of linear educational films or static hypertext. Hypervideo combines dynamic audio-visual presentation formats with great flexibility in terms of the information to be included. Furthermore, users are free to access this information in different ways. According to Guimarães *et al.* (2000), hypervideo, as a videocentric learning tool, provides high authenticity and the possibility of adding emotional components to learning situations. Along with this, hypervideo is a medium which integrates different elements of knowledge presentation (e.g. texts with video material), thus increasing their mutual effectiveness. Additionally, hypervideo, as a flexible interaction environment, has the potential to support both experience-based and reflective modes of cognition, different learning styles, different phases during the learning process, as well as cognitive mapping (for details, see Guimarães *et al.*, 2000). Thus, hypervideos allow learners to build up enriched mental models using different representation modalities synchronously and compose flexible knowledge structures according to their own individual needs. Furthermore, learners may express these internal knowledge structures externally and share and discuss them with other students. All of these factors are assumed to promote learning (Spiro & Jehng, 1990; Mayer & Anderson, 1991; Park & Hopkins, 1993; Wetzel *et al.*, 1994; Guimarães *et al.*, 2000).

However, a more pessimistic perspective would include the notion that these are only potential positive effects, which have not yet been proven empirically. Nothing can be said about the conditions under which these positive effects will, in fact, emerge. And potential negative effects could be predicted, too, because previous research has demonstrated that the presentation of linear multimedia information, such as dynamic visual material with verbal explanations, does not "insure that students will understand the explanation unless research-based principles are applied to design" (Moreno & Mayer, 2000, p. 5).

In addition, multimedia material designed in such a way that it places excessive and unnecessary cognitive load on the learners might inhibit learning (Chandler & Sweller, 1991). Such cognitive load may result from "free linking," which is also accompanied by users' experiencing disorientation (Zhu, 1999). In the case of hypervideos, this kind of problem might be even more pronounced, because the video itself sometimes carries with it the risk of overstraining the cognitive capacities of the learner (Wetzel *et al.*, 1994). Finally, additional cognitive load may result from the dynamic character of nodes and links which puts time pressure on the users when they are required to make navigational decisions. In view of this, questions such as "How can hypervideos be designed so as to unfold their potential in real learning situations?" and "How can unintended negative effects associated with both linear video and hypermedia be circumvented?" become especially interesting.

Related research fields have provided some answers to these questions, but their applicability to hypervideos is far from clear. Despite its non-linearity, hypervideo cannot be equated with hypertext, because of the aforementioned distinctive characteristics (cf. the previous section). Consequently, design principles valid for learning with hypertext may not be applicable to hypervideo. Similarly, hypervideo — although video-based — cannot be classified as a "subcategory" of instructional/educational film. This is due to its non-linearity, which implies a drastically different viewing situation where users can decide what they want to watch. Thus, design principles that might be valid for linear video might not be suitable for hypervideo. In other words, hypervideo should best be considered as an independent new medium with only some functional similarities to linear video and hypertext (Sawhney, 1996). Due to the unique combination of attributes in hypervideos, a set of new design principles is required in order to properly design hypervideos for the purpose of learning. At present we cannot rely on a rich pool of published empirical research to define those principles because literature on hypervideo in general, and on educational hypervideo in particular, is sparse. Nevertheless, in what follows we have derived from existing literature some requirements for the design of educational hypervideos, and we pay attention to how existing examples of hypervideo have addressed these requirements.

According to Guimarães *et al.* (2000), both experience-based and reflective cognitive modes involved in meaningful learning should be addressed by hypervideo design. Whereas experience-based cognitive activities can be supported by linear video (i.e. by following a "narrative sequence" presented by traditional means of audio-visual knowledge communication), for reflection, providing enough time and structuring and organizing the information are necessary prerequisites. As a consequence, hypervideo design has to include both the presentation of coherent audio-visual information as well as possibilities for an organized interactive access to the units of audio-visual information, texts, graphics, photos, etc. Accordingly, two dimensions of hypervideo design are to be distinguished (see also Balcolm, 1996): video production and interface design, the latter including the design of the global hypervideo structure and the design of links.

Producing Hypervideo Scenes for Learning

The basic units of hypervideo systems are single video scenes (Sawhney, 1996). Therefore, hypervideo production generally comprises the preparation of video information for separate scenes or "nodes" that can be arranged in different sequences and be integrated with texts or other symbol systems. Aside from any instructional considerations in this context (as discussed later), the issue of technical constraints has been considered as a primary determinant of video production processes. There are limitations concerning the size (and number) of video scenes in relation to the capacities of the computer hardware used. For example, limited disk space has generally been mentioned as requiring the use of *short* video sequences (Balcolm, 1996). However, as faster processors and extended disk space are developed for computers (including external storage on DVD), the need for short video scenes due to technical limitations will certainly diminish. Accordingly, recent examples of educational hypervideo can easily include longer videos of about 15–20 minutes (Guimarães *et al.*, 2000). Thus, as computer technology offers more flexibility with regard to the length of video scenes, authors of hypervideo are free to establish instructionally based design decisions.

From the instructional perspective, different requirements in relation to video scenes designed to support learning can be defined: Firstly, since the individual scenes are linear, they should convey meaningful information within their time limits, without overstraining the cognitive capacities of the learner. Secondly, sequences of scenes in hypervideo systems may not have one defined beginning and end (or at least we cannot force the learner to start out with a specific beginning). Thus, besides being meaningful, scenes must be more or less independent of each other. Thirdly, a given scene can be part of different sequences. To maintain coherence between scenes, the beginning and end of each scene should eventually make it fit into other scenes, which are then connected to it by links. Finally, for navigational purposes (traversing the scenes and accessing "footnotes," e.g., as texts), the video material needs to contain additional "branching points" within the scenes.

These and similar reflections have led to a reconsideration of traditional video production techniques (all of which serve quite different purposes). Locatis, Charuhas and Banvard (1990), for example, suggest "epitomizing" video for hypermedia, using strategies similar to those present in commercials. "Epitomizing" in this context summarizes several techniques for communicating compact information in short scenes: reduction of episode length to about one minute as long episodes of linear video could suppress interactivity; reduction of dwell time (i.e. the length of time a scene is shown) to a time just long enough to recognize, since users have a number of options for viewing scenes repeatedly, watching them in slow motion, or viewing individual still frames; use of sequences of still frames, like video animations instead of real time presentation to save time; use of asynchronous audio sped up (voice over, only), again to save time and to enhance users' freedom; spending less time on visual transitions, by means of camera and issues of shot progression; and finally, including effects like split screen or other techniques of simultaneous presentation.

In other cases, however, it may be reasonable from the viewpoint of "content perspective" to include larger linear scenes or even base the hypervideo on a single video node e.g., when learners are guided through a procedure (Francisco-Revilla, 1998). In this case, linear video techniques may be a better choice than "non-linear" techniques for producing scenes for a well designed hypervideo.

Generally, the suggested video techniques have not been based on psychological models of media-based knowledge acquisition, neither have they, as yet, been empirically validated. Thus, they should be applied with caution.

Designing Hypervideo Structures for Learning

Certain types of hypervideo are based on a pre-existing linear film. In this case, "non-linear" techniques of video production cannot be applied. Instead, video production mainly consists of re-editing the pre-existing source video, which must be subdivided into scenes. This division must be coordinated with the structure of the source video and with the demands of the resulting hypervideo system. Taking *Citizen Kane* as an example, Spiro and Jengh (1990) used a number of short scenes (called "mini-cases") as their basic units of instruction for the purposes of experience consolidation, early introduction of complexity, for avoiding maladaptive prototype cases, providing cognitive flexibility, retaining openness of interpretation, and avoiding confusion. However, they also offered longer sequences of "mini-cases" where this made sense.

Linear video scenes in hypervideos are generally components of a *non-linear* overall structure. With regard to learning, obviously the central requirement is the production of meaningfulness despite this non-linearity. Therefore, video scenes cannot be arranged and linked arbitrarily. Especially for homogeneous types of hypervideos (and particularly for inducing reflective cognitive modes on the part of the learner), considerable effort is required for establishing coherence and structural unity (Sawhney, 1996). For educational purposes, a primary goal is to generate hypervideo structures that include meaningful paths (with regard to content), meaningful possibilities of interruption, and a comprehensible overall structure of the hypervideo.

To achieve this, notably in those cases where video scenes are originally shot for use in hypervideo, authors must be fully aware of the overall structure of the final hypermedium from the outset (Balcolm, 1996). Accordingly, a "hyperscript" needs to be created that reveals the overall structure of the hypervideo for mapping the connections between related informational units and for visualizing the system's organization (Balcolm, 1996). Sawhney (1996) has proposed that the following aspects be included in such a "grammar of hypervideo": scenes (as basic units of video), narrative sequences (possible threads through linked video scenes or text), temporal and spatio-temporal opportunities for navigation (text- or image-based links to traverse scenes), and navigational bridges (visual effects that smooth transitions from one scene to another, e.g. camera zoom). In other words, general tasks of hypervideo organization involve both the integration of information and the definition of meaningful routes for navigation.

With regard to the integration of information, Guimarães *et al.* (2000) describe different examples of hypervideo for educational purposes, thereby suggesting that there is no general "best way" of conceptualizing the structure of a hypervideo, as this depends heavily on the characteristics of the underlying content. Their examples include an integration of video with text (heterogeneous hypervideo) as well as exclusive uses of video scenes. Furthermore, some cases rely on short video segments, whereas in other cases larger video nodes seem to be more appropriate. Despite this variability, the authors emphasize that in learning situations the hypervideo structure has to be made explicit to the users and, accordingly, they use video-synchronized indexes that both reveal the video structure and serve as tools for navigation.

The design of navigation, which proceeds primarily through links, must take into account the spatial and temporal properties of hypervideos (Sawhney, 1996). In contrast to hypertexts, where links and nodes are static and may co-exist simultaneously, in hypervideo links are not always available to the user. They appear and disappear as the context changes. Sawhney (1996) proposes different opportunities for linking in a hypervideo: temporal and spatio-temporal (see Figure 9.2). Temporal opportunities are time-based references between video scenes. Here, a link, which is available for a limited time can be activated to play back another video scene and can be presented within the frame of the video scene (indicated by a marking or a change of the cursor) or outside the frame (as dynamic previews of the attached material). Spatio-temporal opportunities of navigation are references that, in addition to time, contain a spatial dimension relative to their position within the film space as well as to the "spatial semantics attributed to the nature of their content" (Sawhney, 1996, p. 7). These links are available for a limited amount of time and at a certain position within the video frame. They can be "attached" to the image of a certain object or a person and can be visually marked, for example by a flashing frame. Such opportunities are not confined to video-to-video links, but are also possible for video-to-text references (Francisco-Revilla, 1998).

Guimarães *et al.* (2000) further classify links according to media-specific attributes: They distinguish video-to-video links (that connect single scenes with their position in the source video), video-to-video links of spatio-temporal quality (i.e. content based), video-to-text links of spatio-temporal quality, temporal video-to-text links, text-to-video links, and general navigation tools (e.g. "back"). In addition, they distinguish possibilities of discrete versus continuous access to the source video. Continuous access is made possible by means of a graphic presentation of time progression in the source video (timeline), whereas discrete access occurs through different kinds of video indexes (text, icons, video previews, topics, map). With these various navigational possibilities at their disposal, learners can develop a more flexible mental representation of the system's structure and of the content.

Considering the amount of different linking opportunities with regard to learning, the question of cognitive overload again comes into play: How can users cope with different kinds of dynamic links? Which linking opportunity is more suitable for which purpose? Although these questions still remain open, it may be suggested that to some extent, the decision for specific kinds of links depends on the structure of the content and that, in addition, they can be chosen in accordance with the users' individual preferences or the task demands.

Designing Hypervideos for Learning — an Explorative Study

So far, the question of designing hypervideo for learning has been addressed on a somewhat general or even speculative level. Although many suggestions may seem plausible, they have not been confirmed in terms of empirical research. Indeed, there is an almost complete lack of published studies on the effects of hypervideo design

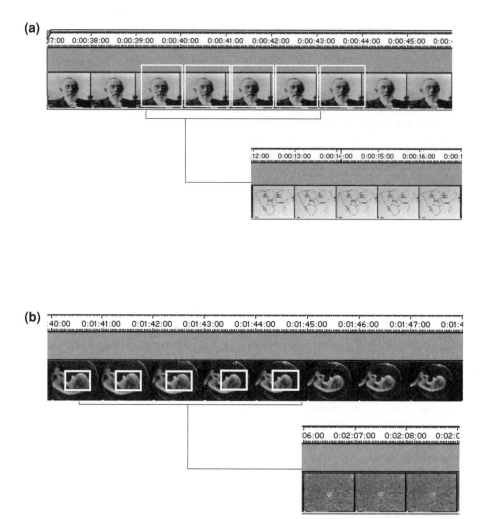

Figure 9.2: (a) Temporal hyperlinks are available during a brief period of time within a video-sequence. If activated they serve to pursue a different path in the hypervideo structure, e.g. to play back another video scene, which refers to the video-context at that point. If not activated, the hyperlink disappears as the source-video continues to play. (b) Spatio-temporal hyperlinks are available during a certain period of time within a video sequence *and* they are spatially located within the frame (e.g. they might be applied to a certain object). If activated, they serve to pursue a different path in the hypervideo structure which semantically refers to their location within the video-frame. If not activated, the hyperlink disappears as the source-video continues to play.

on learning. Even of the approaches presented in the previous paragraphs only a few make reference to having tested the design of their hypervideo systems in educational contexts (i.e. with students working on a certain topic).

Besides the lack of previous research, there appears to be an even greater problem associated with research on hypervideo: the problem of descending from a global level of studying the field of educational hypervideo to a specific level, required for systematic empirical work. We contend that this is due to the complexity of the medium making it difficult to isolate variables of interest for empirical experimentation with regard to learning. Particularly, the interrelations between design strategies and design effects seem far more complex than they are, for example, in linear video: hypervideo systems provide a broader frame of possibilities for users' actions. Within this frame learners "create" their own individual "instantiations" of the hypervideo by following a specific path through it, by revisiting certain parts of the hypervideo, etc. Rather than the general frame, it is these specific decisions of the users (i.e. their concrete instantiations of the hypervideo) that eventually affect knowledge acquisition. Thus, design intentions (of authors) and design effects (in users) "drift apart" as users are presented with higher levels of interactivity. Along with this, the numbers of possible design strategies and possible users' actions rise. As a consequence, learning by working with a hypervideo can take place in different ways while eventually producing similar outcomes in knowledge acquisition.

Considering this, direct investigation of design effects — which can ultimately provide a solid basis for successful authoring — becomes a difficult task for researchers. The selection of variables may become arbitrary because of the huge diversity of possible design strategies, users' behavior and cognitive effects intervening throughout the process.

In our attempts to find a solution to this dilemma, we have developed a preliminary framework to guide our research on designing hypervideo for learning. Due to the aforementioned problem we proceeded by "splitting the field" into research on design strategies and research on design effects. In our definition, design strategies consist of principles that are applied by hypervideo authors according to their design intentions for the purpose of supporting learning. They depend either on the structure of the content or on formal features of the materials that constitute the hypervideo. They may also be determined by individual characteristics of hypervideo authors, for example, their professional knowledge background. By empirically studying design strategies, a range of possible design criteria is identified on the basis of which their influence on knowledge acquisition can be determined.

A second step addresses the investigation of design effects, which may be defined as the consequence of design strategies on the learners' behavior and cognitive processes and, consequently, on their learning outcomes. The investigation of these effects should be carried out through a controlled variation of specific design principles.

Description of the Study

Our investigation is especially concerned with the design decisions relative to the overall, non-linear structure of hypervideos. Thus, we presented our subjects with pre-existing video material instead of asking them to produce new videos. We selected three different, non-interactive short video clips cut out of a longer instructional video on cellular biology. Clip 1 contained information about the basic structure of human cells, clip 2 showed different types of human cells, clip 3 illustrated details about the history of biological research introducing important persons, instruments and methods. The clips were about one to two minutes long and differed in the video techniques that were used. Clip 1 was a "typical" instructional animation, where objects were faded in and named subsequently. Clip 2 resembled a "scientific" film. It consisted of photos in which entities and processes were shown in great detail. Clip 3 looked like a TV-documentary and included different pictorial materials such as drawings, archive photos, etc.

Three groups of participants were selected for our study according to their specific background knowledge: 10 subjects had a high level of background knowledge in the content domain of biology (biology experts); 10 other subjects had a high level of background knowledge in the field of media production, i.e. video production and editing, web-design, etc. (media experts); and 10 further subjects were students with no special expertise in any of the two domains and who could be considered as typical addressees of an educational hypervideo on the topic (non-expert users).

The task of the subjects was to propose possible spatio-temporal links for the three different instructional video clips. The participants in the groups of biology experts and media experts were required to make their linking proposals pretending they were authors of the instructional hypervideo ("author perspective"); in contrast, the group of non-expert users had to do the same task under the assumption that they were to use the instructional hypervideo to learn about the topic ("user perspective"). For this purpose subjects were presented with template cards on which they had to write for each proposed link: where the link leading to additional information should begin and end (time code of the video image), which entity of the image should be marked as a "hot spot" (i.e. "be clickable"), how long this "hot spot" should remain activated, why there should be a link at the position selected, which feature of the video presentation caused their linking decision (image size, camera movement, beginning or end of a spoken sentence, speech volume, etc.), and whether the link should be explicitly marked (e.g. visually). All subjects worked individually. After they had been read the instruction (including an introduction to the notion of hypervideo), they worked on the three video clips, which were presented on a computer screen in random order. After completing the task, they were asked to fill in a questionnaire, in which they had to briefly describe the "set of rules" they had followed when making their linking decisions. They had also the opportunity to offer their opinion on how suitable the source video scenes were for being supplied with links.

Overall, the study aimed at answering the following questions:

- What design strategies do potential authors with varying background knowledge apply in order to create an "adequate" (heterogeneous) hypervideo for supporting learning?
- Do these authors' design strategies correspond to the design expectations of non-expert users?
- In which way are the decisions of the authors and the expectations of users influenced by formal aspects of the source video clips ?

Results of the Study

Firstly, we were interested in the number of links that the different groups proposed for the different video clips. Because the clips differed in length (8 shots, 14 shots, and 16 shots, respectively), the variable "number of links" was defined as the relative frequency of hyperlinked shots (i.e. shots provided with at least one link proposal) proportional to the total number of shots in the clip. For the total sample, the mean relative number of linked shots were 77 percent for clip 1, 60 percent for clip 2, and 54 percent for clip 3 (see Table 9.1).

A mixed two-way ANOVA was carried out with the between-subjects factor "background knowledge" (biology experts, media experts, non-experts) and the within-subjects factor "video clip" (clips 1, 2, 3). This analysis failed to reveal a significant effect of the factor "background knowledge." Participants with different background knowledge seemed to propose a similar amount of links within each clip. However, a significant main effect of "video clip" was found [$F(2,32) = 15,10$; $p < 0.001$]: the mean proportion of hyperlinked shots differed significantly among the different video clips. Clip 1 received significantly more links than clips 2 and 3, and for clip 2 more links were proposed than for clip 3. No significant interaction between background knowledge and video clip was shown.

In sum, although the subjects did not place links in all shots, the mean proportions of links in the video clips were rather high. In clip 1 more than three-quarters of all shots were provided with links to additional information, and in clip 3 every second

Table 9.1: Mean relative frequencies of hyperlinked shots by knowledge group and video clip (standard deviations in parentheses).

Knowledge group	Video clip			
	Clip 1	Clip 2	Clip 3	Total
Biology experts	0.77 (0.09)	0.79 (0.11)	0.56 (0.20)	0.71 (0.10)
Media experts	0.77 (0.15)	0.49 (0.28)	0.55 (0.15)	0.60 (0.10)
Non-expert users	0.79 (0.17)	0.54 (0.19)	0.50 (0.37)	0.61 (0.21)
Total	0.77 (0.13)	0.60 (0.29)	0.54 (0.17)	

picture would contain a link. Thus, we may conclude that the subjects would provide video scenes with a rather wide range of additional information, offering many "side roads" to potential learners, with the type of film clearly having an influence on the design decisions. The film receiving most linking proposals (clip 1) was an animation with a schematic presentation of the cell structure, where the cell components were progressively emphasized to support learning. This visual simplification and instructional character of the film could have facilitated the subjects' design decision of proposing a link to provide additional information on the cell components.

Secondly, we sought to discover whether subjects with different background knowledge placed their links in the same positions within the video clips. For each shot, the number of subjects from each group who would set the beginning of a link within the shot was recorded. On these data we calculated the correlations between the groups. Significant correlations were found between the biology-expert and the non-expert groups ($r = 0.70$, $p < 0.001$ for clip 2; $r = 0.63$, $p < 0.001$ for clip 3). No other correlations achieved significance. Thus, although two groups (biology experts and non-experts) made approximately the same decisions on the links position in clips 2 and 3, there was no general consistent pattern across all groups in this respect. The correlation between the content experts (biology group) and the potential learners (non-expert users) would suggest an important coincidence between the content-based decisions of potential biology authors and the content-based learning needs of potential users for offering or requesting additional information on the topic.

Thirdly, the mean duration of the links was determined. A mixed two-way ANOVA on background-knowledge and video clip showed no significant primary effect of background knowledge. The effect of video clips was marginally significant [$F(2,32) = 6,30$; $p < 0.1$]. In clip 1 the mean duration of links was higher than in the other clips, and the variability of the duration measures for this clip was very high, too (see Table 9.2). This seems to reflect in some way the reactions of the subjects to the design of the source video. Clip 1 consisted of animated objects being sequentially faded in, but not faded out. Two design strategies were, therefore, possible. Either links could be placed in parallel, i.e. attached to the objects of interest in the image as soon as these appeared and by remaining activated till the end of the clip. Or links could be placed sequentially, i.e. attached to one object only and remaining activated until another interesting object would appear in the clip. For clip 1, and independently of their background knowledge, some subjects seemed to prefer parallel linking, whereas others preferred sequential linking.

Fourthly, with regard to the need of explicitly marking the links, most participants were of the opinion that the links should be marked, so that these could be readily identified as sensitive regions or "clickable" objects. For the total sample, subjects decided that 79 percent of their proposed links (on average) should be visually marked. Different ways of visual marking were proposed: coloring or re-coloring the "clickable" objects, highlighting contours of sensitive regions, inserting symbols (buttons), inserting written text (captions).

These findings were also supported in part by the subjects' answers to the questionnaire on their criteria for adding links to a video. From these answers, three categories of design criteria were derived:

Table 9.2: Mean links duration in seconds by knowledge group and video clip (standard deviations in parentheses).

Knowledge group	Video clip			
	Clip 1	**Clip 2**	**Clip3**	**Total**
Biology experts	13.7 (10.2)	5.4 (1.9)	9.0 (2.6)	9.3 (4.1)
Media experts	11.9 (11.3)	6.9 (2.7)	8.1 (4.0)	9.0 (4.6)
Non-expert users	14.3 (11.2)	6.5 (3.3)	8.3 (4.0)	9.7 (4.9)
Total	13.7 (10.4)	6.3 (2.6)	8.5 (3.4)	

- *Design principles relative to the original video scene (aspects of the material).* A video scene, as basis for a hyperlinked video, should contain shots long enough to show the "clickable" object for a sufficient amount of time. It should also contain meaningful, clearly structured images and show static objects. Images and narration should refer to the same information.
- *Design principles relative to the links.* Video-based hyperlinks should be explicitly marked (or follow a specific scheme for introduction at the beginning of the video) and should appear sequentially. Hyperlinks should be used to specify and explain information given in the video, especially when that information (visual or auditory in terms of narration) is difficult to understand and it is not explained in the video itself. In addition, when clicking on a link, the video should stop.
- *Design principles relative to the to-be-attached information.* The information which appears when clicking on a linked object should provide details which refer to the visual or audio information given in the video at that particular moment. It should not be too extensive in order to avoid distraction from the original video scene.

It should be kept in mind that, because it was mainly explorative in nature, the study suffers some restrictions: We worked with a small number of subjects who, to some degree, lacked feedback with regard to their link proposals because the latter did not materialize in a real interactive hypervideo; there was no controlled variation of the visual features of the scenes as the study was based on existing educational videos.

Nevertheless, as previously outlined, the study was able to identify a complex but reasonable pattern of design strategies for hyperlinking videos, which potential producers and recipients apply. The findings also show that the participants did not apply these strategies in an undifferentiated and unreflective manner. Instead, as the differences between the three video clips make clear, the design decisions were strongly influenced by the content and structure of the videos to-be-linked.

In the present context, another finding of the study also claims special importance, namely, the substantial overlap between the behavior of users and producers. The finding that novice users are able to anticipate some of the linking principles of the experts suggests that the former possess at least some basic skills for producing hypervideos. Thus, the question which now arises is, whether these production skills may be utilized more systematically for purposes of knowledge acquisition. Linking decisions, however, constitute only a small part of the overall process of creating a hypervideo. Therefore, as discussed in the following section, learning by designing hypervideos requires a much broader scope of pedagogical and psychological considerations.

Learning by Designing Hypervideos

In this part of our contribution we propose the use of hypervideos from the instructional perspective of "learning by doing," i.e. learning within the activity context of constructing a hypervideo. We see this as an ideal activity because it integrates the three roles of Dillon's (see Chapter 2 in this volume) three-stakeholder model of hypermedia development and use. First, since students must decide on the content to be presented, they act as *authors*; second, as they also have to decide on how to present and organize that content information for a specific user group, they act as *designers*; and third, since they must evaluate and revise their writing and design work from the perspective of those who will use it, they act as *users*.

The integration of these three roles in the authoring activity and the demands (on thinking, work organization, group coordination, etc.) that this role integration implies make this kind of activity a complex one (cf. Harel & Papert, 1990). This complexity, in turn, constitutes its great learning potential. In what follows, we refer to the cognitive, metacognitive and social skills that the accomplishment of design activities in general, and of designing a hypervideo in particular, require; furthermore, we mention the learning benefits students may derive from those activities; finally, we point out some problems that may appear in the context of authoring activities, and we include some suggestions for aiming at a more successful use of these kinds of activities.

Again, the empirical knowledge concerning learning by designing hypervideos is as lacking as it was for designing hypervideos for learning. Therefore, we may draw some parallels to existing research in related domains: student design of hypertexts (Reimann & Zumbach, 2001; Braaksma, Rijlaarsdam, Couzijn, & van den Bergh, this volume; Bromme & Stahl, this volume; Talamo & Fasulo, this volume), student construction of hypermedia documents or learning programs (Harel & Papert, 1990; Resnick & Ocko, 1991; Carver, Lehrer, Connell, & Erickson, 1992; Lehrer, 1993; Beichner, 1994; Kafai, Ching, & Marshall, 1997; Erickson & Lehrer, 1998; Ching, 1999; Penuel, Korbak, Cole, & Jump, 1999), children making movies (Posner, Baecker, Poplar, & Becker, 1997) and student integration of video in a hyperdocument (Guimarães *et al.*, 2000).

Cognitive, Metacognitive and Social Demands of the Design Activity

In general, the construction of a hypertext document or a software program is a very demanding activity requiring not only a certain level of knowledge of subject matter and technology and a degree of cognitive and metacognitive skilfulness on the part of the student, but also a certain level of social and communication expertise, since the complexity of the activity usually makes it necessary to work cooperatively in a group. This is all the more true in the case of hypervideos since they require a technical apparatus for producing their "raw materials" far more complex than is the case for texts or static illustrations.

In addition to having a degree of prior knowledge on the subject matter to be addressed and on the production technologies required, students need to have developed a variety of cognitive and metacognitive skills (Harel & Papert, 1990; Carver *et al.*, 1992; Lehrer, 1993; Erickson & Lehrer, 1998; Reimann & Zumbach, 2001; cf. Braaksma *et al.*, this volume), which relate to different aspects of the design activity:

- *Relative to what information on the subject matter should be presented*: Identifying the main problem or theme, dividing it into sub-problems or sub-themes, posing questions, searching for information by using different sources, notetaking, summarizing, analyzing and interpreting the information available, evaluating the user's knowledge and needs for selecting relevant information.
- *Relative to how to represent and communicate that information:* Segmenting the information into small units or nodes, establishing meaningful connections or links among those units or nodes, translating their mental representation of the content into valid audio-visual representation, combining it with other types of representation in a meaningful way, organizing and structuring the information to be presented according to the structural complexity of the subject matter, offering clear navigation paths according to the users' needs and expertise.
- *Relative to some instructional aspects of their design constructions:* Including navigational aids, including a number of questions which allow users to test their own understanding, offering feedback and explanations to the users' answers and reactions.
- *Relative to self management of their individual work:* Planning their research and design tasks for achieving their individual goals according to schedule, evaluating their performance, reflecting on their decisions and identifying possible errors, searching for new alternatives, revising and changing their work when necessary, controlling external distractions and avoiding anxiety.

Because these individual skills are insufficient for facing the challenges posed by hypervideo-based authoring activities, students must work in cooperation to accomplish their design projects. Working collaboratively requires of students that they acquire some degree of social expertise and project management ability (cf. Carver *et al.*, 1992; Kafai *et al.*, 1997; Talamo & Fasulo, this volume), such as explaining their own ideas to others with the aim of achieving mutual understanding, seeking agreement in collective decision-making processes, supporting others when necessary, allocating resources and time to specific tasks, assigning roles to group members according to their interests and skills, reflecting on and evaluating their collective products in progress or introducing changes in their design when necessary.

In addition, the production of a hypervideo would require some media-specific abilities: to make decisions regarding how to mark links within a video (auditory or visual marking), how to present those links (either sequentially as the film goes on or partially grouped at the end of several film sequences), how long to maintain activated links and how to present the linked information (i.e. by using additional film sequences, thereby constructing a homogeneous hypervideo or by using texts, graphics, pictures, simulations, etc., and in so doing constructing a heterogeneous hypervideo).

Finally, if the activity of constructing a hypervideo were to become more complex by asking students to produce the source video themselves in addition to preparing the information to be linked to it, the following skills related to video production would be needed (cf. Posner *et al.*, 1997): writing a shooting script of the scenes to be filmed, acting out those scenes if necessary, operating the camera, selecting proper shot varieties, digitizing and compressing video for use in computers, editing script and video segments, adding sound effects, music and audio-text and evaluating the sound and video quality.

Educational Value of the Design Activity

The knowledge and skill requirements of hypervideo-based design activities — and of complex multimedia design activities in general — constitute their educational value, since these complex and rich activities offer beneficial opportunities for further knowledge acquisition and further development of the skills needed (cf. Carver *et al.*, 1992).

More specifically, the goal of having to produce something useful and "real" for a public (other classmates, younger students, external visitors to their school, etc.) confers meaning on what students do (Harel & Papert, 1990; Resnick & Ocko, 1991; Schank, Berman, & Macpherson, 1999; Talamo & Fasulo, this volume). And this experience of meaningful activity enhances their intrinsic motivation to learn and actively participate (Beichner, 1994; Lehrer, 1993; Penuel *et al.*, 1999). The experience of authoring a multimedia product in collaboration with others (peers, teachers, and even researchers) and using a modern and culturally extended technology (computers, software, authoring tools, video) promotes a feeling of ownership of what students do and learn (Carver *et al.*, 1992), improves their conception of themselves as learners (Lehrer, 1993; Resnick & Ocko, 1991) and increases their feeling of becoming a competent member of a "community of practice" (Kafai *et al.*, 1997; Penuel *et al.*, 1999).

Design activities also contribute to a deeper and more flexible understanding and an improved, connected and more applicable knowledge on the content topic (Harel & Papert, 1990; Lehrer, 1993; Kafai *et al.*, 1997; Ching, 1999; Reimann & Zumbach, 2001; Bromme & Stahl, this volume), as students have to work on complex relationships among concepts and phenomena when designing links among information units and structuring their documents, and as they also need to reformulate or "re-represent" their knowledge when having to articulate and externalize their ideas in different forms of representation (texts, graphics, simulation models, video) for the purposes of communicating them to others. By having to use different means of representation with different tools in concrete and diverse tasks, students also have the opportunity to improve their design skills (Ching, 1999) and their "critical standards" or consensually-developed opinions of what constitutes a good design (Erickson & Lehrer, 1998). This is especially true for hypervideos, where even basic skills of "video literacy" cannot be firmly assumed (Messaris, 1994).

Multimedia-based design activities encourage students to reflect on what they need to know, which skills and processes are required to accomplish their tasks and how to activate those skills, to monitor what they do in order to identify possible failures and the reasons for those failures, and to search for new design solutions; in this way, these activities foster the further development of the students' metacognitive skills (Harel & Papert, 1990; Ching, 1999; Talamo & Fasulo, this volume).

Finally, the importance of conferring a collaborative structure to the design activities not only derives from the fact that these activities are too complex to be accomplished by the students individually but it also derives from the opportunities a collaborative context induces: it facilitates the expression of students' communicative intentions and amplifies the communication within the group through members' participation in collective discussion and decision-making processes (Talamo & Fasulo, this volume); it allows students with different skills and strengths to become involved in the group work and to define roles for themselves over time, and it contributes to nurturing a collaborative culture within the classroom, so as to enhance the students' repertoire of social skills for working together (Penuel *et al.*, 1999).

Problems Associated with the Design Activity

Because of the demanding nature of multimedia-based design activities a series of problems may accompany their achievement, thereby hindering the learning effects of those activities. Reimann and Zumbach (2001) point out the following difficulties: students may easily feel themselves overwhelmed, a greater focus on design and production tasks may distract them from paying enough attention to the knowledge content, the group may have difficulties with the organization of its work (cf. Posner *et al.*, 1997), and teachers may also have some problems with "classroom management."

Kafai and colleagues (1997) report on other problems that emerged in their study with 5th and 6th graders having to construct (in groups) an interactive multimedia program about astronomy for younger students (3rd and 4th graders). Their students showed difficulties foreseeing the needs and interests of the intended users of their programs (younger students), and consequently, they tended to create less-demanding pages (those with more appealing elements like titles, navigation aids, quiz questions) and to neglect the construction of more-demanding pages (content pages). In addition, their prior experience with commercial software seemed to influence their design (with the students trying to emulate those programs) and to hinder their learning of new design aspects. Penuel and colleagues (1999) also mention how the previous use of a specific multimedia software program affected their students' initial presentations made with a different program.

Another problem involves the convenience (or otherwise) of using a metaphor to introduce the idea of what a hypervideo is or looks like and, accordingly, the need of finding an appropriate metaphor for each case. Talamo and Fasulo (this volume) consider a spatial metaphor inappropriate for representing what a hyperdocument is and how one can navigate in it, and emphasize the need for authors of hyperspaces to find a proper metaphor that mirrors the anticipated user's control of information. In the case of constructing a hypervideo, as we have seen in the preceding section, authors seem to make their link proposals dependent on the nature of the film and its content; consequently, the decision to provide the students with a metaphor of a hypervideo should depend on whether a suitable metaphor exists for the content structure of the film under consideration.

A final problem refers to assessment issues that researchers interested in the implementation of learning through multimedia-based design activities encounter. Carver and colleagues (1992) point out, on the one hand, the need to assess not only the design products of the students, but also the design process itself (cf. Reimann & Zumbach, 2001), as the students' actions and interactions during this process contribute considerable valuable information. On the other hand, they comment on the need for new and appropriate assessment measures (cf. Lehrer, 1993) that not only take into account the dynamic nature of the learning-through-design process, but also the practical constraints of time and organization in public schooling.

Suggestions for Implementing Design Activities

After having been acquainted with the complex and demanding nature of hypervideo-based design activities (i.e. the cognitive, metacognitive and social demands these activities imply) and having seen some of the problems associated with their implementation in the classroom, we would like to conclude this section with some suggestions on how to implement these rich activities so as to allow the students to obtain the aforementioned learning benefits.

The first point we should consider before deciding whether or not to implement a design activity, is the present environmental conditions: whether there are enough teachers and additional staff available to support students participating in the design activity or project; whether the students have the working materials and resources needed for their activity at their disposal (books, computers, software, video camera, videotapes, etc.); or whether the spatial conditions of the classroom allow students to work collaboratively or independently (according to their needs) without disturbing each other. Once we are able to take the availability of these conditions for granted, the following suggestions, derived from the results of several research projects, would help make the implementation of design activities more successful.

Several authors strongly recommend the simultaneous occurrence or integration of learning both the multimedia design (and programming) and subject matter in the school practice (Harel & Papert, 1990; Kafai *et al.*, 1997; Penuel *et al.*, 1999); in other words, an equilibrated balance between design activity and content knowledge acquisition should be established for avoiding the aforementioned problem of focusing on the former and neglecting the latter (Reimann & Zumbach, 2001).

This recommendation notwithstanding, because students' experience with editing programs and authoring tools may be rather limited (especially with regard to video/

hypervideo), they must be provided with enough time, practice and expert assistance (from teachers, researchers, technicians or professional designers) so as to be in a position to master those tools. This enables them at a later stage to work more independently of adults for their content and design decisions, to help their peers use the software, and to concentrate on the elaboration of the content (Beichner, 1994). Carver and colleagues (1992) also emphasize the importance of providing sufficient exposure to design skills and criteria in the learning environment: in an environment in which the design skills and criteria were made explicit to the students, practiced in different occasions and discussed frequently along the design process, students showed a gradual progression from teacher intervention to more autonomous functioning.

In order to support students' planning of the overall information structure of their hypervideo, several proposals require consideration: encouraging students to plan their pages or screens on paper first, before they begin working on their design with the use of the computer (Beichner, 1994); asking them to make storyboards of their document, i.e. drafts of the nodes (what each page will present and how it will appear) and the links connecting them (Penuel *et al.*, 1999); or providing students with a basic conceptual map of the subject matter that they are progressively required to expand as they work on the content knowledge and on a hyperdocument with integrated video (Guimarães *et al.*, 2000). In addition, Bromme & Stahl (this volume) provide evidence showing that asking students to adopt different user perspectives when constructing a hypertext on the same topic seemed to encourage them to reflect on the structure of their hypertexts and on the content structure of the topic.

As we mentioned earlier, students may have difficulties considering the users' learning experience and interests when designing their programs and, accordingly, they need support for orienting their design and content decisions to the needs of their public (Kafai *et al.*, 1997). This support can be provided through direct feedback from the users addressed or from classmates acting as users (Carver *et al.*, 1992; Erickson & Lehrer, 1998) after having tested the products in progress.

The importance of regular assessment and critique sessions along the design process, in which students evaluate their own and each other's work, is highlighted by several researchers (Harel & Papert, 1990; Erickson & Lehrer, 1998; Penuel *et al.*, 1999), since this evaluation promotes students' reflection on, explanation and revision of their design decisions, the search for design alternatives and the sharing of their own design solutions with others. For the additional support of students' work planning, reflection on their thinking and revision of their decisions, some authors (Harel & Papert, 1990; Resnick & Ocko, 1991) suggest requesting them to keep a "designer's notebook" for documenting their own designs in which for every working session they include what they plan to do, how they plan to do it, which problems they have encountered, what changes they have had to introduce in their designs, etc.

Although these suggestions for improving the implementation of design activities mostly come from investigations in which students were to create a hypertext or a multimedia-based learning program or document, they could also be considered in the research on the implementation of students' construction of hypervideos. It is particularly in this context that we would like to propose the following recommendations: it is of especial importance for students engaging in the design of hypervideos to be instructed in the basic skills of video production because (unlike text writing) the development of these skills seems to have been neglected in our educational systems. One implication of this is that the suggestion of providing students with enough time becomes especially important, since mastery of the tools and design criteria provides a basis for working more independently later on. An additional proposal would be to give students some guidelines relative to the linking varieties available and the possibilities of hypervideo structure that depend on characteristics of the content or subject matter. In this regard, when the content of the source film consists of historical events (as, for instance was the case for our clip 3), where the images of protagonists, places, etc. related to those events only play an illustrative role, and the evolution of the events in time comes to the fore, it seems suitable to use temporal links from scenes of the source film to additional video sequences of the personal history of the protagonists or of other events possibly related to the main event. Conversely, when the source film refers to the structure and functioning processes of mechanisms or artificial systems or to the composition and dynamics of natural systems or entities (as in our clip 1), where the visualization of the system's components helps to understand the system and the image of those components can be spatially marked within the scene framework, it seems appropriate to use spatio-temporal links from those regions of the film to additional information about detail characteristics of those components offered in another coding format (text, picture, graphic). As mentioned earlier, because research in this area is still in its inception, we still await research results that support these and any other new suggestions.

Conclusion

In our contribution we introduced hypervideo as a hypermedia that — in contrast to hypertext — is primarily based on dynamic audio-visual information. We outlined some similarities between hypervideo and hypertexts, on the one hand, and hypervideos and linear video on the other. In addition, we highlighted the unique characteristics of hypervideos (including audio-visual nodes and time-dependent links) and pointed out various consequences for learning derived from such characteristics (offering new interaction possibilities to the learners, but also implying some constraints).

We addressed the issue of learning with hypervideo systems from two perspectives: the first focused on the design aspects which must be considered for learning by working with a hypervideo, while the second focused on the instructional aspects to be considered for learning through the students' construction of a hypervideo. In each perspective, a considerable lack of investigation was evident: from the perspective of "design for learning" this concerns a deficit of research work from educational contexts, in the perspective of "learning through design" research in educational contexts does indeed exist, it is generally limited to the self-construction of other media (hypertexts, multimedia programs and documents) which are different from hypervideo. Thus, in general, we were constrained to pose more questions than we were able to provide answers for and to propose design and instructional suggestions based on previous empirical research.

This notwithstanding, our own explorative study did contribute some findings that, thinking our estimation, represent a good start in this research field. From the results reported here, it is evident that the nature of the source video influences the design decisions as to the number of links to additional information that should be integrated into the video and the duration of time that these links should remain activated. In addition, the importance of considering the content topic when deciding where to establish a link in the video was clear, as the needs for additional information on the part of potential learners seemed to coincide with the proposals for providing that information on the part of content experts acting as potential authors.

Further questions we would propose for future research refer to the following issues: how students actually work with different kinds of dynamic video links in relation to accomplishing different tasks (i.e. not only for information seeking or knowledge acquisition, but also for problem solving); which aspects should be considered when deciding to present or produce a homogeneous hypervideo (where video is combined with more video sequences) versus a heterogeneous hypervideo (where video is combined with other representational forms, such as texts, static pictures, graphics, animations); or which kind of support is necessary to compensate for the cognitive and metacognitive demands associated with the structural and functional complexity of hypervideo systems in order to avoid the hindering effects on learning that may derive from those demands.

Empirically based answers to these questions (and to new ones) could contribute important ideas for the use of hypervideos as powerful educational tools in both perspectives of design for learning and learning through design. With our paper, we hope to have offered some stimulus for further research in this area.

References

Balcolm, D. (1996). *Hypervideo: Notes Toward a Rhetoric*. Retrieved September 2001 from http://www.lcc.gatech.edu/gallery/hypercafe/David_Project96/

Beichner, R. J. (1994). Multimedia editing to promote science learning. *Journal of Educational Multimedia and Hypermedia, 3*(1), 55–70.

Carver, S. M., Lehrer, R., Connell, T., & Erickson, J. (1992). Learning by hypermedia design: Issues of assessment and implementation. *Educational Psychologist, 27*(3), 385–404.

Chandler, P., & Sweller, J. (1991). Cognitive load theory and the format of instruction. *Cognition and Instruction, 8*(4), 293–332.

Ching, C. C. (1999). "It's not just programming": Reflection and the nature of experience in learning through design. In: C. M. Hoadley, and J. Roschelle (eds), *Proceedings of the Computer Support for Collaborative Learning (CSCL) 1999 Conference* (pp. 101–107). Palo Alto, CA: Stanford University.

Erickson, J., & Lehrer, R. (1998). The evolution of critical standards as students design hypermedia documents. *The Journal of the Learning Sciences, 7*(3/4), 351–386.

Francisco-Revilla, L. (1998). *A Picture of Hypervideo Today*. Retrieved September 2001, from http://www.csdl.tamu.edu/~l0f0954/academic/cpsc610/p-1.htm

Guimarães, N., Chambel, T., & Bidarra, J. (2000). From cognitive maps to hypervideo: Supporting flexible and rich learner-centred environments. *Interactive Multimedia Electronic Journal of Computer-Enhanced Learning, 2*(2). Retrieved January 28, 2002, from http://imej.wfu.edu/articles/2000/2/03/index.asp

Harel, I., & Papert, S. (1990). Software design as a learning environment. *Interactive Learning Environments, 1*, 1–32.

Hodges, M. E., & Sasnett, R. M. (1993). *Multimedia Computing*. Reading, MA: Addison-Wesley.

Kafai, Y. B., Ching, C. C., & Marshall, S. (1997). Children as designers of educational multimedia software. *Computers and Education, 29*(2/3), 117–126.

Lang, A. (2000). The limited capacity model of mediated message processing. *Journal of Communication, 50*(4), 46–70.

Lehrer, R. (1993). Authors of knowledge: Patterns of hypermedia design. In: S. P. Lajoie, and S. J. Derry (eds), *Computers as Cognitive Tools* (pp. 197–227). Hillsdale, NJ: Erlbaum.

Locatis, C., Charuhas, J., & Banvard, R. (1990). Hypervideo. *Educational Technology Research and Development*, 41–49.

Mayer, R. E. (1997). Multimedia learning: Are we asking the right questions? *Educational Psychologist, 32*(1), 1–19.

Mayer, R. E., & Anderson, R. B. (1991). Animations need narrations: An experimental test of a dual-coding hypothesis. *Journal of Educational Psychology, 83*(4), 484–490.

Messaris, P. (1994). *Visual Literacy: Image, Mind, and Reality*. Boulder: Westview Press.

Moreno, R. & Mayer, R. E. (2000). A learner-centred approach to multimedia explanations: deriving instructional design principles from cognitive theory. *Interactive Multimedia Electronic Journal of Computer-Enhanced Learning, 2*(2). Retrieved April 6, 2002 from http://imej.wfu.edu/articles/2000/2/index.asp

Park, O., & Hopkins, R. (1993). Instructional conditions for using dynamic visual displays: A review. *Instructional Science, 21*, 427–448.

Penuel, W. R., Korbak, C., Cole, K. A., & Jump, O. (1999). Imagination, production, and collaboration in project-based learning using multimedia. In: C. M. Hoadley, and J. Roschelle (eds), *Proceedings of the Computer Support for Collaborative Learning (CSCL) 1999 Conference* (pp. 445–453). Palo Alto, CA: Stanford University.

Posner, I., Baecker, R., Poplar, S., & Becker, M. (1997). *Children Collaborating in Making Movies Using Computer Based Multimedia: Multimedia Summer Camp Revisited*. Poster session presented at the Computer Support for Collaborative Learning (CSCL) 1997 Conference.

Reimann, P., & Zumbach, J. (2001). Design, Diskurs und Reflexion als zentrale Elemente virtueller Seminare [Design, discourse, and reflection as central elements of virtual seminars]. In: F. W. Hesse, and H. F. Friedrich (eds), *Partizipation und Interaktion im virtuellen Seminar* (pp. 135–163). Münster: Waxmann.

Resnick, M., & Ocko, S. (1991). LEGO/Logo: Learning through and about design. In: I. Harel, and S. Papert (eds), *Constructionism* (pp. 141–150). Norwood, NJ: Ablex.

Sawhney, N. (1996). Authoring and navigating video in space and time. Retrieved September 2001 from http://www.lcc.gatech.edu/gallery/hypercafe/Nick_Project96/hypervideo.html

Sawhney, N., Balcom, D., & Smith, I. (1996). HyperCafe: Narrative and aesthetic properties of hypervideo. Paper presented at Seventh ACM Conference on Hypertext. Retrieved September 2001 from http://www.lcc.gatech.edu/gallery/hypercafe/HT96_HTML/HyperCafe_HT96.html

Schank, R. C., Berman, T. R., & Macpherson, K. A. (1999). Learning by doing. In: C. M. Reigeluth (ed.), *Instructional Design Theories and Models: A New Paradigm of Instructional Theory* (vol. 2) (pp. 161–181). Mahwah, NJ: LEA.

Spiro, R. J., & Jehng, J. C. (1990). Cognitive flexibility, random access instruction, and hypertext: Theory and technology for non-linear and multidimensional traversal of complex subject matter. In: D. Nix, and R. J. Spiro (eds), *Cognition, Education, and Multimedia: Exploring Ideas in High Technology* (pp. 163–205). Hillsdale, NJ: Lawrence Erlbaum.

Wetzel, C. D., Radtke, P. H., & Stern, H. W. (1994). *Instructional Effectiveness of Video Media*. Hillsdale, NJ: Lawrence Erlbaum.

Zhu, E. (1999). Hypermedia interface design: The effects of number of links and granularity of nodes. *Journal of Educational Multimedia and Hypermedia, 8*(3), 331–358.

Chapter 10

Methods for Assessing Cognitive Processes During the Construction of Hypertexts

Elmar Stahl

The paucity of research on writing or constructing hypertexts indicates a strong need to analyze both the cognitive and executive processes in their construction to find out, for example, how they are similar to or differ from writing in other text forms and to study their cognitive demands and potentials for authors. This chapter presents various methods for assessing these cognitive processes and discusses their advantages and disadvantages. It shows that existing methods can be applied to this field, but that ideas on new methods also need to be developed.

Introduction

The present chapter describes methods for assessing the cognitive processes that authors engage in while constructing hypertexts. Whereas assessing process data is a standard procedure for deriving as well as testing models and theories in research on both the production and reception of "traditional" texts (e.g., Kellogg, 1988, 1994; Hayes, 1996; Levy & Ransdell, 1996; Rijlaarsdam, Couzijn, & van den Bergh, 1996), one can find only sporadic attempts to apply it to the reception of hypertexts (see the critiques of Perfetti, 1996; Dillon & Gabbard, 1998), and applications to the writing of hypertexts are almost completely lacking. The chapters in this book from Braaksma, Rijaarsdam, Couzijn, and van den Bergh as well as from Bromme and Stahl are starting to fill in these gaps and reveal how valuable process data are for gaining a better understanding of the prerequisites and effects of hypertext construction.

Because of their structural features of nodes and links and their "non-linearity," hypertexts impose other demands on authors than printed texts in books and articles. It would be good to be able to describe these demands more closely through process analyses. Such analyses might reveal, for example, similarities and differences compared with "traditional" writing, and lead to a more effective design of hypertext construction as a method of knowledge acquisition.

Writing Hypertext and Learning: Conceptual and Empirical Approaches
Copyright © 2002 by Elsevier Science Ltd.
All rights of reproduction in any form reserved.
ISBN: 0-08-043987-X

Depending on the data level, one can distinguish three groups of methods for assessing process data during the construction of hypertexts: activity analyses (see pp. 178–181), assessing verbal data through thinking aloud or retrospection methods (pp. 182–187), and authors' self-ratings during the construction process through, for example, a computer-assisted assessment (pp. 187–193). This chapter will present these groups of methods and discuss their advantages and disadvantages.

Bromme and Stahl's research project on learning through constructing hypertexts (see Bromme & Stahl, this volume; and also Stahl & Bromme, 1997; Bromme & Stahl, 1999, 2001; Stahl, 2001) is performing process analyses on all three data levels. The experiences gained in this project are used here as a basis for presenting category systems for each method that can be used in analyses as well as examples of findings that provide a concrete illustration of which analyses can be carried out with each method.

Activity Analyses

A frequent practice in research on the reception of hypertexts is to assess process data through activity protocols (e.g., log-file analyses) registering the temporal course of navigation through a hypertext (Canter, Rivers, & Storres, 1985; Gay, Trumbull, & Mazur, 1991; Gray, 1990, 1995; Mayes, Kibby, & Anderson, 1990; Hutchings, Hall, & Colbourn, 1993). Such protocols can be used to plot, for example, how often and for how long nodes are opened, the sequences in which links are activated, or how frequently certain help functions are used. The data can be used to draw conclusions on how learners use the system or its individual components.

When applied to the construction of hypertexts, an activity analysis addresses all the learners' actions with the HTML editor that are needed to produce the hypertexts. This includes activities such as setting links or writing new content in nodes; in other words, manipulations of the contents, but not just navigating through unmodifiable documents. Hence, just recording navigation behavior is insufficient. To record these kinds of data, it is necessary to videotape and analyze activities on the computer screen. This requires a graphics board connecting the computer not just to the screen but also to the videotape recorder.

In such an analysis, the type of activities to be performed is linked closely to the various functions available in the HTML editor used to set up the hypertexts. The following presents a category system for common graphics-oriented editors that makes it possible to classify all the actions of participants that are visible on the computer screen while they are constructing a hypertext from existing node texts.

The category system covers eight activities that can be assigned to the three activity areas *navigation in hypertext, linking up nodes,* and *internal activities.*

Navigation in the hypertext is served by three activities: opening a node, activating a link, and activating the back or forward keys. These are used to move between the nodes in the hypertext. *Opening a node* refers to opening a node through the menu bar or through activating the node symbol on the desktop. *Activating the back or forward keys* refers to the activation of the corresponding browser buttons with the mouse. The category *activating a link* refers to using the mouse to activate a link that has already been set.

A fourth navigation activity is to reclose an opened node. This activity was not included in the category system, because of its close relationship to the category *opening a node*. Many editors require previously opened nodes to be closed before a new node can be opened. Therefore the system categorized only opening the nodes to avoid counting one activity twice.

Linking up nodes is served by the four activities: setting a link, writing a link, deleting a previously set link, and breaking off setting a link. These are used to link the individual nodes together into a complete document. *Setting a link* refers to the complete execution of the sequence of commands to set a link. The category *writing a link* refers to the entering of text at the nodes. This always occurs when a participant writes his or her own connection that can be used as a link to another node. *Deleting a previously set link* refers to erasing a link through the commands in the menu bar. As long as the text in the link was written by the participant, it can also be highlighted and deleted. The category *breaking off setting a link* refers to the same sequence of commands as setting a link. However, it is disrupted by the participant at an arbitrary point when he or she decides not to set that link during the current procedure.

Internal activities are defined as time intervals in which no activity can be observed on the screen. These can occur, for example, when participants are reading the content of nodes, taking notes, comparing printed out nodes with each other, or planning their next steps. In our experiments, we decided that these intervals had to last at least 5 s in order to distinguish them from short breaks in work on the screen when participants are, for example, looking for something on the screen or briefly checking their bearings. Research on text production views pauses as indicating cognitive processes in writing (see Flower & Hayes, 1981). The present context also assumes that *internal activities* are intervals that are not used for executive activity but for cognitive processes such as thinking about the contents or the structure of the hypertext. Nonetheless, it is impossible to ascertain whether participants actually use these intervals in this manner.

A further activity is *saving a node*. This involves saving the node via the menu bar. However, if participants forget to do this, some editors will always ask whether alterations should be saved when leaving a node, and this has to be confirmed by clicking an "OK" button. Because no inherent meaning can be assigned to saving text, and the computer always asks participants to do this when they forget to do it themselves, this activity was not included in the category system.

These categories permit an objective classification of all activities needed to construct hypertexts from given nodes. The individual categories are summarized in Table 10.1.

The more degrees of freedom in an experiment, the more comprehensive the system has to be. If, for example, participants have to formulate the node texts themselves, additional categories have to be included for writing, deleting, and altering text. If texts are adopted for the hypertext from various existing text files, categories have to be added for copy and paste.

Table 10.1: Categories for assessing computer screen activities observed during the construction of a hypertext.

Areas of activity	Actions
Navigation in the hypertext	Opening a node through the menu bar Activating the back or forward keys Activating a link
Linking up nodes	Setting a link Deleting a link Writing text for a link Breaking off setting a link
Internal activities	Intervals lasting at least 5 s within which no computer screen activity occurs. It is assumed that these intervals are used for cognitive processes such as thinking about the contents and structure of the hypertext.

When performing an analysis, it seems reasonable to aggregate the number of activities performed. For internal activities, this has to take account of the duration of periods without observable activities, because a simple totaling of how often internal activities could be seen neglects the fact that these phases can vary greatly in length.

In order to compare time courses, these frequencies can be computed separately for specific intervals. In our experiments, for example, we divided the construction phase into 10-minute intervals and compared activities per time interval.

Figure 10.1 presents an example of such a time course for the total number of all linking-up-nodes activities. It is taken from an experiment in which 40 psychology students with no prior experience of hypertexts were asked to construct a hypertext on the topic of the Internet from 16 given node texts (Bromme & Stahl, 2001; Stahl, 2001). Groups of 20 college students received advance instructions on the concept of hypertext based on either a book metaphor comparing hypertexts with books or a space metaphor comparing hypertexts with a virtual space. Activity analyses were used to examine how these different instructions on what constitutes a hypertext influenced construction processes. Participants had 60 minutes to construct their hypertexts, and this time period was divided into six 10-minute intervals. As can be seen in Figure 10.1, the mean number of linking-up-nodes activities per time interval rose continuously in the book-metaphor group, whereas the progression tended to form an inverted U in the space-metaphor group. This curve reflected the fact that the latter group started executing their links more quickly and forged a significantly higher total number of links than the book-metaphor group. Such analyses were able to show that metaphors had a clear influence on the entire construction process.

The advantages of activity analyses are, first, that they permit a very precise

Linking-up-nodes activities

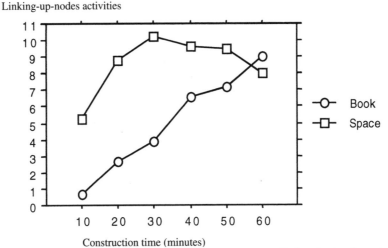

Construction time (minutes)

Figure 10.1: Time distribution of linking-up-nodes activities split for the book and space metaphors. The *y*-axis reports the number of activities; the *x*-axis the time.

documentation of single activities and activity curves. Second, this assessment method — unlike other methods presented below — does not disturb the participants' work, and they do not notice it. This rules out any potential effects elicited particularly by the assessment method itself. Third, it is possible to monitor the participants' technical approach to the HTML editor, and, for example, estimate whether and when technical problems arose. This can be used to test how far certain events can be traced back solely to a better or worse handling of the computer program. Fourth, activities offer a context for interpreting verbal data. When participants have to think aloud while working on tasks or are asked about what they are doing (see pp. 182–187), their statements can be recorded on the same videotape as the activities. Sometimes, imprecise statements only become meaningful through such context information, thus making them easier to classify. Fifth, results can be evaluated objectively, because the classification of an activity to a category can be defined precisely.

Disadvantages of activity analyses are, first, the large amount of effort required to evaluate them. When activities are recorded over the computer screen, they have to be examined by raters and translated into category systems, and this requires a lot of time. Second, technical requirements have to be considered, because special graphics boards are necessary if the video is to be of sufficient quality to recognize something. These two disadvantages impacted particularly on the method presented here. If much of the data can be gathered with log-file analyses, the amount of effort involved in analyzing it can be reduced substantially. Third, activity analyses provide only indirect access to cognitive processes and are difficult to interpret in cognitive terms. Conclusions about the participants' underlying strategies and decisions always remain speculative. There is not enough data for a differentiated analysis of the cognitive processes that have accompanied the activity.

Assessing Verbal Data

A more direct access to the cognitive processes can be obtained by applying procedures in which participants report on what they are doing themselves. Two common methods are thinking aloud (p. 182) and the retrospective interview carried out either at the end of an experiment or — at fixed time intervals — directly during it (pp. 182–184). The presentation of these methods will be followed by two category systems that can be helpful for analyzing the data: first, a categorization based on Hayes and Flower's process model of writing (pp. 184–186) and, second, a more content-focused system that we have found very practical in our experiments (pp. 186–187).

Thinking Aloud

The thinking aloud method requests participants to say everything that comes into their minds while working on a task. This method is based on the idea that participants will particularly verbalize the current contents of their short-term memories (Ericsson & Simon, 1980, 1993). Correspondingly, the data should provide a suitable basis for drawing conclusions on their decisions and cognitive processes while processing a task. Because thinking aloud is one of the standard methods for gathering process data, it does not need to be presented in more detail here.

Instead, a few problems will be addressed that can emerge particularly when the method is applied in the domain of constructing hypertexts. The basic problem has to do with the potentially very high cognitive effort involved in constructing hypertexts. This is the case when, for example, authors are working on a topic about which they know very little in advance, have little prior experience with the hypertext text form, and are also using a rather unfamiliar program (the HTML editor). Confronting participants in such situations with the additional demand to utter all their thoughts aloud requires an additional cognitive effort that may be detrimental to coping with the task (see Kellogg, 1994). It can also be assumed that the procedure can also have a direct impact on coping with the task (Janssen, van Waes, & van den Bergh, 1996). Becker-Mrotzek (1997) proposes that writing processes undergo major assessment-induced changes when thinking aloud, because what are usually routine mental processes are made continuously explicit and conscious. Furthermore, condensing extensive verbal protocols and coding them objectively is very time-consuming (Kluwe, 1988). However, if these problems are accepted, there is certainly no other method with which cognitive processes can be assessed so directly during the construction process.

Retrospection

A further method is retrospective questioning, carried out either after the experiment or through time sampling during it.

Retrospection after the end of the experiment   Retrospective questioning at the end of the experiment asks participants about their strategies, approaches, and decisions after they have completed their task. Retrospection can be supported by showing participants videotape recordings from the experiment, and asking them why they had carried out specific actions. For the construction of hypertexts, one could show videotapes of computer screen activities so that the participants can review their own construction processes (a procedure known as stimulated recall).

One clear advantage of this method is that participants are not interrupted during the experiment itself, ruling out the above-mentioned problems for thinking aloud. A further advantage is that participants can be questioned directly about important passages when, for example, they obviously had problems or made important decisions. Hence, with this method, participants can use a meta-level to report how they view what was happening at that time. In some cases, such a reflection over one's own approach may lead to a deeper understanding of the process than the direct statements obtained with thinking aloud.

Nonetheless, the method also has its disadvantages: First, a great deal of the information in a long-lasting construction process is lost, because retrospective questioning can address only a few areas of such a complex process. Second, it is uncertain how far retrospective statements still reflect true decisions and strategies during task processing or should be viewed as post hoc interpretations (Gerdes, 1997). Third, the method is very time-consuming, because participants need to be questioned in detail after they have probably already spent a lot of time constructing their hypertexts. Particularly when looking at videotapes of the construction process, another problem is that effective use requires prior knowledge about which sections may be important and need to be reviewed. Frequently, such knowledge is not available before an experiment.

Direct retrospection during the experiment   A further method is "direct" retrospection, in which participants are asked about their decisions and thoughts at regular intervals while constructing their hypertexts. This means that they have to stop working for a short time in order to report what they have just been doing.

This method can attenuate some of the above-mentioned disadvantages with thinking aloud and retrospection at the end of an experiment. Asking about decisions and thoughts in a time-sampling form demands less cognitive effort than thinking aloud. Moreover, there are less data to analyze, because, for each participant, it is necessary to classify only a number of statements determined by the frequency of questioning. One advantage compared with retrospection after the end of an experiment is that participants report directly on what they have just been thinking at the time of questioning, reducing distortions of post hoc interpretations and explanations while simultaneously stemming the problem of information being lost through questioning being too fragmentary to cover complex processes.

Disadvantages of direct retrospection can be seen particularly in the type of questioning. Participants may well start to feel a need to justify themselves or give socially desirable answers and thus produce ideas or decisions that they would otherwise not have thought about so thoroughly.

We have applied direct retrospection several times in our experiments (see Bromme & Stahl, this volume; also, Bromme & Stahl, 2001; Stahl, 2001). Specifically, we asked our participants every 2 minutes: "What are you thinking just now?" When answers did *not* refer to internal aspects of compiling hypertexts (e.g., "I'm just wondering what time it is"), we went on to ask: "And with regard to your task?" When responses were too superficial (e.g., "I'm thinking about the hypertext"), we asked: "Could you be more specific?" A microphone connected to the videotape recorder was used to record the statements on the same videotape as that used to record the computer screen activity for an activity analysis. This made it possible to analyze statements within the context of the specific activities being performed at the time of the question (see above).

The following will present two category systems that can be used to analyze verbal data. Although we have used these in conjunction with direct retrospection, they can also be applied to other methods for gathering verbal data.

One problem when using such category systems needs to be mentioned in advance: confounding positive and negative statements within the same category. Let us assume that all the statements participants make on the structure of the hypertexts they are producing are classified to a category labeled "Structure." In this case, Participant A could say that he had major problems in finding a structure for his hypertext, whereas Participant B reports very precise plans on how she intends to design a user-friendly structure. Both participants would be entered into the same category. Any future comparison of just the number of statements in the categories alone would not disclose that one person reported only problems, whereas the other exhibited a good under-standing of how to construct a hypertext. However, simply splitting the category according to whether statements contain problems or not is also not always a mean-ingful solution. Problems may promote learning, because they create a situation in which it is clear that they need to be dealt with. Nonetheless, they may also inhibit learning when participants exhibit difficulties in understanding that they may be unable to overcome. Hence, it is not always possible to predict which effects a reported problem has had. When dealing with such problems, it is always necessary to retain the option of supplementing analyses based on category systems by performing additional qualitative comparisons.

Category Systems Derived From Hayes and Flower's and Kellogg's Process Models

The process of writing can be conceived as a problem-solving process in which authors have to plan the text, translate their ideas into formulated sentences, and revise the text or previously formulated text passages (see Hayes & Flower, 1980, 1986; Kellogg, 1994; Hayes, 1996). These processes may be performed cyclically (e.g., planning, translating, and revising one paragraph, then the second one, and so on) and can proceed recursively (Hayes & Flower, 1986). Kellogg (1994) distinguishes between the writing phases of prewriting activities, producing a first draft, and revising sub-sequent drafts. All the above processes may occur in each of these phases.

Text production research uses such process models (that are now much more differentiated because of the advances in our knowledge in this field of research) as a basis for studying writing processes. Hence, they can also be generalized to the construction of hypertexts. In this field, the categories can be discriminated as follows:

Planning During planning, participants generate ideas about the design of their hypertext. They have to plan its structure and tackle the contents to be processed. As a result, this category includes statements referring not only to familiarization with the contents of the node texts but also to the development of ideas on how to structure and organize the contents/nodes in the hypertext. Computer screen activity is an important aid to raters here. During planning, no computer screen activity is to be seen. This corresponds to the assumption in text production that planning phases can be recognized through pauses in writing (Kellogg, 1994).

Translation During translation processes, plans are put into practice. These include all executive operations in which the hypertext is constructed. Hence, this category includes statements that participants are executing their ideas, either by producing a preliminary sketch or plan — as a kind of first draft — or producing the hypertext directly. Visible activity on the computer screen involves setting links or writing.

Revision During revision processes, the previously produced product (which can be either the hypertext or a sketch from the first phase of planning) is subjected to a critical examination and modified. Accordingly, this category includes statements that participants are checking their hypertext or the parts of it that they have already completed and improving any errors they find (e.g., in the quality of navigation). Activities observable on the computer screen during revision are phases of navigating through the hypertext produced so far and modifying previously set links through deletion, additions of texts, and so forth.

In addition to these three categories, a remainder category labeled *other* is used to classify all statements that cannot be assigned to the three processes. These are mostly statements with no direct reference to writing the hypertext. The category also includes participants' statements on their own procedure, in other words, in which they talk about their strategies on a meta-level.

When categorizing, it is necessary to consider that participants hardly ever plan the complete hypertext first, then implement all their ideas as a final hypertext, before finally revising the entire product. As already mentioned above, repeating subcycles are to be anticipated. Hence, participants often plan a content subdomain, implement it, and control what they have done before moving on to the next topic. Sometimes, one can also find that they first take each single node text and plan how they can fit it into the existing structure, and then execute the corresponding links and revise whether the product so far is in line with their ideas before they move on to the next node text. Likewise, there can be longer phases of switching between processes of planning and execution without outcomes being revised.

This type of categorization is suitable for examining the effects of different treatments on the frequency and also the distribution of processes across the entire construction process; or to compare the construction process with other variables such as knowledge acquisition.

For the space-metaphor group mentioned in the description of the activity analysis above, for example, we found relations between the number of statements categorized as planning processes and the knowledge transfer about the topic being processed that the group acquired during the experiment ($r = 0.51$, $p < 0.05$).

Nonetheless, this categorization following Hayes and Flower's model also has disadvantages. Because of the above-mentioned partial cycles that writing goes through, it is sometimes a major problem for raters to make a clear classification. Our raters frequently found it particularly difficult to discriminate between planning and translation processes (see also Kellogg, 1994). One way of counteracting this problem is always to inspect computer screen activities as well (see above), because we found that the majority of unclear statements could be classified unequivocally after looking at what the participants were actually doing at the time.

A further disadvantage is that the category system in this form permits no statements on which contents are involved in, for example, the planning processes. For example, different groups may exhibit the same number of planning processes, although the contents they were thinking about at the time might have differed greatly. This content level is not taken into account in this category system. Differentiated analyses require content categories to be specified more precisely.

Category Systems for Classifying the Content of the Data

This is why we present a second category system focusing more strongly on the content levels that participants might handle while constructing hypertexts. This system contains 13 individual categories assigned to six topic areas. These six topics that participants may address while constructing hypertexts, are, first, *content-related deliberations*, within which they think about and process the contents to be depicted. Second, participants can also make *deliberations on the structure of their hypertexts*, in other words, think about how they can combine the individual nodes through links to form a final product. Of course, these two topics exert a strong influence on each other, in that the understanding of content influences how the hypertext will be constructed and, vice versa, the concept of the hypertext will influence how intensively individual contents are processed.

Third, these deliberations can be linked to various types of *search processes* in which participants search for concrete options for linking together two nodes. These search processes are viewed as an independent topic, because, first, they follow specific decisions on the content and/or the structure, and, second, attendant statements reveal no intensive consideration of either content-related ideas or ideas on the structure of the hypertext. Fourth, participants may report on activities linked to the *translation* of their ideas. Fifth, they may reflect their *own approach* on a metacognitive level; and, sixth, they may make *content-irrelevant statements*.

Each of these six general topics is assessed with concrete categories. Table 10.2 presents an overview of these categories and illustrates them with statements taken from our experiment.

This category system can be used to classify all the participants' statements in terms of their content. When categorizing, it is recommended that long statements addressing different topic domains should be broken down into individual substatements and categorized separately. Hence, a participant who reports which semantic relation she recognizes between two nodes, and then adds that she is looking for a way to write down this relation in a node, is addressing two categories.

Our experiments showed that this categorization was suitable for comparing the effects of different instructions on the processes. For example, in the above-mentioned experiment comparing the book with the space metaphor, a MANOVA was computed across the number of statements in each group in which the six main themes occurred (Bromme & Stahl, 2001; Stahl, 2001). Results showed that participants working with the book metaphor reported on the structure of their hypertexts significantly more frequently. A more detailed qualitative analysis of the statements in the corresponding categories showed, nonetheless, that they also significantly more frequently reported problems in developing an appropriate structure for their hypertexts, because they had trouble coordinating the idea of sequencing information indicated by the metaphor with the complexity of the topic to be processed.

Authors' Self-Ratings: Computer-Assisted Assessment of Cognitive Processes

A further method for gathering process data is to ask participants to categorize the procedure they have used themselves. Kellogg (1988, 1994) applied this strategy in experiments on text production. He trained participants to handle a category system, and then asked them to use it to report their activities at set time intervals while working on the task. He called this method directed retrospection. Although it can be assigned to the group of retrospective procedures, it is dealt with separately here, because it differs from the procedures reported above in that participants categorize their cognitive processes themselves rather than having them categorized by subsequent raters. Apart from this aspect, category systems like those presented in the last section (p. 186) can also be used for self-ratings — as long as they are not too extensive.

When studying the construction of hypertexts, it seems apt to use a computer-assisted assessment to perform such a self-rating. Through this, participants would not need to interrupt their work on the computer screen in order to complete, for example, a written questionnaire, but could report their judgment by clicking the mouse and continue working on the task without too much distraction. Within our research project, we have devised such a computer-assisted questioning system that is presented in the following as an example of how this method can be applied.

To transfer the method of directed retrospection to a computer-assisted questioning format, a program was written that opened a window on the screen at an interval defined in advance by the experimenter, e.g., every 2 minutes (see Figure 10.2).

Table 10.2: Category system for assessing participants' statements divided into 6 topic domains with a total of 13 categories. In the examples, the headings of nodes are written in uppercase.

Topic domain 1: Content-related deliberations

Category 1: Comprehending separate node contents.
This category includes all statements indicating that, at the time of the question, participants were involved in comprehending the contents of single nodes. Hence, statements refer to the content of one node without relating this to the content of other nodes.

Example: "I am thinking about this network, what you find, well, it's actually like a spider's web: this PACKAGE-ORIENTED COMPUTER NETWORK. The data in it are separated into single data packages, sent individually to the users, and then put back together again."

Category 2: Comprehending relations between the contents of two nodes.
This category covers all statements verbalizing relations between the contents of two nodes. This includes statements comparing the contents of two nodes or expressing an existing relation between them.

Example: "I'm just thinking about linking NCP [first node] and the PACKAGE-ORIENTED COMPUTER NETWORKS [second node]. Well, both texts are dealing with the idea of the data and the distribution of the data packages. NCP is necessary to send the data, and the PACKAGE-ORIENTED COMPUTER NETWORKS are decomposing these data packages."

Category 3: Comprehending relations between the contents of several nodes.
This category includes statements verbalizing relations between the contents of several nodes. However, it only includes statements emphasizing ideas on the structure of the content.

Example: "Yes, well, I think the ARPANET is the beginning, and I've noticed that the extension of the ARPANET, in other words, the NSFNET, also uses the TCP and the IP. Seems to be just like the way it's still done in the INTERNET these days. I'm trying to see how I can link them together."

Topic domain 2: Search processes

Category 4: Searching for links on the basis of common terms.
This category covers statements recognizing that there are unknown terms or terms requiring explanation within the content of a node. This may trigger a search process to see whether these terms are explained in more detail in other nodes. These search processes come to an end when participants find potential starting points and target nodes for links.

Table 10.2: *(continued)*

Example: "About how I should organize which link to take next. ARPA reappears in the NSFNET, I've underlined that, I've underlined this IP, I've underlined TCP."

Category 5: Searching for potential positionings of a node in the existing hypertext.
This category includes statements referring to the search for ways of linking together one or more nodes. Whereas in Category 4, participants start with one node and try to find common terms explained in other nodes, this category contains statements on searching for how a node can be integrated into an existing hypertext.

Example: "Well, I'm still thinking about whether I can fit IRC in somewhere, but I'm no longer sure how. Because that's an Internet service, and, somehow, I don't know how I should fit that in as well."

Category 6: Searching for a starting word (link point) for a link.
This category covers statements about which link point should be used for a link, or at which point within a node a link should be placed.

Example: "I've changed that now, because I found it stupid to start off with "routes," I mean, with the word. Because that will just confuse the reader. I thought that (link) would then fit better in "data transport.""

Topic domain 3: Deliberations on the structure of the hypertext

Category 7: Statements on central nodes.
These categories cover statements on choosing a suitable initial node or a central node from which the later user should enter the hypertext.

Example: "Putting ARPANET right at the beginning, practically as the start, and then going on to the INTERNET."

Category 8: Ideas on the structure of the product.
This category gathers together all statements referring to the structure of the hypertext document. This includes statements on how the nodes should be sequenced or which structure should be given to the hypertext.

Example: "I don't know, . . . well, I was thinking whether it would be a good idea to use NSFNET . . . well, I was at the node ARPANET, and then I wanted to go to the node NSFNET as a side street, so to say. But you can only continue on the main street. Or should I look at the NSFNET as a continuation of the ARPANET, and you can only get any further over the NSFNET, so to say. In other words, apart from the whole link that is still there between the individual nodes, I am thinking about the main way, so to say. Like a core."

Table 10.2: *(continued)*

Topic domain 4: Translation activities

Category 9: Setting a link.
This category includes statements that participants are just setting a link without specifying why they have linked together the header node and the target node.

Example: "Actually, about nothing. I'm working at the moment. I'm just joining up the INTERNET with ARPANET. Through a link."

Category 10: Technical deliberations.
This category includes statements referring to technical aspects of handling the HTML editor.

Example: "How do I open up something completely new, that is, when I don't want to set any more links?"

Category 11: Working with a sketch.
This category includes statements referring to working with a sketch of the hypertext. Mostly, participants talk about entering links they have set in their sketch or using their sketch to set links.

Example: "I was just thinking how practical it is to have it all written down in advance, because then you don't get into such a terrible mess about what you now want to network with what and so forth. You can simply cross out what you've already done so that you don't do it over and over again."

Topic domain 5: Metacognitive statements on one's own approach

Category 12: Statements on one's own approach.
This domain is covered by one single category. It contains statements containing general comments on the task and the approach to it.

Example: "And I was wondering whether I go round the block the wrong way with my ideas. Because linking everything together seems to be such a difficult task, well, sometimes I think my way around three corners, and yet its totally simple, and you can do it in 5 minutes or so. Sometimes I get far too theoretical on such tasks. That's why I'm asking myself whether I'm making it much too complicated or whether it is right."

Topic Domain 6: Other statements

Category 13: Content-irrelevant statements.
This single category covers statements that do not refer to internal aspects of constructing the hypertext. In these cases, the experimenter asked further: "And what are you thinking about as far as the contents of the task are concerned?"

Example: "That the screen saver's gone on again. That made me jump."

This window overrides all the other programs used at the time — in this case, the HTML editor — and blocks their use. The window asks participants to categorize the decisions made at this point in time in terms of a predefined category system.

The current version is using a category system developed from those presented on pp. 184–187. The first step is for participants to report whether they are currently engaged in planning, translation, or revision, or whether they are thinking about something else. To help them decide, short definitions of these categories are given in an extra text window, so that participants can find out more about what is behind the categories should uncertainties arise (see Figure 10.2).

Once participants have selected one of the main categories, a submenu opens in which the choice has to be specified more precisely. Three subcategories are available for each of the categories Planning, Translation, and Revision. These are summarized in Table 10.3.

If, for example, a participant has selected the category *Planning*, he can decide whether he is currently tackling the contents to be processed and their comprehension, working out relations between the contents of node texts, or planning the structure of his hypertext. If this participant clicks one of the categories with the mouse, it will be defined for him briefly in the text window (see Figure 10.2).

Experimenters can use an editor to modify the contents of these categories in line with their research interests. In other words, the main categories and specifications can be adapted to meet the goals of other experiments.

At all times, participants can activate only *one* of the subcategories with the mouse. Should they be uncertain and want to read different definitions, they can, nonetheless, revise their choice as often as they wish.

Once participants are satisfied with their choice, they have to click an "OK" button that appears only after one of the subcategories has been selected. This closes the window and reenables the other programs. Participants can now continue to work on their hypertexts.

This starts off the next 2-minute interval; in other words, the program counts off 2 minutes in the background before the question window reappears. This rhythm is repeated until the length of time predetermined by the researcher (e.g., 1 hour of experimentation) has passed. At this point, a further window opens informing the participant that the time available for the experiment has come to an end.

The results of the self-rating are entered directly into a user-friendly Microsoft Access table so that they are available for immediate analysis (see Figure 10.3). The current program records the participant number, the actual number in the series of questionings, the time of questioning, which main category is selected, and the chosen specification.

We have already tested this system in two experiments on the construction of hypertexts. Initial experiences show that it runs without any error and proves to be user-friendly. Participants reported no problems in using the program or the categories and said that they did not find the questionings distracting.

The advantages of self-rating methods are their great economy. Time-consuming activities such as transcribing data and giving them to two raters to categorize are no longer necessary. Furthermore, unlike the assessment methods using verbal data

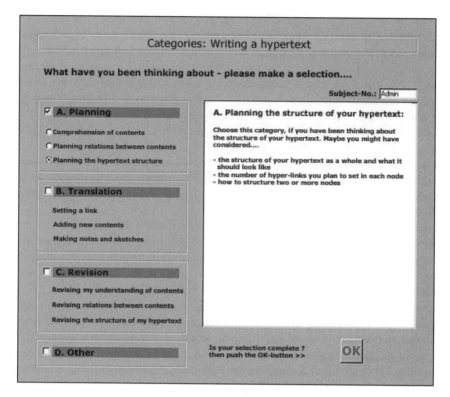

Figure 10.2: Screenshot of the window for categorizing the
construction process.

Table 10.3: Contents of the category system for a computer-assisted questioning of
cognitive processes.

Main category	Specification
A. Planning	Reading and comprehending the contents Planning relations between contents Planning the hypertext structure
B. Translation	Setting a link Adding new contents Making notes and sketches
C. Revision	Revising the comprehension of contents Revising relations between contents Revising the hypertext structure
D. Other	

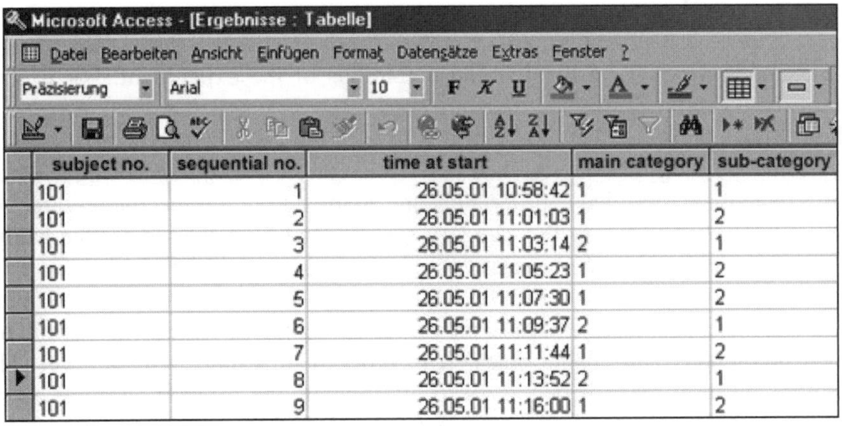

subject no.	sequential no.	time at start	main category	sub-category
101	1	26.05.01 10:58:42	1	1
101	2	26.05.01 11:01:03	1	2
101	3	26.05.01 11:03:14	2	1
101	4	26.05.01 11:05:23	1	2
101	5	26.05.01 11:07:30	1	2
101	6	26.05.01 11:09:37	2	1
101	7	26.05.01 11:11:44	1	2
101	8	26.05.01 11:13:52	2	1
101	9	26.05.01 11:16:00	1	2

Figure 10.3: Screenshot of the analysis window. Data are entered automatically into the predefined columns recording the participant number, the actual number in the series of questionings, the time of questioning, the number of the main category selected, and the number of the chosen sub-category.

described above, they can be applied in group studies. A third advantage is that participants' statements no longer have to be interpreted by raters but are categorized directly. This rules out imprecise categorizations of ambiguous statements. At the same time, it can be assumed that participants are highly capable of categorizing their own approaches (see Kellogg, 1994). It is also conceivable that this type of questioning helps to prevent them from developing a feeling that they need to justify themselves before the experimenter and thus reduces any potential effects of social desirability.

Disadvantages of the method are that the category system cannot be too extensive or participants will no longer be able to learn it. Hence, very differentiated assessments are not possible. Moreover, it is necessary to possess prior knowledge on which categories are decisive before such a system can be developed. A further problem may be that this assessment method encourages certain approaches by giving categories in advance that participants only become aware of through selecting them.

Discussion

The present chapter discusses methods for assessing process data during the construction of hypertexts and presents category systems for analyzing such data. It lists various possible ways of assessing and categorizing process data and discusses their advantages and disadvantages. These possible ways are activity analyses, the assessment of verbal data, and self-ratings of cognitive processes by the participants themselves.

These different methods provide a repertoire for performing a differentiated analysis of the processes that occur while constructing or writing a hypertext. Because each method presented here assesses only a fraction of all the processes that occur, detailed analyses require a combination of several methods. Naturally, the choice of appropriate methods depends on the framing conditions of the experiment. For example, some of them cannot be applied in group sessions.

The methods presented here are oriented toward the usual methods of process data analysis in psychology. However, their application in the domain of writing hypertexts requires them to be modified appropriately and adapted to fit the specific research goal.

This applies, first of all, to the category systems and models used for the analysis. The systems presented here are relatively imprecise. It would be good to be able to assess the processes in more detail. Of course, this is a circular process: new findings on the cognitive processes involved in the construction of hypertexts permit more detailed predictions and enable research to proceed to a more refined level. These predictions, in turn, make it necessary to differentiate the category systems, permitting the acquisition of knowledge on a higher level, and so on.

However, this process could be accelerated if research on hypertexts were to pay more attention to and exploit existing theories, findings, and methods from other domains such as "traditional" text production and reception. Up to now, only sporadic attention has been paid to such findings. In the domain of learning with hypertexts, they have often been used to demarcate hypertext from other forms of text (by those in favor of hypertexts) or to counter the existing arguments on the learning efficacy of working with hypertexts (by those who are critical of hypertexts). However, there has been no serious comparison with related research domains. Vice versa, the idea that hypertexts can be treated as a special text format is gaining acceptance only slowly in the domain of research on text production. Particularly when assessing the individual processes involved in the writing of (hyper-)texts, it can be anticipated that mutual recognition would be advantageous to both sides.

Moreover, this also applies to the development of the methods themselves. The fact that hypertexts are produced on a computer makes it possible to modify existing methods — as shown already in computer-assisted self-ratings or in log file analyses in the field of activity analyses. Accordingly, one goal of future research in this domain should be to improve the methods themselves in order to retain or even strengthen their advantages while attenuating their disadvantages. Another possibility is to consider new methods that may have been technically infeasible before. In this domain, the fact that the computer can be viewed not only as a tool that authors use to produce hypertexts but also as a tool that researchers can use to gather data generates a strong potential for methodological advances.

Author Note

I wish to thank Raphael Jaron for his help in developing of the computer-assisted assessment tool and Jonathan Harrow for native-speaker advice.

References

Becker-Mrotzek, M. (1997). *Schreibentwicklung und Textproduktion: Der Erwerb der Schreibfertigkeit am Beispiel der Bedienungsanleitung.* [Development of writing and text production: The development of writing skills discussed on the example of operating instructions]. Opladen: Westdeutscher Verlag.

Bromme, R., & Stahl, E. (1999). Spatial metaphors and writing hypertexts: Study within schools. *European Journal of Psychology of Education, 14,* 267–281.

Bromme, R., & Stahl, E. (2001). The idea of "hypertext" and its implications on the process of hypertext writing. In: W. Frindte, T. Köhler, P. Marquet, and E. Nissen (eds), *IN-TELE 99 — Internet-Based Teaching and Learning 99: Vol.3. Internet Communication* (pp. 302–308). Frankfurt am Main: Peter Lang.

Canter, D., Rivers, R., & Storres, G. (1985). Characterizing user navigation through complex data structures. *Behavior and Information Technology, 4,* 93–102.

Dillon, A., & Gabbard, R. (1998). Hypermedia as an educational technology: A review of the quantitative research literature on learner comprehension, control, and style. *Review of Educational Research, 68,* 322–349.

Ericsson, K. A., & Simon, H. A. (1980). Verbal reports as data. *Psychological Review, 87,* 215–251.

Ericsson, K. A., & Simon, H. A. (1993). *Protocol Analysis: Verbal Reports as Data (Rev. ed.).* Cambridge, MA: MIT-Press.

Flower, L., & Hayes, R. (1981). The pregnant pause: An inquiry into the nature of planning. *Research in the Teaching of English, 15,* 229–244.

Gay, G., Trumbull, D., & Mazur, J. (1991). Designing and testing navigational strategies and guidance tools for a hypermedia program. *Journal of Educational Computing Research, 7,* 189–202.

Gerdes, H. (1997). *Lernen mit Text und Hypertext.* [Learning with text and hypertext]. Berlin: Pabst.

Gray, S. H. (1990). Using protocol analyses and drawings to study mental model construction. *International Journal of Human Computer Interaction, 2,* 359–378.

Gray, S. H. (1995). Linear coherence and relevance: Logic in computer-human "conversations". *Journal of Pragmatics, 23,* 627–647.

Hayes, J. R. (1996). A new framework for understanding cognition and affect in writing. In: C. M. Levy, and S. Ransdell (eds), *The Science of Writing: Theories, Methods, Individual Differences, and Applications* (pp. 1–27). Mahwah, NJ: Lawrence Erlbaum.

Hayes, J. R., & Flower, L. S. (1980). Identifying the organisation of writing processes. In: L. W. Gregg, and E. R. Steinberg (eds), *Cognitive Processes in Writing* (pp. 3–30). Hillsdale, NJ: Lawrence Erlbaum.

Hayes, J. R., & Flower, L. S. (1986). Writing research and the writer. *American Psychologist, 41,* 1106–1113.

Hutchings, G. A., Hall, W., & Colbourn, C. J. (1993). Patterns of students' interaction with a hypermedia system. *Interacting with Computers, 5,* 295–313.

Janssen, D., van Waes, L., & van den Bergh, H. (1996). Effects of thinking aloud on writing processes. In: C. M. Levy, and S. Randsell (eds), *The Science of Writing: Theories, Methods, Individual Differences, and Applications* (pp. 233–250). Mahwah, NJ: Lawrence Erlbaum.

Kellogg, R. T. (1988). Attentional overload and writing performances: Effects of rough draft and outline strategies. *Journal of Experimental Psychology, 14,* 355–365.

Kellogg, R. T. (1994). *The Psychology of Writing.* New York: Oxford University Press.

Kluwe, R. H. (1988). Methoden der Psychologie zur Gewinnung von Daten über menschliches Wissen [Psychological methods for data capture about human knowledge]. In: H. Spada, & H. Mandl (eds), *Wissenspsychologie* (pp. 359–385). München: Psychologie Verlags Union.

Levy, C. M., & Randsdell, S. (eds) (1996). *The Science of Writing. Theories, Methods, Individual Differences, and Applications*. Mahwah, NJ: Lawrence Erlbaum.

Mayes, T., Kibby, M., & Anderson, T. (1990). Learning about learning from hypertext. In: D. H. Jonassen, and H. Mandl (eds), *Designing Hypermedia for Learning* (pp. 227–250). Berlin: Springer-Verlag.

Perfetti, C. A. (1996). Text and hypertext. In: J.-F. Rouet, J. J. Levonen, A. Dillon, and R. J. Spiro (eds), *Hypertext and Cognition* (pp. 157–161). Mahwah, NJ: Lawrence Erlbaum.

Rijlaarsdam, G., Couzijn, M., & van den Bergh, H. (1996). Current research on effective teaching and learning to write. In: G. Rijlaarsdam, H. van den Bergh, and M. Couzijn (eds), *Effective Teaching and Learning of Writing: Current Trends in Research* (pp. IV-XVIII). Amsterdam: University Press.

Stahl, E. (2001). *Hyper-Text-Schreiben: Die Auswirkungen verschiedener Instruktionen auf Lernprozesse beim Schreiben von Hypertext* [Writing-Hyper-Text: Effects of different instructions on learning processes during the writing of hypertext]. Münster: Waxmann.

Stahl, E., & Bromme, R. (1997). Verständnis von Hypertext-Strukturen durch die Konstruktion von Hypertexten? Beobachtungen zum Umgang mit Hypertexten im Schulunterricht [Understanding of hypertext structures through constructing hypertexts? Observations of the use of hypertexts in school lessons]. In: D. Janetzko, B. Batinic, M. Mattingley-Scott, and G. Strube (eds), *CAW-97: Beiträge zum Workshop "Cognition & Web"* (pp. 158–175). Freiburg i.Br.: IIG-Berichte 1/97.

Index